PostgreSQL 9 Administration Cookbook

Solve real-world PostgreSQL problems with over 100 simple, yet incredibly effective recipes

Simon Riggs

Hannu Krosing

PUBLISHING

BIRMINGHAM - MUMBAI

PostgreSQL 9 Administration Cookbook

First published: October 2010

Production Reference: 1191010

Published by Packt Publishing Ltd.
32 Lincoln Road
Olton
Birmingham, B27 6PA, UK.

ISBN 978-1-849510-28-8

www.packtpub.com

Cover Image by John M. Quick (john.m.quick@gmail.com)

Credits

Authors
Simon Riggs
Hannu Krosing

Reviewers
Gabriele Bartolini
Dimitri Fontaine

Acquisition Editor
Sarah Cullington

Development Editor
Eleanor Duffy

Technical Editor
Azharuddin Sheikh

Copy Editor
Neha Shetty

Indexer
Hemangini Bari

Editorial Team Leader
Akshara Aware

Project Team Leader
Ashwin Shetty

Project Coordinator
Zainab Bagasrawala

Proofreader
Clyde Jenkins

Production Coordinator
Kruthika Bangera

Cover Work
Kruthika Bangera

About the Authors

Simon Riggs is a major developer and one of the few committers on the PostgreSQL database project, as well as CTO of 2ndQuadrant, providing 24x7 support and services to PostgreSQL users worldwide.

Simon works actively as a database architect and support troubleshooter, skills which drive and shape his contributions to the development of operational features for PostgreSQL. Feature credits include Point in Time Recovery, Warm Standby replication, Hot Standby, Asynchronous Commit, Partitioning and many other performance and tuning features. His designs and solutions can be found throughout the PostgreSQL code and documentation.

Simon has also previously worked with Oracle, Teradata, and DB2 and holds multiple certifications. His previous experience covers management and senior technical roles in the banking, telecommunications and software industries. Simon's early research work has been published by the Royal Society.

Hannu Krosing is a principal consultant at 2ndQuadrant and a Technical Advisor at Ambient Sound Investments. As the original database architect at Skype Technologies, Hannu was responsible for designing the Skytools suite of replication and scalability technologies. Hannu has more than 12 years experience working with and contributing to the PostgreSQL project.

About the Reviewers

Gabriele Bartolini is a long time open-source programmer, writing Linux/Unix applications in C and C++ for over 10 years, specializing in search engines and web analytics with large databases.

Gabriele has a degree in Statistics from the University of Florence. His areas of expertise are data mining and data warehousing, having worked on web traffic analysis in Australia and Italy.

Gabriele is a consultant with 2ndQuadrant and an active member of the international PostgreSQL community.

Gabriele currently lives in Prato, a small but vibrant city located in the northern part of Tuscany, Italy. His second home is Melbourne, Australia, where he has studied at Monash University and worked in the ICT sector.

His hobbies include "calcio" (football or soccer, depending on which part of the world you come from) and playing his Fender Stratocaster electric guitar.

Thanks to my family, in particular Cathy who encourages me by saying there is always something new to learn.

Dimitri Fontaine is part of the PostgreSQL community and has been contributing to open source for more than 10 years. He is the lead developer of enterprise ready solutions such as pgloader (ETL), PostgreSQL prefix indexing (telephony routing), pg_staging (development environment maintenance from production backups), preprepare (allow easy usage of prepare statements behind a connection pooler), and some backports of recent PostgreSQL features

He also contributed to Skytools and the Londiste replication system and, authored a PHP layer for the PGQ event handler, allowing for robust asynchronous processing and code reuse.

Dimitri's passion is system architecture & design, with the goals of reduced maintenance time and very high availability

Professional experience, community involvement, and PostgreSQL expertise have led Dimitri to now work as a principal consultant at 2ndQuadrant, France.

Table of Contents

Preface

PostgreSQL is an advanced SQL database server, available on a wide range of platforms and is fast becoming one of the world's most popular server databases with an enviable reputation for performance, stability, and an enormous range of advanced features. PostgreSQL is one of the oldest open source projects, completely free to use, and developed by a very diverse worldwide community. Most of all, it just works!

One of the clearest benefits of PostgreSQL is that it is open source, meaning that you have a very permissive license to install, use, and distribute PostgreSQL without paying anyone any fees or royalties. On top of that, PostgreSQL is well-known as a database that stays up for long periods, and requires little or no maintenance in many cases. Overall, PostgreSQL provides a very low total cost of ownership.

PostgreSQL Administration Cookbook offers the information you need to manage your live production databases on PostgreSQL. The book contains insights direct from the main author of the PostgreSQL replication and recovery features, and the database architect of the most successful startup using PostgreSQL, Skype. This hands-on guide will assist developers working on live databases, supporting web or enterprise software applications using Java, Python, Ruby, .Net from any development framework. It's easy to manage your database when you've got PostgreSQL 9 Administration Cookbook at hand.

This practical guide gives you quick answers to common questions and problems, building on the author's experience as trainers, users, and core developers of the PostgreSQL database server.

Each technical aspect is broken down into short recipes that demonstrate solutions with working code, and then explain why and how that works. The book is intended to be a desk reference for both new users and technical experts.

The book covers all the latest features available in PostgreSQL 9. Soon you will be running a smooth database with ease!

What this book covers

Chapter 1, First Steps, covers topics such as an introduction to PostgreSQL 9, downloading and installing PostgreSQL 9, connecting to a PostgreSQL server, enabling server access to network/remote users, using graphical administration tools, using psql query and scripting tools, changing your password securely, avoiding hardcoding your password, using a connection service file, and troubleshooting a failed connection.

Chapter 2, Exploring the Database, helps you identify the version of the database server you are using and also the server uptime. It helps you locate the database server files, database server message log, and database's system identifier. It lets you list a database on the database server, contains recipes that let you know the number of tables in your database, how much disk space is used by the database and tables, which are the biggest tables, how many rows a table has, how to estimate rows in a table, and how to understand object dependencies.

Chapter 3, Configuration, covers topics such as reading the fine manual (RTFM), planning a new database, changing parameters in your programs, the current configuration settings, parameters that are at non-default settings, updating the parameter file, setting parameters for particular groups of users, basic server configuration checklist, adding an external module into the PostgreSQL server, and running the server in power saving mode.

Chapter 4, Server Control, provides information about starting the database server manually, stopping the server quickly and safely, stopping the server in an emergency, reloading the server configuration files, restarting the server quickly, preventing new connections, restricting users to just one session each, and pushing users off the system. It contains recipes that help you decide on a design for multi-tenancy, how to use multiple schemas, giving users their own private database, running multiple database servers on one system, and setting up a connection pool.

Chapter 5, Tables & Data, guides you through the process of choosing good names for database objects, handling objects with quoted names, enforcing same name, same definition for columns, identifying and removing duplicate rows, preventing duplicate rows, finding a unique key for a set of data, generating test data, randomly sampling data, loading data from a spreadsheet, and loading data from flat files.

Chapter 6, Security, provides recipes on revoking user access to a table, granting user access to a table, creating a new user, temporarily preventing a user from connecting, removing a user without dropping their data, checking whether all users have a secure password, giving limited superuser powers to specific users, auditing DDL changes, auditing data changes, integrating with LDAP, connecting using SSL, and encrypting sensitive data.

Chapter 7, Database Administration, provides recipes on useful topics such as writing a script wherein either all succeed or all fail, writing a psql script that exits on the first error, performing actions on many tables, adding/removing columns on tables, changing the data type of a column, adding/removing schemas, moving objects between schemas, adding/removing tablespaces, moving objects between tablespaces, accessing objects in other PostgreSQL databases, and making views updateable.

Chapter 8, Monitoring and Diagnosis, provides recipes that answer questions such as is the user connected?, what are they running?, are they active or blocked?, who is blocking them?, is anybody using a specific table?, when did anybody last use it?, how much disk space is used by temporary data?, and why are my queries slowing down? It also helps you in investigating and reporting a bug, producing a daily summary report of logfile errors, killing a specific session, and resolving an in-doubt prepared transaction.

Chapter 9, Regular Maintenance, provides useful recipes on controlling automatic database maintenance, avoiding auto freezing and page corruptions, avoiding transaction wraparound, removing old prepared transactions, actions for heavy users of temporary tables, identifying and fixing bloated tables and indexes, maintaining indexes, finding unused indexes, carefully removing unwanted indexes, and planning maintenance.

Chapter 10, Performance & Concurrency, covers topics such as finding slow SQL statements, collecting regular statistics from pg_stat* views, finding what makes SQL slow, reducing the number of rows returned, simplifying complex SQL, speeding up queries without rewriting them, why is my query not using an index?, how do I force a query to use an index?, using optimistic locking, and reporting performance problems.

Chapter 11, Backup & Recovery, most people admit that backups are essential, though they also devote only a very small amount of time to thinking about the topic. So, this chapter provides useful information about backup and recovery of your PostgreSQL database through recipes on understanding and controlling crash recovery, planning backups, hot logical backup of one database, hot logical backup of all databases, hot logical backup of all tables in a tablespace, backup of database object definitions, standalone hot physical database backup, hot physical backup & continuous archiving. It also includes topics such as recovery of all databases, recovery to a point in time, recovery of a dropped/damaged table, recovery of a dropped/damaged database, recovery of a dropped/damaged tablespace, improving performance of backup/recovery, and incremental/differential backup and restore.

Chapter 12, Replication & Upgrades, replication isn't magic, though it can be pretty cool. It's even cooler when it works, and that's what this chapter is all about. This chapter covers topics such as replication concepts, replication best practices, setting up file-based log shipping replication, setting up streaming log replication, managing log shipping replication, managing Hot Standby, selective replication using Londiste 3.0, selective replication using Slony 2.0, load balancing with pgpool II 3.0, upgrading to a new minor release (for example, 9.0.0 to 9.0.1), in-place major upgrades (for example, 8.4 to 9.0, or 9.0 to 9.1), and major upgrades online using replication tools.

What you need for this book

We need the following software for this book:

▶ PostgreSQL 9.0 Server Software

▶ psql client utility (part of 9.0)

▶ pgAdmin3 1.12

Who this book is for

This book is for system administrators, database administrators, architects, developers, and anyone with an interest in planning for or running live production databases. This book is most suited to those who have some technical experience.

Conventions

In this book, you will find a number of styles of text that distinguish between different kinds of information. Here are some examples of these styles, and an explanation of their meaning.

Code words in text are shown as follows: "In PostgreSQL 9.0, the utility `pg_standby` is no longer required, as many of its features are now performed directly by the server."

A block of code is set as follows:

```
CREATE USER repuser
        SUPERUSER
        LOGIN
        CONNECTION LIMIT 1
        ENCRYPTED PASSWORD 'changeme';
```

When we wish to draw your attention to a particular part of a code block, the relevant lines or items are set in bold:

```
SELECT *
FROM mytable
WHERE   (col1, col2, … ,colN) IN
(SELECT col1, col2, … ,colN
 FROM mytable
 GROUP BY
                    col1, col2, … ,colN
 HAVING count(*) > 1);
```

Any command-line input or output is written as follows:

```
$ postgres --single -D /full/path/to/datadir postgres
```

New terms and **important words** are shown in bold. Words that you see on the screen, in menus or dialog boxes for example, appear in the text like this: " The Query tool has a good looking visual explain feature as well as a **Graphical Query Builder**, as shown in the following screenshot".

 Warnings or important notes appear in a box like this.

Tips and tricks appear like this.

Reader feedback

Feedback from our readers is always welcome. Let us know what you think about this book—what you liked or may have disliked. Reader feedback is important for us to develop titles that you really get the most out of.

To send us general feedback, simply send an e-mail to feedback@packtpub.com, and mention the book title via the subject of your message.

If there is a book that you need and would like to see us publish, please send us a note in the **SUGGEST A TITLE** form on www.packtpub.com or e-mail suggest@packtpub.com.

If there is a topic that you have expertise in and you are interested in either writing or contributing to a book, see our author guide on www.packtpub.com/authors.

Customer support

Now that you are the proud owner of a Packt book, we have a number of things to help you to get the most from your purchase.

 Downloading the example code for this book

You can download the example code files for all Packt books you have purchased from your account at http://www.PacktPub.com. If you purchased this book elsewhere, you can visit http://www.PacktPub.com/support and register to have the files e-mailed directly to you.

Errata

Although we have taken every care to ensure the accuracy of our content, mistakes do happen. If you find a mistake in one of our books—maybe a mistake in the text or the code—we would be grateful if you would report this to us. By doing so, you can save other readers from frustration and help us improve subsequent versions of this book. If you find any errata, please report them by visiting http://www.packtpub.com/support, selecting your book, clicking on the **errata submission form** link, and entering the details of your errata. Once your errata are verified, your submission will be accepted and the errata will be uploaded on our website, or added to any list of existing errata, under the Errata section of that title. Any existing errata can be viewed by selecting your title from http://www.packtpub.com/support.

Piracy

Piracy of copyright material on the Internet is an ongoing problem across all media. At Packt, we take the protection of our copyright and licenses very seriously. If you come across any illegal copies of our works, in any form, on the Internet, please provide us with the location address or website name immediately so that we can pursue a remedy.

Please contact us at copyright@packtpub.com with a link to the suspected pirated material.

We appreciate your help in protecting our authors, and our ability to bring you valuable content.

Questions

You can contact us at questions@packtpub.com if you are having a problem with any aspect of the book, and we will do our best to address it.

1
First Steps

In this chapter, we will cover the following:

- ▶ Introducing PostgreSQL 9
- ▶ Getting PostgreSQL
- ▶ Connecting to PostgreSQL
- ▶ Enabling server access to network/remote users
- ▶ Using graphical administration tools
- ▶ Using psql query and scripting tools
- ▶ Changing your password securely
- ▶ Avoiding hardcoding your password
- ▶ Using a connection service file
- ▶ Troubleshooting a failed connection

Introduction

PostgreSQL is a feature-rich general purpose database management system. It's a complex piece of software, but every journey begins with the first step.

We start with your first connection. Many people fall at the first hurdle, so we try not to skip too swiftly past that. We move on quickly to enabling remote users, and from there to access through GUI administration tools.

We also introduce the psql query tool, which is the tool used for loading our sample database, as well as many other examples in the book.

For additional help, we include a few useful recipes that you may need for reference.

Introducing PostgreSQL 9

PostgreSQL is an advanced SQL database server, available on a wide range of platforms.

One of the clearest benefits of PostgreSQL is that it is open source, meaning that you have a very permissive license to install, use, and distribute PostgreSQL without paying anyone fees or royalties. On top of that, PostgreSQL is well-known as a database that stays up for long periods, and requires little or no maintenance in many cases. Overall, PostgreSQL provides a very low total cost of ownership.

PostgreSQL is also noted for its huge range of advanced features, developed over the course of more than 20 years continuous development and enhancement. Originally developed by the Database Research group at the University of California, Berkeley, PostgreSQL is now developed and maintained by a huge army of developers and contributors. Many of those contributors have full-time jobs related to PostgreSQL, working as designers, developers, database administrators, and trainers. Some, but not many, of those contributors work for companies that specialize in services for PostgreSQL, such as *Hannu* and me. No single company owns PostgreSQL, nor are you required, or even encouraged, to register your usage.

PostgreSQL has the following main features:

- ▶ Excellent SQL Standards compliance up to SQL 2008
- ▶ Client-server architecture
- ▶ Highly concurrent design where readers and writers don't block each other
- ▶ Highly configurable and extensible for many types of application
- ▶ Excellent scalability and performance with extensive tuning features

What makes PostgreSQL different?

The PostgreSQL project focuses on the following objectives:

- ▶ Robust, high-quality software with maintainable, well-commented code
- ▶ Low maintenance administration for both embedded and enterprise use
- ▶ Standards-compliant SQL, interoperability, and compatibility
- ▶ Performance, security, and high availability

What surprises many people is that PostgreSQL's feature set is more comparable with Oracle or SQL Server than it is with MySQL. The only connection between MySQL and PostgreSQL is that those two projects are open source; apart from that, the features and philosophies are almost totally different.

One of the key features of Oracle since Oracle 7 has been "snapshot isolation", where readers don't block writers, and writers don't block readers. You may be surprised to learn that PostgreSQL was the first database to be designed with this feature, and offers a full and complete implementation. PostgreSQL names this Multi-Version Concurrency Control (MVCC), and we will discuss this in more detail later in this book.

PostgreSQL is a general-purpose database management system. You define the database that you would like to manage with it. PostgreSQL offers you many ways to work. You can use a "normalized database model", you can utilize extensions such as arrays and record subtypes, or you can use a fully dynamic schema using an extension named **hstore**. PostgreSQL also allows you to create your own server-side functions in one of a dozen different languages.

PostgreSQL is highly extensible, so you can add your own datatypes, operators, index types, and functional languages. For example, you can override different parts of the system using plugins to alter the execution of commands or add a new optimizer.

All of these features offer a huge range of implementation options to software architects. There are many ways out of trouble when building applications and maintaining them over long periods of time. Regrettably, we simply don't have space in this book for all of the cool features for developers—this book is about administration, maintenance, and backup.

In the early days, when PostgreSQL was still a research database, the focus was solely on cool new features. Over the last 15 years, enormous amounts of code have been rewritten and improved, giving us one of the most stable, large, software servers available for operational use.

You may also read that PostgreSQL was, or is, slower than My Favorite DBMS, whichever one that is. It's been a personal mission of mine over the last six years to improve server performance and the team have been successful in making the server highly performant and very scalable. That gives PostgreSQL enormous headroom for growth.

Who is using PostgreSQL? Prominent users include Apple, BASF, Genentech, IMDB.com, Skype, NTT, Yahoo, and The National Weather Service. PostgreSQL receives well in excess of 1 million downloads per year, according to data submitted to the European Commission, who concluded "...PostgreSQL, is considered by many database users to be a credible alternative...

We need to mention one last thing. When PostgreSQL was first developed, it was named Postgres, and so many aspects of the project still refer to the word "postgres". For example, the default database is named postgres, and the software is frequently installed using the postgres userid. As a result, people shorten the name PostgreSQL to simply Postgres, and in many cases people use the two names interchangeably.

PostgreSQL is pronounced as "post-grez-q-l". Postgres is pronounced as "post-grez".

Some people get confused, and refer to "Postgre", which is hard to say, and likely to confuse people. Two names are enough, so please don't use a third name!

Getting PostgreSQL

PostgreSQL is 100% open source software.

PostgreSQL is freely available to use, alter, or redistribute in any way you choose. PostgreSQL's license is an approved open source license very similar to the **BSD (Berkeley Distribution Software)** license, though only just different enough that it is now known as **TPL (The PostgreSQL License)**.

How to do it...

PostgreSQL is already in use by many different application packages, and so you may already find it installed on your servers. Many Linux distributions include PostgreSQL as part of the basic installation, or include it with the installation disk.

One thing to be wary of is that the version of PostgreSQL included may not be the latest release. It will typically be the latest major release that was available when that operating system release was published. There is usually no good reason to stick at that level—there is no increased stability implied there and later production versions are just as well-supported by the various Linux distributions.

If you don't yet have a copy, or you don't have the latest version, you can download the source code or download binary packages for a wide variety of operating systems from the following URL:

```
http://www.postgresql.org/download/
```

Installation details vary significantly from platform-to-platform and there aren't any special tricks or recipes to mention. Please, just follow the installation guide, and away you go. We've consciously avoided describing the installation processes here to make sure we don't garble or override the information published to assist you.

If you would like to receive e-mail updates of the latest news, then you can subscribe to the PostgreSQL announce mailing list, which contains updates from all the vendors that support PostgreSQL. You'll get a few e-mails each month about new releases of core PostgreSQL and related software, conferences, and user group information. It's worth keeping in touch with developments.

 For more information about the PostgreSQL announce mailing list, visit the following URL:

```
http://archives.postgresql.org/pgsql-announce/
```

How it works...

Many people ask questions, such as "How can this be free?", "Are you sure I don't have to pay someone?", or "Who gives this stuff away for nothing?"

Open source applications such as PostgreSQL work on a community basis, where many contributors perform tasks that make the whole process work. For many of those people, their involvement is professional, rather a hobby, and they can do this because there is generally a great value for both contributors and their employers alike.

You might not believe it. You don't have to because It Just Works.

There's more...

Remember that PostgreSQL is more than just the core software. There is a huge range of websites offering add-ons, extensions, and tools for PostgreSQL. You'll also find an army of bloggers describing useful tricks and discoveries that will help you in your work.

And, there is a range of professional companies able to offer you help when you need it.

Connecting to PostgreSQL server

How do we access PostgreSQL?

Connecting to the database is most people's first experience of PostgreSQL, so we want to make it a good one. So, let's do it, and fix any problems we have along the way. Remember that a connection needs to be made securely, so there may be some hoops for us to jump through to ensure that the data we wish to access is secure.

Before we can execute commands against the database, we need to connect to the database server, giving us a **session**.

Sessions are designed to be long-lived, so you connect once, perform many requests, and then eventually disconnect. There is a small overhead during connection. That may become noticeable if you connect/disconnect repeatedly, so you may wish to investigate the use of connection pools. Connection pools allow pre-connected sessions to be served quickly to you when you wish to reconnect.

Getting ready

First, catch your database. If you don't know where it is, we'll probably have difficulty accessing it. There may be more than one, and you'll need to know the right database to access, and have the authority to connect to it.

How to do it...

You need to specify the following five parameters to connect to PostgreSQL:

- ▸ host or host address
- ▸ port
- ▸ database name
- ▸ user
- ▸ password (or other means of authentication, if any)

To connect, there must be a PostgreSQL server running on *host*, listening on port number *port*. On that server, a database named *dbname* and *user* must also exist. The host must explicitly allow connections from your client—this is explained in the next recipe, and you must also pass authentication using the method the server specifies. For example, specifying a password won't work if the server has requested a different form of authentication.

Almost all PostgreSQL interfaces use the **libpq** interface library. When using libpq, most of the connection parameter handling is identical, so we can just discuss that once.

If you don't specify the preceding parameters, we look for values set through environment variables, which are as follows:

- ▸ PGHOST or PGHOSTADDR
- ▸ PGPORT (or set to 5432 if this is not set)
- ▸ PGDATABASE
- ▸ PGUSER
- ▸ PGPASSWORD (though this one is definitely not recommended)

If you specify the first four parameters somehow, but not the password, then we look for a password file, discussed in a later recipe.

Some PostgreSQL interfaces use the client-server protocol directly, so the way defaults are handled may differ. The information we need to supply won't vary significantly, so please check the exact syntax for that interface.

How it works...

The PostgreSQL server is a client-server database. The system it runs on is known as the host. We can access the PostgreSQL server remotely through the network. However, we must specify the host, which is a hostname, or a hostaddr, which is an IP address. We can specify a host of "localhost" if we wish to make a TCP/IP connection to the same system. It is often better to use a Unix socket connection, which is attempted if the host begins with a slash (/) and the name is presumed to be a directory name (default is /tmp).

On any system, there can be more than one database server. Each database server listens on exactly one "well-known" network port, which cannot be shared between servers on the same system. The default port number for PostgreSQL is 5432, which has been registered with **IANA**, and is uniquely assigned to PostgreSQL. (You can see it used in the /etc/services file on most *nix servers). The port number can be used to uniquely identify a specific database server if many exist.

A database server is also sometimes known as a "database cluster", because the PostgreSQL server allows you to define one or more databases on each server. Each connection request must identify exactly one database identified by its dbname. When you connect, you will only be able to see database objects created within that database.

A database user is used to identify the connection. By default, there is no limit on the number of connections for a particular user, though there is a later recipe to restrict that. In more recent versions of PostgreSQL, users are referred to as login roles, though many clues remind us of the earlier naming, and it still makes sense in many ways. A login role is a role that has been assigned the CONNECT privilege.

Each connection will typically be authenticated in some way. This is defined at the server, so is not optional at connection time if the administrator has configured the server to require authentication.

Once you've connected, each connection can have one active transaction at a time and one fully active statement at any time.

The server will have a defined limit on the number of connections it can serve, so a connection request can be refused if the server is oversubscribed.

Inspecting your connection information

If you want to confirm you've connected to the right place and in the right way, you can execute some or all of the following commands:

```
SELECT inet_server_port();
```

This shows the port on which the server is listening.

```
SELECT current_database();
```

Shows the current database.

```
SELECT current_user;
```

This shows the current userid.

```
SELECT inet_server_addr();
```

Shows the IP address of the server that accepted the connection.

A user's password is not accessible using general SQL for obvious reasons.

You may also need the following:

```
SELECT version();
```

See also

There are many other snippets of information required to understand connections. Some of those are mentioned in this chapter, although others are discussed in the chapter on *Security*. For further details, please consult the PostgreSQL server documentation.

Enabling access for network/remote users

PostgreSQL comes in a variety of distributions. In many of these, you will find that remote access is initially disabled as a security measure.

How to do it...

▸ Add/edit the following line in your `postgresql.conf`:

```
listen_addresses = '*'
```

▸ Add the following line as the first line of `pg_hba.conf`, to allow access to all databases for all users with an encrypted password:

# TYPE	DATABASE	USER	CIDR-ADDRESS	METHOD
host	all	all	0.0.0.0/0	md5

How it works...

The `listen_addresses` parameter specifies on which IP addresses to listen. This allows you to have more than one network card (NICs) per system. In most cases, we want to accept connections on all NICs, so we use "*", meaning "all IP addresses".

The `pg_hba.conf` contains a set of host-based authentication rules. Each rule is considered in sequence until one rule fires, or the attempt is specifically rejected with a `reject` method.

The preceding rule means a remote connection that specifies any user, or any database, on any IP address will be asked to authenticate using an **md5** encrypted password.

`Type = host` means a remote connection.

`Database = all` means "for all databases". Other names match exactly, except when prefixed with a plus (+) symbol, in which case we mean a "group role" rather than a single user. You can also specify a comma-separated list of users, or use the @ symbol to include a file with a list of users. You can also specify "sameuser", so that the rule matches when we specify the same name for the username and database name.

`User = all` means "for all users." Other names match exactly, except when prefixed with a plus (+) symbol, in which case we mean a "group role" rather than a single user. You can also specify a comma-separated list of users or use the @ symbol to include a file with a list of users.

`CIDR-ADDRESS` consists of two parts: IP-address/sub-net mask. The subnet mask is specified as the number of leading bits of the IP-address that make up the mask. Thus `/0` means 0 bits of the IP address, so that all IP addresses will be matched For example, 192.168.0.0/24 would mean match the first 24 bits, so any IP address of the form 192.168.0.x would match. You can also use "samenet" or "samehost".

 Don't use the setting "password", as this allows a password in plain text.

`Method = trust` effectively means "no authentication". Other authentication methods include GSSAPI, SSPI, LDAP, RADIUS, and PAM. PostgreSQL connections can also be made using SSL, in which case client SSL certificates provide authentication.

There's more...

In earlier versions of PostgreSQL access through the network was enabled by adding the `-i` command line switch when you started the server. This is still a valid option, though now it means the following:

```
listen_addresses = '*'
```

So, if you're reading some notes about how to set things up, and this is mentioned, then be warned that those notes are probably long out of date. Not necessarily wrong, though worth looking further to see if anything else has changed.

See also

Look at installer- and/or operating system-specific documentation to find the standard location of files.

Using graphical administration tools

Graphical administration tools are often requested by system administrators.

PostgreSQL has a range of tool options. The two most popular options are as follows:

- pgAdmin3
- phpPgAdmin

We're going to describe pgAdmin3 in more detail here, because it is installed by default with the PostgreSQL Windows installer. That most likely makes it the most popular interface, even if many people choose to use server software running on Linux or variants.

How to do it...

pgAdmin3 is a client application that sends and receives SQL to PostgreSQL, displaying the results for you to browse. One pgAdmin client can access many PostgreSQL servers, and a PostgreSQL server can be accessed by many pgAdmin clients.

pgAdmin3 is usually named just pgAdmin. The *3* at the end has a long history, but isn't that important. It is not the release level. Current release level is 1.12 at time of writing.

When you start pgAdmin, you will be prompted to register a new server, as shown in the following screenshot:

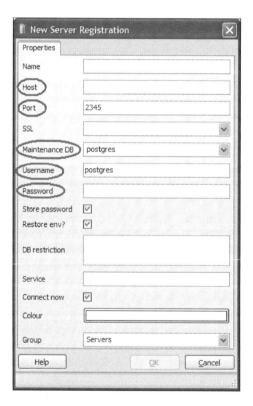

As shown in the preceding screenshot, note the five basic connection parameters, as well as other information.

The port number prompted is **2345**, though this is deliberately not the default PostgreSQL port of *5432*, presumably to force you to think about what setting should be used.

You should uncheck the **Store password** box.

If you have many database servers, you can group them together. Personally, I would avoid giving each server a **colour**, as green, yellow, and red are usually taken to mean status, which could easily be misinterpreted. Just give each server a sensible name.

You will then get access to the main browser screen, with the object tree view on the left, and properties on the top-right, as shown in the following screenshot:

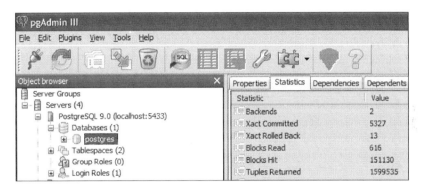

pgAdmin easily displays much of the data that is available from PostgreSQL. The information is context sensitive, allowing you to browse around and see everything quickly and easily. The information is not dynamically updated; this will only occur when you click to refresh, so keep function key *F5* in mind when using the application.

You'll also find pgAdmin provides a **TIP of the Day**, though I would turn those off. Keep the **Guru Hints** option on, though luckily no chirpy paperclips offering suggestions.

pgAdmin also provides an **Object Report** generator and a **Grant Wizard**. These are useful for DBAs for review and immediate maintenance.

pgAdmin Query tool allows you to have multiple active sessions. The Query tool has a good-looking *Visual Explain* feature, as well as a **Graphical Query Builder**, as shown in the following screenshot:

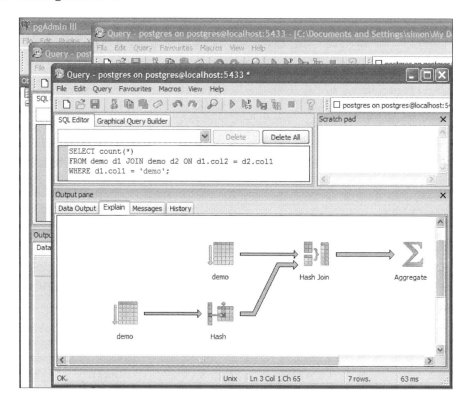

How it works...

pgAdmin provides a wide range of features, many of which are provided by other tools as well. That gives us the opportunity to choose which of those tools we like or dislike, and for many reasons, it is best to use the right tool for the right job, and that is always a matter of expertise, experience, and personal taste.

 pgAdmin submits SQL to the PostgreSQL server, and displays the results quickly and easily. As a browser, it is fantastic. For performing small DBA tasks, it is ideal. As you might guess from these comments, I don't recommend pgAdmin for *every* task.

Scripting is an important technique for DBAs: you keep a copy of the task executed, and you can edit and resubmit if problems occur. It's also easy to put all the tasks in a script into a single transaction, which isn't possible using current GUI tools. pgAdmin provides pgScript, which only works with pgAdmin, so is much less easily ported. For scripting, I strongly recommend the psql utility, which has many additional features you'll grow to appreciate over time.

Although I use psql as a scripting tool, I also find it convenient as a query tool. Some people may find this strange, and assume it is a choice for experts only. Two great features of psql are the online help for SQL and "tab completion", that allows you to build up SQL quickly without having to remember the syntax. See the recipe on *Using psql and scripting tool* for more.

pgAdmin also provides pgAgent, a task scheduler. Again, more portable schedulers are available, and you may wish to use those instead. Schedulers aren't covered in this book.

Also, a quick warning: when you create an object in pgAdmin, and if you use capitals anywhere in the object name, the object will be created with a mixed case name. If I ask for a table named MyTable, then the only way to access that table is by referring to it in double quotes as "MyTable". See the recipe about Handling objects with quoted names.

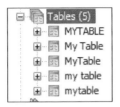

There's more...

phpPgAdmin is available at the following URL:

```
http://phppgadmin.sourceforge.net/
```

There is an online demonstration of the software, so you can try it out yourself, and see if it does the job you want done. The following screenshot shows phpPgAdmin 4 displayed on a Windows Internet Explorer browser. Version 5 is available and works with PostgreSQL 9.

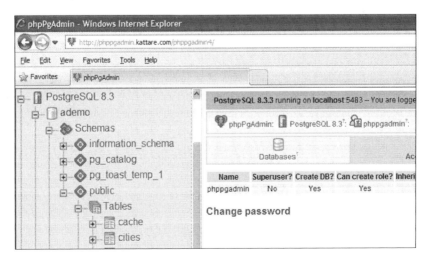

One of the big contrasts with pgAdmin is that phpPgAdmin is browser-based, so it may be easier to provide secure access to administrators this way.

phpPgAdmin provides the familiar left-hand tree view of the database, and also provides a simple SQL query tool. Those are the basics for which you should be looking. Many additional features in pgAdmin3 aren't available, though if you follow my advice you will be doing much of your work using scripts, so this may not be a problem.

See also

You may also be interested in commercial tools of various kinds for PostgreSQL. A full listing is given in the PostgreSQL software catalogue at the following URL:

```
http://www.postgresql.org/download/products/1
```

The following tools cover general administration, though other products not listed here specialize in development, data modeling, or model administration:

- Navicat

  (`http://pgsql.navicat.com/`)
- EMS SQLManager

  (`http://www.sqlmanager.net/products/studio/postgresql`)
- Lightning Admin

  (`http://www.amsoftwaredesign.com/`)

Using psql query and scripting tool

psql is the query tool supplied as part of the core distribution of PostgreSQL, so it is available and works similarly in all environments. This makes it an ideal choice for developing portable applications and techniques.

psql provides features for use as both an interactive query tool and as a scripting tool.

Getting ready

From here on, we will assume that "psql" is a sufficient command to allow you access to the PostgreSQL server. That assumes that all of your connection parameters are defaults, which may not be true.

Written out in full, the connection parameters would be as follows:

```
psql -h hostname -p 5432 -d dbname -U username -W
```

How to do it...

The easiest command is the one that executes a single SQL command and prints the output as:

```
$ psql -c "SELECT current_time"
     timetz
------------------
 18:48:32.484+01
(1 row)
```

The `-c` command is non-interactive. If we want to execute multiple commands, we can write those commands in a text file, and then execute them using the `-f` option. The following command loads a very small and simple set of examples:

$ psql -f examples.sql

which produces the following output when successful:

```
SET
SET
SET
SET
SET
SET
CREATE SCHEMA
SET
SET
SET
DROP TABLE
CREATE TABLE
DROP TABLE
CREATE TABLE
```

The script `examples.sql` is very similar to a dump file produced by PostgreSQL backup tools, so this type of file, and the output it produces, are very common. PostgreSQL produces the name of the command as a "command tag" when it executes successfully, which is what produces the preceding output.

psql can also be used in interactive mode, which is the default, so requires no option:

```
$ psql
postgres=#
```

The first interactive command you'll need is the following:

```
postgres=# help
```

You can then type in SQL or other commands.

The last interactive command you'll need is:

```
postgres=# \quit
```

Unfortunately, you cannot type "quit" on its own, nor can you type "\exit" or other options. Sorry, just "\quit" or "\q" for short.

How it works...

psql allows you to enter the following two types of command:

  ▶ psql "meta-commands"
  ▶ SQL

A meta-command is a command for psql client, whereas SQL is sent to the database server. An example of a meta-command is "\q", that tells the client to disconnect. All lines that begin with "\" (backslash) as the non-blank first character are presumed to be meta-commands of some kind.

If it isn't a meta-command, then it's SQL. We keep reading SQL until we find a semicolon, so we can spread SQL across many lines and format it any way we find convenient.

The help command is the only exception. We provide this for people who are completely lost, which is a good thought, so let's start there ourselves:

There are two types of help, which are as follows:

  ▶ \? provides help on psql meta-commands
  ▶ \h provides help on specific SQL commands

For example:

```
postgres=# \h DELETE
Command:      DELETE
Description: delete rows of a table
Syntax:
DELETE FROM [ ONLY ] table [ [ AS ] alias ]
    [ USING usinglist ]
    [ WHERE condition | WHERE CURRENT OF cursor_name ]
    [ RETURNING * | output_expression [ AS output_name ] [,]]
```

I find this a great way to discover or remember options and syntax.

You'll also like the ability to scroll back through the previous command history.

You'll get a lot of benefit from tab completion, which will fill in the next part of syntax just by pressing the *Tab* key. This also works for object names, so you can type in just the first few letters, and then press *Tab*; all of the options will be displayed, so you can type in just enough letters to make the object name unique and then hit *Tab* to get the rest.

One-line comments are double-dash as follows:

```
-- This is a single-line comment
```

And multiline comments are like C and Java:

```
/*
 * Multi-line comment
 */
```

You'll probably agree that psql looks a little daunting at first, with strange backslash commands. I do hope you'll take a few moments to understand the interface, and to keep digging for more. psql is one of the most surprising parts of PostgreSQL, and the tool is incredibly useful for database administration tasks when used alongside other tools.

There's more...

psql works across releases, though you may see a message like the following if you do so:

```
SQL Shell (psql)
Server [localhost]:
Database [postgres]:
Port [5433]: 5432
Username [postgres]:
Active code page: 1252
Password for user postgres:
psql (9.0.0, server 8.3.5)
WARNING: psql version 9.0, server version 8.3.
         Some psql features might not work.
Type "help" for help.

postgres=#
```

psql on Windows can be a little problematic. I'd recommend you use a terminal emulator to connect to your server, and access psql from there.

See also

Check out some other useful features of psql, which are as follows:

- Information functions
- Output formatting

- ▸ Execution timing by using the `\timing` command
- ▸ Input/Output and editing commands
- ▸ Automatic startup files: `.psqlrc`
- ▸ Substitutable parameters ("variables")
- ▸ Access to the OS command line

Changing your password securely

If you are using password authentication, then you may wish to change your password from time to time.

How to do it...

The most basic method is to use psql. The `\password` command will prompt you for a new password, and then again to confirm. Connect to psql, and type the following:

`\password`

Enter new password.

This causes psql to send an SQL statement to the PostgreSQL server containing an already encrypted password string. An example of the SQL statement sent is as follows:

```
ALTER USER postgres PASSWORD ' md53175bce1d3201d16594cebf9d7eb3f9d';
```

Whatever you do, don't use "postgres" as your password. This will make you vulnerable to idle hackers, so make it a little more difficult than that, please.

Make sure you don't forget it either. It could prove difficult to maintain your database if you can't get access to it later.

How it works...

As changing the password is just an SQL statement, any interface can do this. Other tools also allow this, such as:

- ▸ pgAdmin3
- ▸ phpPgAdmin

If you don't use one of the main password changes routes, you can still do this yourself using SQL from any interface. Note that you need to encrypt your password, because if you do submit a password in plaintext, like the following:

```
ALTER USER myuser PASSWORD 'secret'
```

then it will be shipped to the server in plaintext, though luckily will still be stored in an encrypted form.

PostgreSQL doesn't enforce a password change cycle, so you may wish to use more advanced authentication mechanisms, such as **GSSAPI**, **SSPI**, **LDAP**, **RADIUS**, and so on.

Avoiding hardcoding your password

We all agree that hardcoding your password is a bad idea. This recipe shows us how to keep the password in a secure password file.

Getting ready

Not all database users need passwords; some databases use other means of authentication. Don't do this step unless you know you will be using password authentication, and you know your password.

First, remove the hardcoded password from where you'd set it previously. Completely remove the `password = xxxx` text from the connection string in a program. Otherwise, when you test the password file, the hardcoded setting will override the details you are just about to place in the file. Having the password hardcoded *and* in the password file is not any better.

Using `PGPASSWORD` is not recommended either, so remove that also.

If you think someone may have seen the password, then change your password before placing it in the secure password file.

How to do it...

A password file contains the usual five fields that we need to connect, so that we can use file permissions to make the password more secure:

```
            host:port:dbname:user:password
such as     myhost:5432:postgres:sriggs:moresecure
```

The password file is located using an environment variable named `PGPASSFILE`. If `PGPASSFILE` is not set, then a default filename and location is searched, which:

- ▶ On *nix systems, check for `~/.pgpass`.
- ▶ On Windows systems, check `%APPDATA%\postgresql\pgpass.conf`, where `%APPDATA%` is the Application Data subdirectory in the path. (For me, that would be `C:\`)

Don't forget: Set the file permissions on the file, so that security is maintained. The file permissions are not enforced on Windows, though the default location is secure. On *nix systems, you must issue the following:

```
chmod 0600 ~/.pgpass
```

If you forget to do this, the PostgreSQL client will *ignore* the `.pgpass` file silently. So don't forget!

How it works...

Many people name the password file as `.pgpass`, whether or not they are on Windows, so don't get confused if they do this.

The password file can contain multiple lines. Each line is matched against the requested `host:port:dbname:user` combination until we find a line that matches, and then we use that password.

Each item can be a literal value or `*` a wildcard that matches anything. There is no support for partial matching. With appropriate permissions, a user could potentially connect to any database. Using the wildcard in the dbname and port fields makes sense, though is less useful in other fields.

Here are a few examples:

- `myhost:5432:*:sriggs:moresecurepw`
- `myhost:5432:perf:hannu:okpw`
- `myhost:*:perf:gabriele:maggioresicurezza`

There's more...

This looks like a good improvement if you have a small number of database servers. If you have many different database servers, you may want to think about using a connection service file instead, or perhaps even storing details on an LDAP server.

Using a connection service file

When the number of connection options gets too much, you may want to think about using a **connection service file**.

The connection service file allows you to give a single name to a set of connection parameters. This can be accessed centrally to avoid the need for individual users to know the host and port of the database, and is more resistant to future change.

How to do it...

First, create a file named `pg_service.conf` with the following contents:

```
[dbservice1]
host=postgres1
port=5432
dbname=postgres
```

You can then either copy it into place at `/etc/pg_service.conf` or another agreed central location. You can then set the environment variable `PGSYSCONFDIR` to that directory location.

Now, you can then specify a connection string like the following:

```
service=dbservice1 user=sriggs
```

The service can also be set using an environment variable named `PGSERVICE`.

How it works...

This applies to libpq connections only, so does not apply to JDBC.

The connection service file can also be used to specify the user, though that would mean that the username would be shared.

`pg_service.conf` and `.pgpass` can work together, or you can use just onr or the other, as you choose. Note that the `pg_service.conf` file is shared, and so is not a suitable place for passwords.

Troubleshooting a failed connection

This section is all about what you should do when things go wrong.

Bear in mind that 90% of problems are just misunderstandings, and you'll be on track again fairly quickly.

How to do it...

- ► Check whether the database name and username are accurate: You may be requesting a service on one system when the database you require is on another system. Recheck your credentials. Check especially that you haven't mixed things up so that you are using the database name as the username and/or the username as the database name. If you receive "too many connections", then you may need to disconnect another session before you can connect, or wait for the administrator to re-enable the connections.

- Check for explicit rejections: If you receive the following error message:

  ```
  pg_hba.conf rejects connection for host …
  ```

  then your connection attempt has been explicitly rejected by the database administrator for that server. You will not be able to connect from the current client system using those credentials. There is little point attempting to contact the administrator, as you are violating an explicit security policy in what you are attempting to do.

- Check for implicit rejections: If the error message you receive is:

  ```
  no pg_hba.conf entry for …
  ```

  then there is no explicit rule that matches your credentials. This is likely an oversight on the part of the administrator, and is common in very complex networks. Please contact the administrator, and request a ruling on whether your connection should be allowed (hopefully) or explicitly rejected in the future.

- Check whether the connection works with psql: If you're trying to connect to PostgreSQL from anything other than the psql command-line utility, switch to that now. If you can make psql connect successfully, yet cannot make your main connection work correctly, then the problem *may* be in the local interface you are using.

- Check whether the server is up: If a server is shut down, then you cannot connect. The typical problem here is simply mixing up to which server you are connecting. You need to specify the hostname and port, so it's possible you are mixing up those details.

- Check whether the server is up and accepting new connections: A server that is shutting down will not accept new connections, apart from superusers. Also, a standby server may not have the `hot_standby` parameter enabled, preventing you from connecting.

- Check whether the server is listening correctly.

- Check the port on which the server is actually listening: Confirm that the incoming request is arriving on interface listed in the `listen_addresses` parameter, or whether it is set to * for remote connections, or `localhost` for local connections.

- Check whether the database name and username exist: It's possible the database or user no longer exists.

- Check the connection request: Check whether the connection request was successful, yet was somehow dropped after connection. You can confirm this by looking at the server log when the following parameters are enabled:

  ```
  log_connections = on
  log_disconnections = on
  ```

- Check for other disconnection reasons: If you are connecting to a standby server, it is possible that you have been disconnected because of hot standby conflicts. See the section on *Replication and Upgrades*.

There's more...

Client authentication and security are the rapidly changing areas between releases. You will also find differences between maintenance-release levels.

The PostgreSQL documents can be viewed at the following URL:

```
http://www.postgresql.org/docs/current/interactive/
client-authentication.html
```

Always check which release levels you are using before consulting the manual or asking for support. Many problems are caused simply by confusing the capabilities between release levels.

2
Exploring the Database

This chapter contains the following recipes:

- ► What version is the server?
- ► What is the server uptime?
- ► Locate the database server files
- ► Locate the database server message log
- ► Locate the database's system identifier
- ► List databases on this database server
- ► How many tables in a database?
- ► How much disk space does a database use?
- ► How much disk space does a table use?
- ► Which are my biggest tables?
- ► How many rows in a table?
- ► Fast estimate of rows in a table
- ► Understanding object dependencies

Introduction

To understand PostgreSQL you need to see it in use. An empty database is like a ghost town without houses.

For now, we're going to assume that you've got a database already. There are already a 1000 books on how to design your own database from nothing. So here we aim to help the people who already have access to a PostgreSQL database yet are still learning to use the PostgreSQL database management system.

The best way to start is by asking some simple questions to orientate yourself, and begin the process of understanding. Incidentally, these are also questions you'll need to answer if you ask someone else for help.

What version is the server?

If you experience problems, then you'll need to double-check which version of the server you have. This will help you report a fault or to consult the correct version of the manual.

How to do it...

Connect to the database, and then issue the following:

```
postgres # SELECT version();
```

You'll get a response with something like the following:

```
PostgreSQL 9.0 on x86_64-unknown-linux-gnu,
compiled by GCC gcc (Ubuntu 4.3.3-5ubuntu4) 4.3.3, 64-bit
```

That's probably too much information all at once!

How it works...

PostgreSQL server version's format is **Major.Minor.Maintenance**

In some other software products, the **Major** release number is all you need to know, but with PostgreSQL the feature set and compatibility relates to the **Major.Minor** release level. What that means is that 8.4 contains more additional features and compatibility changes than 8.3. There is also a separate version of the manual, so if something doesn't work exactly the way you think it should, you must consult the *correct* version of the manual.

Maintenance software releases are identified by the full three-part numbering scheme. **8.4.0** was the initial release of **8.4**, and **8.4.1** is a later maintenance release.

The release support policy for PostgreSQL is available at the following URL:

```
http://wiki.postgresql.org/wiki/PostgreSQL_Release_Support_Policy
```

This explains that each release will be supported for a period of 5 years.

All releases up to and including 8.1 will be de-supported as of November 2010. So by the time you're reading this only PostgreSQL 8.2 or higher will be supported. Those early versions are still robust, though many performance and enterprise features will be missing from those releases. Later de-support dates are as follows:

Version	Last supported date
PostgreSQL 8.2	December 2011
PostgreSQL 8.3	February 2013
PostgreSQL 8.4	July 2014
PostgreSQL 9.0	Aug 2015 (approximately)

There's more...

Some other ways of checking the version number are as follows:

```
bash # psql --version
psql (PostgreSQL) 9.0
```

However, be wary that this shows the client software version number that might differ from the server software version number. You check the server version directly using the following:

```
bash # cat $PGDATADIRECTORY/PG_VERSION
```

Although neither of these show the maintenance release number.

Why is the database version important?

PostgreSQL has internal version numbers for the data file format, the database catalog layout, and the crash recovery format. Each of these is checked as the server runs, to ensure that the data isn't corrupted. PostgreSQL doesn't change these internal formats for a single release, they only change across releases.

From a user perspective, each release differs in terms of the way the server behaves. If you know your application well, then it should be possible to assess the differences just by reading the release notes for each version. In many cases, a retest of the application is the safest thing to do.

What is the server uptime?

Or: How long is it since the server started?

How to do it...

Issue the following SQL from any interface:

```
postgres=# SELECT date_trunc('second',
current_timestamp - pg_postmaster_start_time()) as uptime;
   uptime
_____
 00:38:15
```

How it works...

Postgres stores the server start time, so we can access it directly as follows:

```
postgres=# SELECT pg_postmaster_start_time();
   pg_postmaster_start_time
─────────────────────────────
 2009-11-26 09:39:23.354208+00
```

then we can do some SQL to get the uptime as follows:

```
postgres=# SELECT current_timestamp - pg_postmaster_start_time();
   ?column?
───────────────
 00:35:30.22868
```

and then do some formatting, such as:

```
postgres=# SELECT date_trunc('second',
current_timestamp - pg_postmaster_start_time()) as uptime;
  uptime
──────────
 00:38:15
```

See Also

This is just simple stuff. Further monitoring and statistics are covered in later chapters.

Locate the database server files

Database server files are initially stored in a location referred to as the `data directory`. Additional data files may also be stored in `tablespaces`, if any exist.

Getting ready

You'll need to get an operating system access to the database system, which is what we call the platform on which the database runs.

How to do it...

On **Debian** or **Ubuntu** systems, the default data directory location is as follows:

▶ `/var/lib/postgresql/R.r/main`

Here, `R.r` is the major and minor release number of the database server software, such as 9.0. The configuration files are located in:

- `/etc/postgresql/R.rNn/main/`

In both cases, `main` is just the name of a database server. Other names are also possible. For the sake of simplicity, the rest of the book assumes that you have only a single installation.

On **Red Hat RHEL**, **CentOS**, or **Fedora** the default data directory location is as follows:

- `/var/lib/pgsql/data/`

This also contains, by default, the configuration files (`*.conf`).

Again, `data` is just the default location. You can create additional data directories by using the `initdb` utility.

On Windows and OS X, the default data directory location is as follows:

- `C:\Program Files\PostgreSQL\R.r\data`

How it works...

Even though the Debian/Ubuntu and Red Hat file layouts are different, they both follow the Linux **Filesystem Hierarchy Standard** (**FHS**), so neither layout is *wrong*.

The **Red Hat** layout is simpler and easier to understand. The Debian/Ubuntu layout is more complex, though it has different and more adventurous goals. The Debian/Ubuntu layout is similar to the **Optimal Flexible Architecture** (**OFA**) of other database systems. The goals are to provide a file layout that will allow you to have multiple PostgreSQL database servers on one system, and to allow many versions of the software to exist at once in the filesystem.

The layout for the Windows and OS X installers is different again. Multiple database clusters are possible, but are also more complex than on Debian/Ubuntu.

I recommend that you follow the Debian/Ubuntu layout, on whichever platform you are using. It doesn't really have a name, so I call it the **PostgreSQL Flexible Architecture** (**PFA**). If you do this, you'll need to lay things out yourself, but it does pay off in the long run. PFA uses the following environment variables to name parts of the file layout:

- export PGROOT=/var/lib/pgsql/
- export PGRELEASE=9.0
- export PGSERVERNAME=mamba
- export PGDATADIR=$PGROOT/$PGRELEASE/$PGSERVERNAME
- example, PGDATADIR is /var/lib/pgsql/9.0/mamba

There's more...

Once you've located the data directory, you can look for the files that comprise the PostgreSQL database server. The layout is as follows:

Subdirectory	Purpose
base	Main data directory. Beneath this directory each database has its own directory within which are the files for each database table or index.
global	Database server catalog tables that are shared across all databases.
pg_clog	Transaction status files.
pg_multixact	Row-level lock status files
pg_subtrans	Subtransaction status files
pg_tblspc	Links to external tablespaces
pg_twophase	"2-phase commit", or Prepared transaction status
pg_xlog	Transaction log (or Write Ahead Log - WAL)

None of the aforementioned directories contain user-modifiable files, nor should any of the files be manually deleted, to save space or for any reason. Don't touch it, because you'll break it, and you may not be able to fix it. It's not even sensible to copy files in those directories without carefully following the procedures described in the *Backup* chapter. Keep Off the Grass!

We'll talk about table spaces again elsewhere in the Cookbook. We'll also discuss a performance enhancement, which is to put the transaction log on its own set of disk drives (that's covered in the *Performance* chapter).

The only things you are allowed to touch are Configuration files, which are all `*.conf` files, or Server message log files. Server message log files may or may not be in the data directory.

Locate the database server message log

The database server log is the record of all messages recorded by the database server. This is the first place to look if you have server problems, and a good place to check regularly.

It will have messages in it that look something like the following:

```
2010-01-19 21:23:52 GMT LOG:  database system was not properly shut
down; automatic recovery in progress
2010-01-19 21:23:52 GMT LOG:  record with zero length at 0/49AF90
2010-01-19 21:23:52 GMT LOG:  redo is not required
2010-01-19 21:23:52 GMT LOG:  autovacuum launcher started
```

```
2010-01-19 21:23:52 GMT LOG:   database system is ready to accept
connections
```

We'll explain some more about it once we've located the files.

Getting ready

You'll need to get operating system access to the database system, which is what we call the platform on which the database runs.

How to do it...

The server log can be in a few different places, so first let's list all of those, so that we can locate the log, or decide where we want it to be placed:

- ► Server log may be in a directory beneath the data directory
- ► Server log may be in a directory elsewhere on the file system
- ► Server log may be redirected to **syslog**
- ► There may be no server log at all – time to add one soon

If not redirected to syslog, the server log consists of one or more files. You can change the name of these files, so it may not always be the same on every system.

On Debian or Ubuntu systems the default server log location is as follows:

- ► `/var/log/postgresql`

The current server log file is named `postgresql-N.n-main.log`, where `N.n` is the major and minor release number of the server, for example 9.0. Older log files are numbered as `postgresql-8.3-main.log.1`, the higher the number, the older the file.

On Red Hat, RHEL, CentOS, or Fedora the default server log location is a subdirectory of the data directory as follows:

- ► `/var/lib/pgsql/data/pg_log`

On Windows systems the messages are sent to the Windows Eventlog by default.

How it works...

The server log is just a file that records messages from the server. Each message has a severity level, the most typical one being LOG, though there are others, as shown in the following table:

PostgreSQL Severity	Meaning	Syslog Severity	Windows eventlog
DEBUG 1 through DEBUG 5	Internal diagnostics	DEBUG	INFORMATION
INFO	Command output for user	INFO	INFORMATION
NOTICE	Helpful information	NOTICE	INFORMATION
WARNING	Warns of likely problems	NOTICE	WARNING
ERROR	Current command aborted	WARNING	ERROR
LOG	For sysadmins	INFO	INFORMATION
FATAL	Event that disconnects one session only	ERR	ERROR
PANIC	Event that crashes server	CRIT	ERROR

Watch for FATALs and PANICs. They shouldn't happen in most cases during normal server operation, apart from certain cases related to Replication, so check out that chapter also.

You can adjust the number of messages that appear in the log by changing the `log_min_messages` server parameter. You can also change the amount of information that is displayed for each event by changing the `log_error_verbosity`. If the messages are sent to a standard log file, then each line in the log will have a prefix of useful information that can also be controlled by the system administrator, named `log_line_prefix`. Locate the database's system identifier???

Each database server has a system identifier assigned when the database is initialized (created). The server identifier remains the same if the server is backed up, cloned, and so on.

Many actions on the server are keyed to the system identifier, and you may be asked to provide this information when you report a fault.

Getting ready

Connect as the postgres OS user, or another user with execute privileges on the server software.

How to do it...

```
pg_controldata <data-directory> | grep "system identifier"
Database system identifier:        5558338346489861223
```

 Don't use -D in front of the data directory name. This is the only PostgreSQL server application where you don't need to do that.

How it works...

pg_controldata is a PostgreSQL server application that shows the contents of a server's control file. The control file is located within the data directory of a server, and is created at database initialization time. Some of the information within it is updated regularly, or when certain major events occur.

The full output of pg_controldata looks like the following. (The bold values are ones that may change over time as the server runs):

```
pg_control version number:              851
Catalog version number:                 200911051
Database system identifier:             5408338346412861210
Database cluster state:                 in production
pg_control last modified:               Thu 26 Nov 2009 09:39:23
GMT
Latest checkpoint location:             0/53D8E0
Prior checkpoint location:              0/53D840
Latest checkpoint's REDO location:      0/53D8E0
Latest checkpoint's TimeLineID:         1
Latest checkpoint's NextXID:            0/649
Latest checkpoint's NextOID:            11565
Latest checkpoint's NextMultiXactId:    1
Latest checkpoint's NextMultiOffset     0
Latest checkpoint's oldestXID:          641
Latest checkpoint's oldestXID's DB:     1
Time of latest checkpoint:              Thu 26 Nov 2009 09:15:02 GMT
Minimum recovery ending location:       0/0
Maximum data alignment:                 8
Database block size:                    8192
Blocks per segment of large relation:   131072
WAL block size:                         8192
Bytes per WAL segment:                  16777216
Maximum length of identifiers:          64
Maximum columns in an index:            32
```

```
Maximum size of a TOAST chunk:          1996
Date/time type storage:                 64-bit integers
Float4 argument passing:                by value
Float8 argument passing:                by value
```

There's more...

Never, ever edit the PostgreSQL control file. If you do, the server probably won't start correctly, or you may mask other errors. If you do, people will be able to tell, so fess up as soon as possible!!!

List databases on this database server?

When we connect to PostgreSQL, we always connect to just one specific database on any database server. If there are many databases on a single server, it can get confusing, so sometimes you just want to find out which databases are part of the database server.

It's also confusing because we can use the word database in two different but related contexts. Initially, we start off by thinking that PostgreSQL is a "database" in which we put data, referring to the whole database server just as the word "database". In PostgreSQL, a database server is potentially split into multiple individual databases, so as you get more used to working with PostgreSQL, you'll start to separate the two concepts.

Also note that in some other RDBMS, such as SQLServer, the term "database" is more similar to a "schema" in PostgreSQL.

How to do it...

If you have access to `psql` you can type the following command:

```
bash $ psql -l
                        List of databases
    Name     | Owner  | Encoding |  Collation   |    Ctype     | Access
privileges
-----------+--------+----------+--------------+--------------+---------
----------
  postgres  | sriggs | UTF8     | en_GB.UTF-8  | en_GB.UTF-8  |
  template0 | sriggs | UTF8     | en_GB.UTF-8  | en_GB.UTF-8  | =c/sriggs
+
            |        |          |              |              |
sriggs=CTc/sriggs
  template1 | sriggs | UTF8     | en_GB.UTF-8  | en_GB.UTF-8  | =c/sriggs
+
            |        |          |              |              |
sriggs=CTc/sriggs
(3 rows)
```

You can also get the same information when running `psql` by just typing `\l`

The information at which we just looked is stored in a PostgreSQL catalog table named `pg_database`. We can issue an SQL query directly against that table from any connection to get a simpler result as follows:

```
postgres=# select datname from pg_database;
  datname
-----------
  template1
  template0
  postgres
(3 rows)
```

How it works...

PostgreSQL starts with 3 databases, namely, template0, template1, and **postgres.** The main user database is postgres.

You can create your own databases as well, using the following:

```
CREATE DATABASE my_database;
```

or you can do that from the command line using:

```
bash $ createdb my_database
```

After you've created your databases, make sure you secure them properly as discussed in the *Security* chapter.

When you create another database it actually takes a *copy* of an existing database. Once created, there is no further link between the two databases.

Template0 and template1 are known as template databases. Template1 can be changed to allow you to create a localized template for any new databases that you create. Template0 exists so that when you alter Template1 you still have a pristine copy on which to fall back.

You can drop the database named postgres. But don't, OK? Similarly, don't touch template0. Template1 exists to be modified, so feel free to change that.

There's more...

The information at which we just looked is stored in a PostgreSQL catalog table named `pg_database`. We can look at this directly to get some more information. In some ways the output is less useful as well, as we need to look up some of the codes in other tables:

```
postgres=# \x
postgres=# select * from pg_database;
-[ RECORD 1 ]-+-----------------------------
datname       | template1
datdba        | 10
encoding      | 6
datcollate    | en_GB.UTF-8
datctype      | en_GB.UTF-8
datistemplate | t
datallowconn  | t
datconnlimit  | -1
datlastsysoid | 11620
datfrozenxid  | 644
dattablespace | 1663
datacl        | {=c/sriggs,sriggs=CTc/sriggs}
-[ RECORD 2 ]-+-----------------------------
datname       | template0
datdba        | 10
encoding      | 6
datcollate    | en_GB.UTF-8
datctype      | en_GB.UTF-8
datistemplate | t
datallowconn  | f
datconnlimit  | -1
datlastsysoid | 11620
datfrozenxid  | 644
dattablespace | 1663
datacl        | {=c/sriggs,sriggs=CTc/sriggs}
-[ RECORD 3 ]-+-----------------------------
datname       | postgres
datdba        | 10
encoding      | 6
datcollate    | en_GB.UTF-8
datctype      | en_GB.UTF-8
datistemplate | f
datallowconn  | t
datconnlimit  | -1
datlastsysoid | 11620
datfrozenxid  | 644
dattablespace | 1663
datacl        |
```

First of all, look at the use of the `\x` command. That makes the output in `psql` appear as one column per line, rather than one row per line.

This output raises many questions, I know. We've discussed templates already. Other interesting things are that we can turn connections on and off for a database, and we can set connection limits for them as well.

Also, you can see that each database has a default tablespace. So, data tables get created inside one specific database, and the data files for that table get placed in one tablespace.

We can also see that each database has a collation sequence, which is the way various language features are defined. More on that in other sections.

How many tables in a database?

The number of tables in a relational database is a good measure of the complexity of a database, so it is a simple way to get to know any database.

How to do it...

From any interface, type in the following SQL command:

```
SELECT count(*) FROM information_schema.tables
WHERE table_schema NOT IN ('information_schema',
                           'pg_catalog');
```

You can also look at the list of tables directly and judge whether that is a small or large number.

In psql, you can see your own tables using the following:

```
postgres@ebony:~/8.3/main$ psql -c "\d"
          List of relations
 Schema  |   Name    | Type  |  Owner
---------+-----------+-------+----------
 public  | accounts  | table | postgres
 public  | branches  | table | postgres
```

or in pgadmin3 you can see the tables in the tree view on the right-hand side as shown in the following screenshot:.

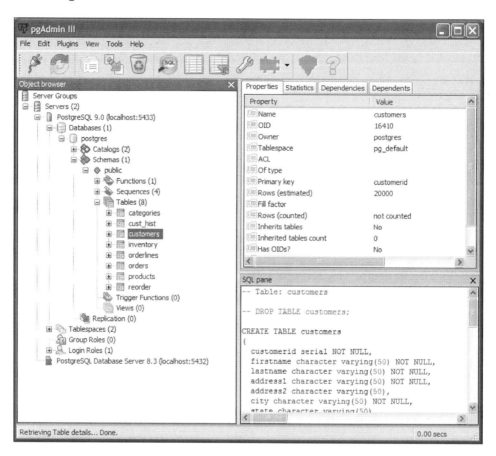

How it works...

PostgreSQL stores information about the database in "catalog tables", which describe every aspect of the way the database has been defined. There is a main set of catalog tables stored in a schema, named pg_catalog. There is a second set of catalog objects named the Information Schema, which are the SQL standard way of accessing information in a relational database. We want to exclude both of those schemas from our query, otherwise we'll get too much information. We excluded those in the preceding query using the NOT IN phrase in the WHERE clause.

Note that this query only shows you the number of rows in one of the databases on the PostgreSQL server. You can only see the tables in the database to which you are currently connected, so you would need to run the same query on each database in turn.

There's more...

As I said, the number of tables in a relational database is a good measure of the complexity. Complexity of what? Well, a complex database might be designed to be deliberately flexible in order to cover a variety of business situations, or a complex business process might have a limited portion of its details covered in the database. So, a large number of tables might reveal a complex business process or maybe just a complex piece of software.

The most distinct major tables I've ever seen in a database is 20,000, not counting partitions, views, or work tables. That clearly rates as a very complex system.

Number of distinct tables ("entities")	Complexity rating
20,000	Incredibly complex. You're either counting wrong or you have a big team to manage this
2,000	Complex business database, not many seen
200	Typical modern business database
20	Simple business database
2	Database with a single clear purpose, tightly designed for performance or some other goal
0	You haven't loaded any data yet...

Of course, you can't always easily tell which tables are entities, so we need to just count the tables. Some databases use a lot of partitions, or similar tables, so the numbers can grow beyond that dramatically. I've seen databases with up to 200,000 tables (of any kind). That's not recommended though, as the database catalog tables then begin to be non-trivially large.

How much disk space does a database use?

For planning or space monitoring, we often need to know how big the database is.

How to do it...

We can do this in the following two ways:

▸ Look at the size of the files that make up the database server
▸ Run an SQL request to confirm database size

If you look at the size of the actual files, you'll need to make sure that you include the data directory and all subdirectories, as well as all other directories that contain tablespaces. That can be tricky, and it is also difficult to break out all the different pieces.

The easiest way is to just ask the database a simple query, such as the following:

```
SELECT pg_database_size(current_database());
```

However, this is limited to only the current database. If you want to find out the size of all databases together, then you'll need a query such as the following:

```
SELECT sum(pg_database_size(datname)) from pg_database;
```

How it works...

The database server knows which tables it has loaded. It also knows how to calculate the size of each table, so the `pg_database_size()` function just goes and looks at the filesizes.

How much disk space does a table use?

How big is a table? What is the total of all the parts of a table?

How to do it...

We can find out the size of a table using the following query:

```
postgres=# select pg_relation_size('accounts');
 pg_relation_size
------------------
                0
(1 row)
```

We can also find out the total size of a table including indexes and other related space using the following query:

```
postgres=# select pg_total_relation_size('accounts');
 pg_total_relation_size
------------------------
                      0
(1 row)
```

or we can also use a psql command as follows:

```
postgres=# \dt+ accounts
                        List of relations Schema |      Name
 | Type  | Owner  | Size    | Description ------------+---------------
--------+--------+---------+----------+--------------- public    |
 pgbench_accounts | table  | sriggs  | 13 MB |
(1 row)
```

How it works...

In PostgreSQL, a table is made up of many "relations". The main relation is the data table. In addition, there are a variety of additional data files. Each index created on a table is also a relation. Long data values are placed in a secondary table named a TOAST table, so in most cases, each table also has a TOAST table and a TOAST index.

Each relation consists of multiple data files. The main data files are broken up into 1 GB pieces. The first file has no suffix, others have a numbered suffix (such as .2). There are also files marked .vm and .fsm, which represent the Visibility Map and FreeSpaceMap respectively. Those are used as part of maintenance operations. They stay fairly small, even for very large tables.

There's more...

TOAST stands for The Outsized Attribute Storage Technique. As the name implies, it's a mechanism for storing long column values. PostgreSQL allows many data types to store values up to 1 GB in size. PostgreSQL transparently stores large data items in many smaller pieces, so the same data type can be used for data from 1 byte to 1 GB.

Which are my biggest tables?

We've looked at how to get the size of a specific table, so now it's time to widen the problem to related areas. Rather than an absolute value for a specific table, let's look at the relative sizes.

How to do it...

The following basic query will tell us the "Top 10 Biggest Tables":

```
SELECT     table_name
                 ,pg_relation_size(table_name) as size
FROM information_schema.tables
WHERE table_schema NOT IN ('information_schema',
                 'pg_catalog')
ORDER BY size DESC
LIMIT 10;
```

Tables are shown in descending order of size, with at most 10 rows displayed. In this case, we look at all tables in all schemas, apart from tables in the information_schema or in pg_catalog. These latter two schemas are the locations where Postgres keeps its own internal data.

How many rows in a table?

Counting is one of the easiest SQL statements, so it is also many people's first experience of a Postgres query.

How to do it...

From any interface the SQL command is, as follows:

```
SELECT count(*) FROM table;
```

which returns a single integer value as the result.

In psql this looks like the following:

```
postgres=# select count(*) from orders;
 count
--------
   345
(1 row)
```

How it works...

The SQL `count(*)` function will scan every row in the table using a technique named a Sequential Scan. We access every data block in the table one after the other, reading the number of rows in each block. If the table is on disk, then this will cause a beneficial disk access pattern, and the statement will be fairly fast.

Some people think that the count SQL statement is a good test of the performance of a database management system (DBMS). Some DBMS have specific tuning features for the `count` SQL statement, though Postgres does not optimizes this SQL. The PostgreSQL project has talked about this many times, but few people think we should try to optimize this. Yes, the "count" function is frequently used within applications, but the count function without any WHERE clause is not that useful. So, we have not yet chosen to optimize this form of SQL specifically.

The reason we scan every block of the table is because of a major feature of Postgres named **MVCC**, which stands for **Multi-Version Concurrency Control**. MVCC allows us to run the count SQL statement at the same time that we are inserting, updating, or deleting data from the table. That's a very cool feature, and we go into a lot of trouble in Postgres to provide that to you.

MVCC requires us to record information on each row of a table, stating when that change was made. If the changes were made after the SQL statement begins to execute, then we just ignore those changes. This means that we need to make "visibility checks" on each row in the table to allow us to work out the result to the `count` SQL statement.

If you think a little deeper about this, you'll see that the result of the count SQL statement is just the value at a moment in time. Depending on what happens to the table, that value could change a little, or a lot, while the count SQL statement is executing. So, once you've executed this, all you really know is that at some point in the *past* there were "X" rows in the table.

Quick estimate of the number of rows in a table

We don't always want an exactly accurate count of rows, especially on a large table, since that may take a long time to execute. Administrators often need to estimate how big a table is so that they can estimate how long other operations may take.

How to do it...

We can get a quick estimate of the number of rows in a table by using roughly the same calculation that the Postgres optimizer uses:

```
SELECT (CASE WHEN reltuples > 0 THEN
            pg_relation_size('mytable')/(8192*relpages/reltuples)
        ELSE 0
        END)::bigint AS estimated_row_count
FROM pg_class
WHERE oid = 'mytable'::regclass;
```

which gives:

```
 estimated_count
─────────────────
             293
(1 row)
```

which returns a row count very quickly, no matter how large the table that we are examining is.

How it works...

We saw the `pg_relation_size()` function earlier, so we know it brings back an accurate value for the current size of the table.

When we **vacuum** a table in Postgres, we record two pieces of information in the `pg_class` catalog entry for the table. These two items are the number of data blocks in the table (relpages) and the number of rows in the table (reltuples). Some people think they can use the value of relpages in pg_class as an estimate, but if you use that it could be severely out of date. You will also be fooled if you use information in another table named `pg_stat_user_tables`, which is discussed more in the chapter *Performance*.

The Postgres optimizer uses the relpages and the reltuples values to calculate the average rows per block, also known as the average tuple density.

If we assume that the average tuple density remains constant over time, then we can calculate the number of rows by using the following formula:

Row Estimate = Number of Data Blocks * Rows per Block

We put in a little code to handle the case that the `reltuples` or `relpages` fields are zero. The Postgres optimizer actually works a little harder than we do in that case, so our estimate isn't a very good one.

There's more...

The good thing about the aforementioned recipe is that it returns a value in about the same time no matter how big the table is. The bad thing about it is that `pg_relation_size()` requests a lock on the table, and so if any other user has an `AccessExclusiveLock` on the table, then the table size estimate will wait for the lock to be released before returning a value.

Err... so what is an AccessExclusiveLock? When an SQL maintenance action, such as changing the datatype of a column, PostgreSQL will lock out all other actions on that table. The typical case for me is where I issue some form of SQL maintenance action, such as an **ALTER TABLE**, and then the statement takes much longer than I thought it would. At that point, I think, "Oh, was that table bigger than I thought? How long will I be waiting?". Yes, it's better to calculate that beforehand, but hindsight doesn't get you out of the hole you are in right now. So we need a way to calculate the size of a table without needing the lock.

So my solution is to look at the operating system files that Postgres uses to store data, and figure out how large they are.

Now, this can get somewhat difficult. If the table is locked, it's probably doing something to the table, and so trying to look at the files might well be fruitless, or might give wrong answers. Anyway, here goes:

First, get some details on the table from `pg_class`

```
SELECT reltablespace, relfilenode FROM pg_class
WHERE oid = 'orders'::regclass;
```

Second, confirm the `databaseid` in which the table resides

```
SELECT oid as databaseid FROM pg_database
WHERE datname = current_database();
```

Together `reltablespace`, `databaseid`, and `relfilenode` are the three things we need to locate the underlying data files within the data directory.

If `tablespaceid` is zero, then the files will be

```
$PGDATADIR/base/{databaseid}/{relfilenode}*
```

The bigger the table, the more files you'll see.

If `reltablespace` is not zero then the files will be in:

```
$PGDATADIR/pg_tblspc/{reltablespace}/
{databaseid}/{relfilenode}*
```

Each file should be 1GB in size, apart from the last file.

The preceding discussion glossed over a few other points, as follows:

- Postgres uses the terms data blocks and pages to refer to the same concept. Postgres also does that with the terms tuple and row.
- A datablock is 8192 bytes in size, by default, though you can change that if you re-compile the server yourself, and create a new database.

Function 1

You may want to create an SQL function for this calculation, so you won't need to re-type it constantly.

```
CREATE OR REPLACE FUNCTION estimated_row_count(text)
RETURNS bigint
LANGUAGE sql
AS $$
SELECT (CASE WHEN reltuples > 0 THEN
            pg_relation_size($1)/(8192*relpages/reltuples)
        ELSE 0
        END)::bigint
FROM pg_class
WHERE oid = $1::regclass;
$$;
```

Function 2

```
CREATE OR REPLACE FUNCTION
    pg_relation_size_nolock(tablename regclass)
RETURNS BIGINT
LANGUAGE plpgsql
AS $$
DECLARE
    classoutput   RECORD;
    tsid          INTEGER;
    rid           INTEGER;
    dbid          INTEGER;
    filepath      TEXT;
```

```
    filename      TEXT;
    datadir       TEXT;
    i             INTEGER := 0;
    tablesize     BIGINT;
BEGIN
  --
  -- get data directory
  --
  EXECUTE 'SHOW data_directory' INTO datadir;
  --
  -- get relfilenode and reltablespace
  --
  SELECT
   reltablespace as tsid
  ,relfilenode as rid
          INTO classoutput
  FROM pg_class
  WHERE oid = tablename
  AND relkind = 'r';
  --
  -- Throw an error if we can't find the tablename specified
  --
  IF NOT FOUND THEN
          RAISE EXCEPTION 'tablename % not found', tablename;
  END IF;
  tsid := classoutput.tsid;
  rid := classoutput.rid;
  --
  -- get the database object identifier (oid)
  --
  SELECT oid INTO dbid
  FROM pg_database
  WHERE datname = current_database();
  --
  -- Use some internals knowledge to set the filepath
  --
  IF tsid = 0 THEN
          filepath := datadir || '/base/' || dbid || '/' || rid;
  ELSE
          filepath := datadir || '/pg_tblspc/'
                              || tsid || '/'
                              || dbid || '/'
                              || rid;
  END IF;
```

```
    --
    -- Look for the first file. Report if missing
    --
    SELECT (pg_stat_file(filepath)).size
    INTO tablesize;
    --
    -- Sum the sizes of additional files, if any
    --
    WHILE FOUND LOOP
        i := i + 1;
        filename := filepath || '.' || i;
        --
        -- pg_stat_file returns ERROR if it cannot see file
        -- so we must trap the error and exit loop
        --
        BEGIN
            SELECT tablesize + (pg_stat_file(filename)).size
            INTO tablesize;
        EXCEPTION
            WHEN OTHERS THEN
                EXIT;
        END;
    END LOOP;
    RETURN tablesize;
END;
$$;
```

which can also work on Windows with a few minor changes, left as an exercise for the reader.

Understanding object dependencies

In most databases, there will be dependencies between objects in the database. Sometimes, we need to understand those dependencies to figure out how to perform certain actions. Let's look at this in detail.

Getting ready

We'll use the following simple database to understand the issues and to investigate them. There are two tables, as follows:

```
CREATE TABLE orders (
orderid integer PRIMARY KEY
);
```

```
CREATE TABLE orderlines (
  orderid   integer
,lineid    smallint
,PRIMARY KEY (orderid, lineid)
);
```

Now we add a link between them, to enforce what is known as "Referential Integrity" as follows:

```
ALTER TABLE orderlines ADD FOREIGN KEY (orderid)
REFERENCES orders (orderid);
```

If we try to DROP the "referenced" table, we get the following message:

```
DROP TABLE orders;
ERROR: cannot drop table orders because other objects depend on it
DETAIL: constraint orderlines_orderid_fkey on table orderlines depends
on table orders
HINT: Use DROP ... CASCADE to drop the dependent objects too.
```

Be very careful! If you follow the hint, you could accidentally remove all the objects that have any dependency on the orders table. You might think that would be a great idea, but to me it seems lazy and foolish. It might work, but we need to make sure it will work.

So we need to know what dependencies there are on the orders table, and then review them. Then we can decide whether it is OK to issue the CASCADE version of the command, or whether we should reconcile the situation manually.

How to do it...

You can use the following command from psql to display full information about a table, the constraints that are defined upon it, and the constraints that reference it.

```
\d+ orders
```

You can also get the specific details of the constraints by using the following query:

```
SELECT * FROM pg_constraint
WHERE confrelid = 'orders'::regclass;
```

Unfortunately, that's not the end of the story, so read the *There's More* section also.

How it works...

When we create a Foreign Key, we add a constraint to the catalog table known as `pg_constraint`. So the query shows us how to find out all of the constraints that depend upon the `orders` table.

The syntax:

```
WHERE confrelid = 'orders'::regclass;
```

introduces the concept of object identifier types. They are just a short-hand trick for converting from the name of an object through to the object identifier number for that object. The best way to understand this is if you think of that syntax as meaning the same thing as a function named `relname2relid()`.

There's more...

With Postgres, there's always a little more when you look beneath the surface. In this case, there's a lot more, and it's important.

The aforementioned queries only covered constraints between tables. We didn't discuss dependencies with other kinds of objects. Two important types of objects that might have dependencies to tables are Views and Functions.

If you issue the following:

```
DROP TABLE orders;
```

the dependency on any of the views will prevent the table from being dropped. Thus, you can then remove those views, and then drop the table.

The story with function dependencies is not as useful. Relationships between functions and tables are not recorded in the catalog, nor is dependency information between functions and functions. This is partly due to the fact that most function languages allow dynamic query execution, so you wouldn't be able to tell which tables or functions that a function would access until it executes. That's only partly the reason why most functions clearly reference other tables and functions, so it ought to be possible to identify and store those dependencies. However, right now, we don't do that. So make a note that you need to record the dependency information for your functions manually, so that you'll know when and if it's OK to remove or alter a table or other objects the functions depend upon.

3
Configuration

In this chapter, we will cover the following:

- ▶ Reading the Fine Manual (RTFM)
- ▶ Planning a new database
- ▶ Changing parameters in your programs
- ▶ The current configuration settings
- ▶ Parameters that are at non-default settings
- ▶ Updating the parameter file
- ▶ Setting parameters for particular groups of users
- ▶ Basic server configuration checklist
- ▶ Adding an external module into PostgreSQL server
- ▶ Running server in power saving mode

Introduction

I get asked many questions about parameter settings in PostgreSQL.

Everybody's busy and most people want the five minute tour of how things work. That's exactly what a Cookbook does, so we'll do our best.

Some people believe that there are some magic parameter settings that will improve their performance, spending hours combing the pages of books to glean insights. Others already feel comfortable because they found some website somewhere that "explains everything", and they "know" they have their database configured OK.

For the most part, the settings are easy to understand. Finding the best setting can be difficult, and the optimal setting may change over time in some cases. This section is mostly about knowing how, when, and where to change parameter settings.

Reading the Fine Manual (RTFM)

RTFM is often used rudely, meaning "don't bother me, I'm busy", or is used as a stronger form of abuse. The strange thing is that asking you to read the manual is most often very good advice. Don't flame them back, take the advice. The most important point to remember is that you should refer to a manual whose release version matches the server on which you are operating

The PostgreSQL manual is very well written, and is comprehensive in its coverage of specific topics. One of its main failings is that the "documents" aren't organized in a way that helps somebody who is trying to learn PostgreSQL. They are organized from the perspective of people checking specific technical points, so that they can decide whether their difficulty is user error or not. It sometimes answers "What?", but seldom "Why?', or 'How?"

I've helped write sections of the PostgreSQL documents as well, so I'm not embarrassed to steer you towards reading them. There are still many things to read here that are useful.

How to do it...

The main documents for each release are available at the following website:

```
http://www.postgresql.org/docs/manuals/
```

The most frequently accessed parts of the documents are as follows:

- ▶ SQL Command Reference, Client, and Server tools reference (`http://www.postgresql.org/docs/9.0/interactive/reference.html`)
- ▶ Configuration (`http://www.postgresql.org/docs/9.0/interactive/runtime-config.html`)
- ▶ Functions (`http://www.postgresql.org/docs/9.0/interactive/functions.html`)

You can also grab yourself a PDF version of the manual, which can allow easier searching in some cases. Don't print it! The documents are more than 2000 pages of A4-size sheets.

How it works...

The PostgreSQL documents are written in SGML, which is similar to, but not quite XML. These files are then processed to generate HTML or PDFs, and so on.

There's more...

There's a Wiki site on `postgresql.org` that is worth a look at as well. More information is also available at `http://wiki.postgresql.org`

Planning a new database

Planning a new database can be a daunting task. It's easy to get overwhelmed by it, so here we present some planning ideas. It's also easy to charge headlong at the task as well, thinking that the parts you know are all the things you'll ever need to consider.

Getting ready

You are ready. Don't wait to be told what to do. If you haven't been told what the requirements are, then write down what you think they are, clearly labeling them as "Assumptions" rather than "Requirements"—we mustn't confuse the two things.

Iterate until you get some agreement, and then build a prototype.

How to do it...

Write a document that covers the following items:

- **Database design**: Plan your database design.
    - Calculate the initial database sizing
- **Transaction analysis**: How will we access the database?
    - Look at the most frequent access paths
    - What are the requirements for response times?
- **Hardware configuration**
    - Initial performance thoughts—will all data fit into RAM?
- **Localization plan**
    - Decide server encoding, locale, and time zone
- **Access and security plan**
    - Identify client systems and specify required drivers
    - Create roles according to a plan for access control
    - Specify `pg_hba.conf`
- **Maintenance plan**: Who will keep it working? How?
- **Availability plan**: Consider the Availability requirements
    - `checkpoint_timeout`
    - Plan your backup mechanism, and test them

▶ **High-availability plan**

      ❑ Decide what form of replication you'll need, if any

How it works...

One of the most important reasons for planning your database ahead of time is that retrofitting some things is difficult. This is especially true of server encoding and locale, which can cause much downtime and exertion if we need to change them later. Security is also much more difficult to set up after the system is live.

There's more...

Planning always helps. You may know what you're doing, but others may not. Tell everybody what you're going to do before you do it, to avoid wasting time. If you're not sure yet, then build a prototype to help decide—approach the administration framework as if it were a development task. Make a list of things you don't know yet, and work through them, one by one.

This is deliberately a very short recipe. Everybody has their own way of doing things, and it's very important not to be too prescriptive about how to do things. If you already have a plan, great. If you don't, think about what you need to do, make a checklist, and then do it.

Changing parameters in your programs

PostgreSQL allows you to set some parameter settings for each session or for each transaction.

How to do it...

You can change the value of a setting during your session, such as the following:

```
SET work_mem = '16MB';
```

This value will then be used for every future transaction. You can also change it only for the duration of the "current transaction"

```
SET LOCAL work_mem = '16MB';
```

The setting will last until or if you issue the following:

```
RESET work_mem;
```
or
```
RESET ALL;
```

SET and RESET are SQL commands that can be issued from any interface. They apply only to PostgreSQL *server* parameters, by which we mean parameters that affect the server, but not necessarily the whole server. There may be other parameters, such as JDBC driver parameters, that cannot be set in this way. Refer to the *Connections* chapter for help with those.

How it works...

When you change the value of a setting during your session, such as:

```
SET work_mem = '16MB';
```

then this will show up in the catalog view pg_settings as follows:

```
postgres=# SELECT name, setting, reset_val, source
                  FROM pg_settings WHERE source = 'session';
   name     | setting | reset_val | source
----------+---------+-----------+---------
 work_mem | 16384   | 1024      | session
```

until you issue:

```
RESET work_mem;
```

after which the setting returns to the reset_val, and the source returns to default.

```
   name     | setting | reset_val | source
---------+---------+-----------+---------
 work_mem | 1024    | 1024      | default
```

There's more...

You can change the value of a setting during your transaction as well, as follows:

```
SET LOCAL work_mem = '16MB';
```

then this will show up in the catalog view pg_settings as follows:

```
postgres=# SELECT name, setting, reset_val
                  FROM pg_settings WHERE source = 'session';
   name     | setting | reset_val | source
----------+---------+-----------+---------
 work_mem |  1024   | 1024      | session
```

Huh? What happened to my parameter setting? SET LOCAL takes effect only for the transaction in which it was executed, which, in our case, was just the SET LOCAL command. We need to execute it inside a transaction block to be able to see the setting take hold as follows:

```
BEGIN;
SET LOCAL work_mem = '16MB';
```

then this will show up in the catalog view `pg_settings` as follows:

```
postgres=# SELECT name, setting, reset_val, source
                 FROM pg_settings WHERE source = 'session';
    name    | setting | reset_val | source
-----------+---------+-----------+---------
 work_mem  | 16384   | 1024      | session
```

You should also note that the value of source is "session" rather than "transaction", as you might have been expecting.

What are the current configuration settings?

At some point it will occur to you to ask, "What are the *current* configuration settings?"

How to do it...

Your first thought is probably "look in `postgresql.conf`". That works, but only as long as there is only one parameter file. If there are two, then maybe you're reading the wrong file! (How do you know?). So the cautious and accurate way is not to trust a text file, but to trust the server itself.

Also, we learned in the recipe *When to set parameters* that each parameter has a scope that determines when it can be set. Some parameters can be set through `postgresql.conf`, but others can be changed afterwards also. So the current value of configuration settings may have been subsequently changed.

We can use the SHOW command, such as the following:

```
postgres=# SHOW work_mem;
work_mem
----------
1MB
(1 row)
```

though remember that it reports the current setting at the time when it is run, and that can be changed in many places.

Another way of finding current settings is to access a PostgreSQL catalog view named `pg_settings`.

```
postgres=# \x
Expanded display is on.
postgres=# SELECT * FROM pg_settings WHERE name = 'work_mem';
[ RECORD 1 ] -------------------------------------------------
----
name          | work_mem
```

```
setting      | 1024
unit         | kB
category     | Resource Usage / Memory
short_desc   | Sets the maximum memory to be used for query workspaces.
extra_desc   | This much memory can be used by each internal sort
operation and hash table before switching to temporary disk files.
context      | user
vartype      | integer
source       | default
min_val      | 64
max_val      | 2147483647
enumvals     |
boot_val     | 1024
reset_val    | 1024
sourcefile   |
sourceline   |
```

So, you can use the SHOW command to retrieve the value for a setting, or you can access the full detail via the catalog table.

How it works...

Each parameter setting is cached within each session so that we have fast access to the parameter settings. That allows us to access the parameter settings with ease.

Remember that the values displayed are not necessarily settings for the server as a whole; many of those parameters will be specific to the current session. That's different in many other databases and is also very useful.

Which parameters are at non-default settings?

Often, we need to check which parameters have been changed already or whether our changes have correctly taken effect.

How to do it...

```
postgres=# SELECT name, source, setting
                FROM pg_settings
                WHERE source != 'default
                   AND source != 'override'
                ORDER by 2, 1;
............name ...........|........source.......|..setting
---------------------------+--------------------+---------
```

```
application_name         | client                 | psql
log_timezone             | command line           | GB
TimeZone                 | command line           | GB
timezone_abbreviations   | command line           | Default
archive_command          | configuration file     | (disabled)
archive_mode             | configuration file     | off
archive_timeout          | configuration file     | 5
bgwriter_delay           | configuration file     | 10
checkpoint_timeout       | configuration file     | 30
log_checkpoints          | configuration file     | on
log_destination          | configuration file     | stderr
log_filename             | configuration file     | log%Y
logging_collector        | configuration file     | on
log_line_prefix          | configuration file     | %t [%p]
log_min_messages         | configuration file     | log
max_prepared_transactions | configuration file    | 5
max_standby_delay        | configuration file     | 90
port                     | configuration file     | 5443
max_stack_depth          | environment variable   | 2048
work_mem                 | session                | 204800
(29 rows)

('Override' is excluded just for display purposes.)
```

How it works...

You can see from `pg_settings` which values have non-default values, and what the source of the current value is.

The `SHOW` command doesn't tell you whether a parameter is set at a non-default value. It just tells you the value, which isn't much help if you're trying to understand what is set and why.

If the source is a configuration file, then the two columns `sourcefile` and `sourceline` are also set. These can be useful in understanding where the configuration came from.

There's more...

The `setting` column of `pg_settings` shows the current value, though you can also look at `boot_val` and `reset_val`; `boot-val`, which show the value assigned when the PostgreSQL database cluster was initialized ("initdb"), while `reset_val` shows the value that the parameter will return to if you issue the `RESET` command.

Who set that?

`max_stack_depth` is an exception because `pg_settings` says it is set by the environment variable, though it is actually set by `ulimit -s` on Linux/Unix systems. `max_stack_depth` only needs to be set directly on Windows.

The timezone settings are also picked up from the OS environment, so you shouldn't need to set those directly. `pg_settings` shows this as a "command-line" setting.

Updating the parameter file

The parameter file is the main location for defining parameter values for the PostgreSQL server. All of the parameters can be set in the parameter file, which is known as the `postgresql.conf`.

There are also two other parameter files, `pg_hba.conf` and `pg_ident.conf`. Both of these relate to connections and security, so we cover them in the appropriate chapters that follow.

Getting ready

First, locate the `postgresql.conf` as described earlier.

How to do it...

All of the parameters can be set in the parameter file, which is known as the `postgresql.conf`. Some of the parameters take effect only when the server is first started. A typical example might be `shared_buffers`, which defines the size of the shared memory cache.

Many of the parameters can be changed while the server is still running. After changing the required parameters, we issue a `reload` operation to the server, forcing PostgreSQL to re-read the `postgresql.conf`.

```
pg_ctl -D data reload
```

The `postgresql.conf` is a normal text file that can be simply edited. Most of the parameters are listed in the file, so you can just search for them, and then overtype the desired value.

How it works...

If you set the same parameter twice in different parts of the file, the last setting is the one that applies. This can cause lots of confusion if you add settings to the bottom of the file, so you are advised against doing that.

Best practice is to either leave the file as it is and edit the values, or to start with a blank file and just include the values that you wish to change. I personally prefer a file with only the non-default values. That makes it easier to see what's happening.

Whichever method you use, you are strongly advised to keep all of the previous versions of your `.conf` files. You can do this by copying, or you can use a version control system, such as SVN.

There's more...

`postgresql.conf` also supports an include directive. This allows the postgresql.conf file to reference other files, which can then reference other files, and so on. That might help you organise your parameter settings better, if you don't make it too complicated.

Setting parameters for particular groups of users

PostgreSQL supports a variety of ways of defining parameter settings for various user groups.

How to do it...

For all users in database `saas`:

```
ALTER DATABASE saas
SET configuration_parameter = value1;
```

For a user named `simon` connected to any database, use the following:

```
ALTER ROLE saas
SET configuration_parameter = value2;
```

or set a parameter for a user only when connected to a specific database, as follows:

```
ALTER ROLE simon
IN DATABASE saas
SET configuration_parameter = value3;
```

The user won't know that these have been executed specifically for him. These are default settings, and in most cases can be overridden if the user requires non-default values.

How it works...

You can set parameters for each of the following:

- ▶ Database
- ▶ User (named "Roles" by PostgreSQL)
- ▶ Database / User combination

Each of the parameter defaults is overridden by the one below it.

In the preceding three SQL statements if:

- ▶ user hannu connects to database saas, then value1 will apply

> ▶ user simon connects to a database other than saas, then value2 will apply

> ▶ user simon connects to database saas, then value3 will apply

PostgreSQL implements this in exactly the same way as if the user had manually issued the equivalent SET statements immediately after connecting.

Basic server configuration checklist

PostgreSQL arrives configured for use on a shared system, though many people want to run dedicated database systems. The PostgreSQL project wishes to ensure that PostgreSQL will play nicely with other server software, and should not assume it has access to the full server resources. If you, as the system administrator, know that there is no other important server software running on this system, then you can crank up the values much higher.

Getting ready

Before we start, we need to know two sets of information:

First, we need to know the size of the physical RAM that will be dedicated to PostgreSQL.

Second, we need to know something about the types of applications for which PostgreSQL will be used.

How to do it...

If your database is larger than 32MB, then you'll probably benefit from increasing `shared_buffers`. You can increase this to much larger values, though remember that on Linux systems this memory can be swapped out if not in use, so it's better to be conservative. A new value can be set in your `postgresql.conf` and incremented slowly to ensure you get benefits from each change.

If you increase `shared_buffers`, and you're running on a non-Windows server, you will almost certainly need to increase the value of the OS parameter SHMMAX (and on some platforms others as well).

On Linux/Mac OS/FreeBSD, you will need to either edit the `/etc/sysctl.conf` file or use `sysctl -w` with the following values:

> ▶ Linux: `kernel.shmmax=value`

> ▶ Mac OS: `kern.sysv.shmmax=value`

> ▶ FreeBSD `kern.ipc.shmmax=value`

`http://www.postgresql.org/docs/8.4/static/kernel-resources.html#SYSVIPC`

For example on Linux, add the following line to `/etc/sysctl.conf`:

```
kernel.shmmax=value
```

Don't worry about setting `effective_cache_size`. It is much less important a parameter than you might think; no need for too much fuss selecting the value.

If you're doing heavy write activity, then you may want to set `wal_buffers` to a much higher value than the default.

If you're doing heavy write activity and/or large data loads, you then may want to set `checkpoint_segments` higher than the default.

If your database has many large queries, you may wish to set `work_mem` to a value higher than the default.

Make sure `autovacuum` is turned on, unless you have a very good reason to turn it off. Most people don't. Please see later chapters for more information on autovacuum.

To simplify some of this, I recommend that you refer to the following URL:

```
http://pgfoundry.org/projects/pgtune/
```

Leave the settings at that for now. Don't fuss too much about getting the exact settings right. You can change most of them later, so you can take an iterative approach to improving things.

Get the basics right, and keep it simple and solid. Then buy Greg Smith's book on PostgreSQL performance

Especially, don't touch `fsync` parameter. It's keeping you safe.

Adding an external module to PostgreSQL

Another one of PostgreSQL's strengths is its extensibility. Extensibility was one of the original design goals, stretching back to the late 1980s. Now, in PostgreSQL 9.0, there are many additional modules that plug into the core PostgreSQL server.

There are many kinds of additional module offerings, such as the following:

- additional functions
- additional datatypes
- additional operators
- additional indexes

Note that many tools and client interfaces work with PostgreSQL without any special installation. Here, we are discussing modules that extend and alter the behavior of the server beyond its normal range of SQL standard syntax, functions, and behaviors.

Getting ready

First, you'll need to select an appropriate module to install.

There isn't yet an automated package management system for PostgreSQL, so modules are located in a range of places, such as the following:

- Contrib— PostgreSQL "core" includes many functions. There is also an official section for add-in modules, known as "contrib" modules. These are documented at the following URL:

  - ❏ `http://www.postgresql.org/docs/9.0/static/contrib.html`

- pgFoundry— an open source development website created specifically to allow PostgreSQL modules and tools to be shared. PgFoundry uses the same software as SourceForge.net. Take a look at the following URL:

  - ❏ `http://pgFoundry.org/`

- Separate projects— large external projects, such as PostGIS, offer extensive and complex PostgreSQL modules. Take a look at the following URL:

  - ❏ `http://www.postgis.org/`

How to do it...

In some cases, modules can be added during installation if you're using a stand-alone installer application, for example, **OneClick** installer.

In other cases, you'll be able to install from a package, such as with the Oracle compatibility module `http://www.postgres.cz/index.php/Oracle_functionality`

First, we get

`http://pgfoundry.org/frs/download.php/2420/orafce-3.0.1-1.pg82.rhel5.i386.rpm`

then install using commands, such as the following:

```
rpm -ivh orafce-3.0.1-1.pg90.rhel5.i386.rpm
sudo apt-get install postgresql-8.4-orafce
```

In many cases useful modules may not have full packaging. In these cases you may need to install the module manually. This isn't very hard and is a useful exercise to help you understand what happens.

Each module will have different installation requirements. There are generally two aspects to installing a module. They are as follows:

- ▶ Installing the SQL objects for the module
- ▶ Installing the dynamic load libraries for the module

Most of the more useful modules require you to handle both of the aforementioned aspects. There are a couple of examples, such as AutoExplain, that only has dynamic load libraries.

- ▶ Build the libraries

Follow instructions for that module

- ▶ Install the library where the server can find it:

```
shared_preload_libraries = '$libdir/modlib'
Create the database objects
psql -d dbname -f SHAREDIR/contrib/module.sql
```

How it works...

PostgreSQL can dynamically load libraries in the following three ways:

- ▶ By using the explicit LOAD command in a session
- ▶ By using shared_preload_libraries parameter in postgresql.conf at server start
- ▶ At session start, using local_preload_libraries parameter for a specific user, as set using ALTER ROLE

PostgreSQL functions and objects can reference code in these libraries, allowing extensions to be bound tightly into the running server process. The tight binding makes this method suitable for use even in very high-performance applications, and there's no significant difference between additional supplied features and native ones.

Running server in power saving mode

Power consumption is a hot topic. Everybody is looking for ways to do their bit for the environment. The same is true for PostgreSQL users.

Getting ready

If your PostgreSQL server is only used very sporadically, or has periods of total inactivity, then you may be able to benefit from some of the advice given here. That could be a laptop, or it could be a somewhat inactive virtual server.

How to do it...

PostgreSQL is a server-based database, so it mostly does nothing at all if there are no active clients. To minimize server activity, set the following parameters in the `postgresql.conf` file:

- `autovacuum = off`
- `wal_writer_delay = 10000`
- `bgwriter_delay = 10000`

These settings are not optimal for many uses and should only be used when it is known that the server will be quiet. They should be reset to previous values when the server becomes busy again.

How it works...

There are a couple of processes that stay active continually, on the expectation that they will be needed should clients become active. These processes are as follows:

- Writer process (also known as the "Background writer")
- WAL writer process
- Archiver, which will be active if WAL archiving is enabled.
- WAL receiver process, which will be active if streaming replication is in use.
- Autovacuum process

The Background writer process wakes up by default every 200ms to do its work. The maximum setting is 10s, which isn't very long, though the Background writer can be disabled by the setting, `bgwriter_lru_maxpages = 0`.

The WAL writer process wakes up by default every 200ms. The maximum setting is also 10s. This cannot be disabled. If there is no write activity, then no work will be performed, other than the wakeup and check.

The Archiver process will wake up every 15s and check whether any new WAL files have been written. This will cause some activity against the filesystem directory. That time cannot be changed by a parameter.

The WAL receiver process will wake up every 100ms to check if new replication data has arrived. If no new data has arrived, it will sleep again. That time cannot be changed by a parameter.

Autovacuum will wake up every 60s by default. This can be changed by altering the setting of `autovacuum_naptime`. Autovacuum can be disabled completely by setting `autovacuum = off`.

So, if you are using Streaming Replication, then the server will wake up every 100ms. If not, then you can reduce the wakeup time to every 10s rather than every 200ms, which is the default setting.

4
Server Control

In this chapter, we will cover the following:

- ▶ Starting the database server manually
- ▶ Stopping the server quickly and safely
- ▶ Stopping the server in an emergency
- ▶ Reloading the server configuration files
- ▶ Restarting the server quickly
- ▶ Preventing new connections
- ▶ Restricting users to just one session each
- ▶ Pushing users off the system
- ▶ Deciding on a design for multi-tenancy
- ▶ Using multiple schemas
- ▶ Giving users their own private database
- ▶ Running multiple database servers on one system
- ▶ Setting up a connection pool

Introduction

PostgreSQL consists of a set of server processes, the group leader of which is named the postmaster. Starting the server is the act of creating these processes, and stopping the server means to terminate those processes.

Each postmaster listens for client connection requests on one defined port number. Multiple concurrently running postmasters cannot share that port number. The port number is often used to identify a particular postmaster uniquely, and so also the database server that it leads.

When we start a database server, we refer to one **data directory**, which contains the heart and soul, or at least the data for our database. Subsidiary tablespaces may contain some data outside of the main data directory, so the data directory is just the main central location, and not the only place where data for that database server is held. Each running server has one data directory, and one data directory can have at the most one running server (or "instance").

To perform any action for a database server, we must know the data directory for that server. The basic actions we can perform on the database server are starting and stopping. We can also perform a restart, though that is just a stop, followed by a start. In addition, we can reload the server, meaning to reread the server's configuration files.

We should also mention a few other points:

The default port number for PostgreSQL is **5432**. That has been registered with **Internet Assigned Numbers Authority** (**IANA**), and so should already be reserved for PostgreSQL's use in most places. Because each PostgreSQL server requires a distinct port number, the normal convention is to use subsequent numbers for any additional server, for example, 5433, 5434, and so on. Subsequent port numbers might not be as easily recognized by the network infrastructure, which might in some cases make life more difficult for you in larger enterprises, especially more security-conscious ones.

The database server is also sometimes referred to as a database cluster. I don't recommend the term for normal usage because it makes people think about multiple nodes, not just one database server on one system.

Starting the database server manually

Typically, the PostgreSQL server will start automatically when the system boots. You may have opted to stop and start the server manually, or you may need to start up/shut down for various operational reasons.

Getting ready

First, we need to understand the difference between the service and the server. The word server refers to the database server and its processes. The word service refers to the operating system wrapper by which the server gets called. The server works in essentially the same way on every platform, whereas each operating system and distribution has its own concept of a service.

How to do it...

On all platforms, there is a specific command to start the server, which is as follows:

UBUNTU/DEBIAN	`pg_ctlcluster 9.0 main reload`
RED HAT/FEDORA	`pg_ctl -D /var/lib/pgsql/data start`
SOLARIS	`pg_ctl -D /var/lib/pgsql/data start`
MAC OS	`pg_ctl -D /var/lib/pgsql/data start`
FREEBSD	`pg_ctl -D /var/lib/pgsql/data start`

although on some platforms, the service can be started in various ways such as:

RED HAT/FEDORA	`service postgresql start`
WINDOWS	`net start postgres`

How it works...

On Ubuntu/Debian, the `pg_ctlcluster` wrapper is a convenient utility that allows multiple servers to coexist more easily, which is especially good when you have servers with different versions. Very useful.

Stopping the server safely and quickly

Let's do it!

How to do it...

You can issue a database server stop using fast mode as follows:

```
pg_ctl -D datadir -m fast stop
```

You must use `-m fast` if you wish to shut down as soon as possible. Normal shutdown means "wait for all users to finish before we exit". That can take a very long time, though all the while new connections are refused.

On other systems, this command might be as follows:

DEBIAN/UBUNTU	`pg_ctlcluster 9.0 main stop --force`

How it works...

When you do a fast stop, all users have their transactions aborted and all connections are disconnected. It's not very polite to users, but it still treats the server and its data with care, which is good.

PostgreSQL is similar to other database systems, in that it does do a shutdown checkpoint before it closes. This means that the startup that follows will be quick and clean. The more work the checkpoint has to do, the longer it will take to shut down.

One difference between PostgreSQL and some other RDBMS such as Oracle, DB2, or SQLServer is that the transaction rollback is very fast. On those other systems, if you shut down the server in a mode that rolls back transactions, then this can cause the shutdown to take a while, possibly a very long time. This difference is for internal reasons, and isn't in any way unsafe.

The Debian/Ubuntu `--force` option is rather nice, because it first attempts a fast shutdown, and then if that fails, it performs an immediate shutdown, and then after that kills the postmaster.

Stopping the server in an emergency

If nothing else is working, we may need to stop the server quickly.

"Break glass in case of emergency."

How to do it...

The basic command to perform an emergency restart on the server is the following:

```
pg_ctl -D datadir stop -m immediate
```

We must use an `immediate stop` mode.

How it works...

When you do an immediate stop, all users have their transactions aborted, and all connections are disconnected. There is no clean shutdown, nor politeness of any kind.

An immediate mode stop is similar to a database crash. Some cached files will need to be rebuilt, and the database itself needs to undergo crash recovery when it comes back up.

Note that for DBAs with Oracle experience, immediate mode is the same thing as a **shutdown abort**. PostgreSQL immediate mode stop is not the same thing as shutdown immediate on Oracle.

Reloading the server configuration files

Some PostgreSQL configuration parameters can only be changed by "reloading" the whole configuration file.

How to do it...

On all platforms, there is a specific command to reload the server, which is as follows:

UBUNTU/DEBIAN	`pg_ctlcluster 9.0 main reload`
RED HAT/FEDORA	`service postgresql reload` `pg_ctl -D /var/lib/pgsql/data reload`
SOLARIS	`pg_ctl -D /var/lib/pgsql/data reload`
MAC OS	`pg_ctl -D /var/lib/pgsql/data reload`
FREEBSD	`pg_ctl -D /var/lib/pgsql/data reload`

You can also reload the configuration files while still connected to PostgreSQL. This can be done from the command line as follows, if you are a superuser:

```
postgres=# select pg_reload_conf();
 pg_reload_conf
----------------
 t
```

which is also often executed from an admin tool, such as pgAdmin3

If you do this, you should realize that it's possible to implement a new authentication rule that is violated by the current session. It won't force you to disconnect, but when you do disconnect, you may not be able to reconnect.

How it works...

To reload the configuration files, we send the SIGHUP signal to the postmaster, which then passes that on to all connected backends. That's why some people call reloading the server "sigh-up-ing".

If you look at the catalog table `pg_settings`, you'll see that there is a column named `context`. Each setting has a time and a place where it can be changed. Some parameters can only be reset by a server reload, and so the value of context for those parameters will be a "sighup". Here are a few of the ones you'll want to change sometimes during server operation (there are others!):

```
postgres=#  SELECT name, setting, unit
                      ,(source = 'default') as is_default
            FROM pg_settings
            WHERE context = 'sighup'
            AND     (name like '%delay' or name like '%timeout')
            AND setting != '0';
```

name		setting	unit	is_default
authentication_timeout		60	s	t
autovacuum_vacuum_cost_delay		20	ms	t
bgwriter_delay		10	ms	f
checkpoint_timeout		32	s	f
deadlock_timeout		1000	ms	t
max_standby_delay		30		t
wal_sender_delay		200	ms	t
wal_writer_delay		200	ms	t

(8 rows)

There's more...

As reloading the configuration file is achieved by sending the SIGHUP signal, we can reload the configuration file just for a single backend using the `kill` command. As you might expect, you can get some strange results from doing this, so don't try this at home.

First, find out the `pid` of the backend using `pg_stat_activity`.

Then, from the OS prompt, issue the following:

```
kill    -SIGHUP    pid
```

Or we can do both at once, as in the following command:

```
kill -SIGHUP \
`psql -t -c "select procpid from pg_stat_activity limit 1"`
```

though that is only useful with a sensible WHERE clause.

Restarting the server quickly

Some of the database server parameters require you to stop and start the server again fully. Doing this as quickly as possible can be very important in some cases. The best time to do this is usually a quiet time, with lots of planning, testing, and forethought. Sometimes, not everything goes according to plan.

How to do it...

The basic command to restart the server is the following:

```
pg_ctl -D datadir restart -m fast
```

A restart is just a stop followed by a start, so it sounds very simple. In many cases, it will be simple, but there are times when you'll need to restart the server while it is fairly busy. That's when we need to start pulling some tricks to make that restart happen faster.

First, the stop performed needs to be a fast stop. If we do a default or "smart" stop, then the server will just wait for everyone to finish. If we do an immediate stop, then the server will crash, and we will need to crash recover the data, which will be slower overall.

The running database server has a cache full of data blocks, many of them dirty. PostgreSQL is similar to other database systems, in that it does a shutdown checkpoint before it closes. This means that the startup that follows will be quick and clean. The more work the checkpoint has to do, the longer it will take to shut down.

The actual shutdown will happen much faster if we issue a normal checkpoint first, as the shutdown checkpoint will have much less work to do. So, flush all dirty `shared_buffers` to disk with the following command issued by a database superuser:

```
psql -c "CHECKPOINT"
```

The next consideration is that once we restart, the database cache will be empty again and will need to refresh itself. The larger the database cache, the longer it takes for the cache to get warm again, and 30 to 60 minutes is not uncommon before returning to full speed. So what was a simple restart can actually have a large business impact if handled badly.

I've written a utility named `pg_cacheutils` to record the contents of the database cache prior to shutdown. This can then be used to prime or warm the cache again immediately after restart.

```
psql -c "select pg_cache_save('mycache')"
```

Then, you can issue a database server stop using immediate mode, so that we stop quickly and start up again cleanly as follows:.

```
pg_ctl -D datadir -m immediate restart
```

One we're up, we can connect and warm the cache again as follows:

```
psql -c "select pg_cache_warm('mycache')"
```

It's not magic, so it will still take some time to be at full speed.

How it works...

`pg_cache_save()` will save the set of disk blocks in a table named `mycache`. That allows you to have several sets of caches for various purposes if you need them. If you don't supply a name, it will just use `saved_cache`.

`pg_cache_warm()` will read the saved cache information and perform a prefetch operation on each block. This will bring the information back into cache using OS prefetch, if available. Any non-existent blocks will be ignored.

`http://projects.2ndQuadrant.com/pg_cacheutils/`

Preventing new connections

In certain emergencies, you may need to lock down the server completely, or just prevent specific users from accessing the database. It's hard to foresee all the situations in which you might need to do this, so we present a range of options.

How to do it...

Connections can be prevented in a number of ways as follows:

- ▶ Pause/Resume the session pool. See recipe on controlling connection pools

- ▶ Stop the server! See the earlier recipe, but it is not recommended.

- ▶ Restrict connections to zero for a specific database by setting the connection limit to zero.

  `ALTER DATABASE foo_db CONNECTION LIMIT 0;`

  This will limit normal users from connecting to that database, though it will still allow superuser connections.

- ▶ Restrict connections to zero for a specific user by setting the connection limit to zero. (See also later recipe.)

  `ALTER USER foo CONNECTION LIMIT 0;`

  This will limit normal users from connecting to that database, though it will still allow connection if the user is a superuser, so luckily you cannot shut yourself out accidentally.

- ▶ Change host-based authentication (HBA) file to refuse all incoming connections, and then reload the server:

  - ❏ Create a new file named `pg_hba_lockdown.conf`, and add the following two lines to the file. This puts rules in place that will completely lock down the server, including superusers. Please have no doubt that this is a serious and drastic action.

# TYPE	DATABASE	USER	CIDR-ADDRESS	METHOD
local	all	all	reject	
host	all	all	0.0.0.0/0	reject

If you still want superuser access, then try something like the following:

```
# TYPE   DATABASE   USER        CIDR-ADDRESS   METHOD
  local  all        postgres                   ident
  local  all        all                        reject
  host   all        all         0.0.0.0/0      reject
```

which will prevent connection to the database by any user except the postgres operating system userid connecting locally to the postgres database. Be careful not to confuse the second and third columns: the second column is the database and the third column is the username. It's worth keeping the header line just for that reason. The method "ident" should be replaced by other authentication methods if a more complex configuration is in use.

- ❏ Copy the existing pg_hba.conf to pg_hba_access.conf, so that it can be replaced again later, if required.
- ❏ Copy pg_hba_lockdown.conf to pg_hba.conf
- ❏ Reload the server following the recipe earlier in this chapter.

How it works...

The pg_hba.conf is where we specify the host-based authentication rules. We do not specify the authentications themselves, but just specify which authentication mechanisms will be used. This is the top-level set of rules for PostgreSQL authentication. The rules are specified in a file, and applied by the postmaster process when connections are attempted. To prevent denial of service attacks, the HBA rules never involve database access, so we do not know whether a user is a superuser or not. As a result, you can lock out *all* users. But note that you can always re-enable access by editing the file and reloading.

Restricting users to just one session each

If resources need to be closely controlled, you may wish to restrict users so that they can only connect at most once to the server. The same technique can be used to prevent connections entirely for that user.

How to do it...

We can restrict users to just one connection by using the following command:

```
postgres=# ALTER ROLE fred CONNECTION LIMIT 1;
ALTER ROLE
```

This will then cause any additional connections to receive the error message:

FATAL: too many connections for role "fred".

 You can eliminate this restriction by setting the value to -1.

It's possible to set the limit to zero or any positive integer. You can set this to a number other than `max_connections`, though it is up to you to make sense of that if you do.

Setting the value to zero will completely restrict normal connections. Note that even if you set connection limit to zero for superusers, they will still be able to connect.

How it works...

The connection limit is applied during session connection. Raising this limit would never affect any connected users. Lowering the limit doesn't have any effect either, unless they try to disconnect and reconnect.

So if you lower the limit, you should immediately check to see whether there are more sessions connected than the new limit you just set, otherwise there may be some surprises if there is a crash.

```
postgres=> SELECT rolconnlimit
                   FROM pg_roles
                   WHERE rolname = 'fred';

 rolconnlimit
--------------
            1
(1 row)
postgres=> SELECT count(*)
                   FROM pg_stat_activity
                   WHERE usename = 'fred';

 count
-------
     2
(1 row)
```

If you have more connected sessions than the new limit, you can ask them politely to disconnect, or apply the recipe *Pushing users off the system*.

Users can't raise or lower their own connection limit, in case you were worried they might be able to override this somehow.

Pushing users off the system

Sometimes we may need to remove groups of users from the database server for various operational reasons. Here's how.

How to do it...

You can terminate a user's session with the `pg_terminate_backend()` function included with PostgreSQL. That function takes the `pid`, or the process ID, of the user's session on the server. This is known as the backend, and is a different system process from the program that runs the client.

To find out the `pid` of a user, we can look at the view `pg_stat_activity`. We can use that in a query like the following:

SELECT pg_terminate_backend(procpid)
FROM   pg_stat_activity
WHERE ...

There's a couple of things to note if you run that query, which are as follows:

- If the WHERE clause matches no sessions, then you won't get anything back from the query. Similarly, if it matches multiple rows, you will also get a fairly useless result.

- If you are not careful enough to include your own session in the query, then you will disconnect yourself! What's even funnier is that you'll disconnect yourself halfway through disconnecting the other users, as the query will run `pg_terminate_backend()` in the order that sessions are returned from the outer query.

So as a more useful query, I suggest a safer query that gives a useful response in all cases, which is as follows:

```
postgres=# SELECT count(pg_terminate_backend(procpid))
FROM pg_stat_activity
WHERE usename NOT IN
(SELECT usename
  FROM pg_user
WHERE usesuper);
 count
-------
     1
```

assuming that superusers are performing administrative tasks.

Other good filters might be:

- ▶ WHERE application_name = 'myappname'
- ▶ WHERE waiting
- ▶ WHERE current_query = '<IDLE> in transaction'
- ▶ WHERE current_query = '<IDLE>'

How it works...

pg_terminate_backend() sends a signal directly to the operating system process for that session.

It's possible that the session may have closed by the time pg_terminate_backend() is named. As pid numbers are assigned by the operating system, it might be possible that a session with that pid number closed, and then a new session started with that exact same number gets cancelled instead. So, be careful.

It's also possible that new sessions could start after we get the list of active sessions. There's no way to prevent that other than by following the recipe *Preventing new connections*.

Deciding on a design for multi-tenancy

There are many reasons why we might want to split up groups of tables or applications: security, resource control, convenience. Whatever the reason, we often need to separate groups of tables (I avoid saying the word "database" just to avoid various confusions).

This topic is frequently referred to as **multi-tenancy**, though that is not a fully accepted term as yet.

The purpose of this recipe is to discuss the options and lead into other more detailed recipes.

How to do it...

If you want to run multiple physical databases on one server, then you have four main options, which are as follows:

1. Run multiple sets of tables in different schemas in one database of a PostgreSQL instance
2. Run multiple databases in the same PostgreSQL instance
3. Run multiple PostgreSQL instances on the same virtual/physical system
4. Run separate PostgreSQL instances in separate virtual machines on the same physical server

Option 1 is covered in the recipe *Using multiple schemas*.

Option 2 is covered in the recipe *Giving users their own private database*.

Option 3 is covered in the recipe *Running multiple servers on one system*.

Which is best? Well, it's certainly a topic many people ask, and something on which many views exist. The answer lies in looking at the specific requirements, which are as follows:

- If our goal is the separation of physical resources, then options 3 or 4 work best. Separate database servers can be easily assigned different disks, individual memory allocations can be assigned, and we may take the servers up or down without impacting the other.

- If our goal is security, then Option 2 may be sufficient.

- If our goal is merely the separation of tables for administrative clarity, then options 1 or 2 may also be useful.

Option 2 allows complete separation for security purposes. That does also prevent someone with privileges on both groups of tables from performing a join between those tables. So, if there is a possibility of future cross-analytics, it might be worth considering option 1, though it might also be argued that such analytics should be carried out on a separate data warehouse, not by co-locating production systems.

Option 3 has one simple difficulty in many of the PostgreSQL distributions. The default installation uses a single location for the database, making it a little harder to configure that option. Ubuntu/Debian handles that aspect particularly well, making it more attractive in that environment.

Option 4 can be arranged using virtualization technology, though outside of the scope of this book.

I've seen people who use PostgreSQL with thousands of databases, though it would be my opinion that the majority of people use just one database, such as postgres (or at least only a few). I've also seen people with a great many schemas.

One thing you will find is that almost all of the admin GUI tools become significantly less useful with 100s or 1000s of items to display. In most cases, admin tools use a tree-view, which doesn't cope gracefully with large numbers of items.

Using multiple schemas

We can separate groups of tables into their own "namespaces", referred to as "schemas" by PostgreSQL. In many ways they can be thought of as being similar to directories, though that is not a precise description.

Getting ready

Make sure you've read the recipe *Deciding on a design for multi-tenancy*, so that you're certain this is the route you wish to take. Other options exist, and it is possible that they may be preferable in some cases.

How to do it...

Schemas can be created easily by using the following:

```
CREATE SCHEMA finance;
CREATE SCHEMA sales;
```

We can then create objects directly within those schemas by using "fully qualified" names, for example:

```
CREATE TABLE finance.month_end_snapshot (....)
```

The default schema into which an object is created is known as the current schema. We can find out which is our current schema by using the following query:

```
postgres=# select current_schema;
 current_schema
----------------
 public
(1 row)
```

When we access database objects, we use the user-settable parameter `search_path` to identify which schemas to search. The current schema is the first schema in the `search_path`—there is no separate parameter for the current schema.

So, if we want to have only a specific user look at certain sets of tables, we can modify his/her `search_path`. The parameter can be set for each user, so that the value will be set when he/she connects. The SQL for this would be something like the following:

```
ALTER ROLE fiona SET search_path = 'finance';
ALTER ROLE sally SET search_path = 'sales';
```

Note that the "public" schema is not mentioned on the `search_path`, and so would not be searched. All tables created by `fiona` would go into the finance schema by default, whereas all tables created by `sally` would go into the sales schema by default.

The users for finance and sales would be able to see that the other schema existed, though we would be able to grant/revoke privileges such that they could neither create objects nor read data in the others' schema.

```
REVOKE ALL ON SCHEMA finance FROM public;
GRANT ALL ON SCHEMA finance TO fiona;
REVOKE ALL ON SCHEMA sales FROM public;
GRANT ALL ON SCHEMA sales TO sally;
```

An alternate technique would be to allow one user to create privileges on only one schema, but usage rights on all other schemas. We would set up that arrangement like the following:

```
REVOKE ALL ON SCHEMA finance FROM public;
GRANT USAGE ON SCHEMA finance TO public;
GRANT CREATE ON SCHEMA finance TO fiona;
REVOKE ALL ON SCHEMA sales FROM public;
GRANT USAGE ON SCHEMA sales TO sally;
GRANT CREATE ON SCHEMA sales TO sally;
```

Note that you need to grant the privileges for usage on the schema, as well as specific rights on the objects in the schema. So, you will also need to issue specific grants for objects, such as:

```
GRANT SELECT ON month_end_snapshot TO public;
```

or set default privileges so that they are picked up when objects are created using:

```
ALTER DEFAULT PRIVILEGES FOR USER fiona IN SCHEMA finance
GRANT SELECT ON TABLES TO PUBLIC;
```

How it works...

Earlier, I said that schemas work like directories, a little at least.

The PostgreSQL concept of `search_path` is similar to the concept of a PATH environment variable.

The PostgreSQL concept of the current schema is similar to the concept of the current working directory. There is no "cd" command to change directory. The current working directory is changed by altering `search_path`.

A few other differences exist, for example, PostgreSQL schemas are not arranged in a hierarchy, as are filesystem directories.

Many people create a user of the same name as the schema to make this work in a similar way to other RDBMS, such as Oracle.

Note that both the finance and sales schemas exist within the same PostgreSQL database, and run on the same database server. They use a common buffer pool, and there are many global settings that tie the two schema fairly closely together.

Giving users their own private database

Separating data and users is a key part of administration. There will always be a need to give users a private, secure, or simply risk-free area ("sandpit") to use the database. Here's how.

Getting ready

Make sure you've read the recipe *Deciding on a design for multi-tenancy*, so that you're certain this is the route you wish to take. Other options exist, and it is possible they may be preferable in some cases.

How to do it...

We can create a database for a specific user with some ease. From the command line, as a superuser, these actions would be as follows:

```
postgres=# create user fred;
CREATE ROLE
postgres=# create database fred owner = fred;
CREATE DATABASE
```

As the database owner:

Users have login privilege, so can connect to any database by default. There is a command named ALTER DEFAULT PRIVILEGES though, that does not currently apply to databases, tablespaces, or languages. ALTER DEFAULT PRIVILEGES also currently applies only to roles (that is, users) that already exist.

So, we need to revoke privilege to connect to our new database from everybody except the designated user. There isn't a REVOKE ... FROM PUBLIC EXCEPT command, so we need to revoke everything, and then just re-grant everything we need all in one transaction, such as the following:

```
postgres=# BEGIN;
BEGIN
postgres=# REVOKE connect ON DATABASE  fred FROM public;
REVOKE
postgres=# GRANT connect ON DATABASE fred TO fred;
GRANT
postgres=# COMMIT;
COMMIT
postgres=# create user bob;
CREATE ROLE
```

Then, try to connect as `bob` to the `fred` database

```
os $ psql -U bob fred
psql: FATAL:  permission denied for database "fred"
DETAIL:  User does not have CONNECT privilege.
```

which is exactly what we wanted.

How it works...

If you didn't catch it before, PostgreSQL allows transactional DDL in most places, so the REVOKE and GRANT in the preceding either both work or neither actions take place. So user `fred` never at any point loses the ability to connect to the database. Note that CREATE DATABASE cannot be performed as part of a transaction, though nothing serious happens as a result.

There's more...

Note that _superusers_ can still connect to the new database, and there is no way to prevent them from doing so.

No other users can see tables created in the new database, nor can they find out the names of any of the objects.

The new database can be seen to exist by other users, and they can also see the name of the user who owns the database.

See also

See the _Security_ section for more details on these issues.

Running multiple servers on one system

Running multiple PostgreSQL servers on one physical system is possible if this is more convenient for your needs.

Getting ready

Make sure you've read the recipe _Deciding on a design for multi-tenancy_, so that you're certain this is the route you wish to take. Other options exist, and it is possible they may be preferable in some cases.

How to do it...

Core PostgreSQL easily allows multiple servers running on the same system. There are a few wrinkles of which to be aware.

Some installer versions create a PostgreSQL data directory named "data". It then gets a little difficult to have more than one data directory without different directory structures and names.

The Debian/Ubuntu layout is specifically designed to allow multiple servers, potentially running with different software release levels.

To create an additional data directory, run the following:

```
sudo pg_createcluster 9.0 database2
```

which can then be started using the following:

```
sudo pg_createcluster 9.0 database2
```

which will create an additional database cluster at version 9.0, named "database2", with files stored in /var/lib/postgresql/9.0/database2.

With Red Hat systems, you will need to run initdb directly, selecting your directories carefully. Something like the following:

```
initdb -D /var/lib/pgsql/database2
```

then, modify the port parameter in the postgresql.conf, and then start using:

```
pg_ctl -D /var/lib/pgsql/database2 start
```

which will create an additional database cluster at the default server version with files stored in /var/lib/pgsql/database2.

You can set up the server with chkconfig also.

How it works...

PostgreSQL servers are controlled using pg_ctl. Everything else is a wrapper of some kind around it. The only constraints on running multiple versions of PostgreSQL come from file locations and naming conventions. Everything else is straightforward. Having said that, the Debian/Ubuntu design is currently the only one that makes it actually easy to run multiple servers.

Set up a Connection Pool

A Connection Pool is the term used for a collection of already connected sessions that can be used to reduce the overhead of connection and reconnection.

There are various ways that connection pools can be provided, depending upon the software stack in use. Probably the best option is to look at "server side" connection pool software, because that works for all connection types, not just within a single software stack.

Here we're going to look at pgbouncer, which is designed as a very lightweight connection pool. The name comes from the idea that the pool can be paused/resumed to allow the server to be restarted or bounced.

Getting ready

First of all, decide where you're going to store the pgbouncer parameter files, log files, and pid files.

pgbouncer can manage more than one database server's connections at same time, though that probably isn't wise. If you keep pgbouncer files associated with the database server, then it should be easy to manage.

How to do it...

Carry out the following steps to configure pgbouncer:

1. Create a pgbouncer.ini file

   ```
   ;
   ; pgbouncer configuration example
   ;
   [databases]
   postgres = port=5432 dbname=postgres
   [pgbouncer]
   listen_port = 6543
   listen_addr = 127.0.0.1
   admin_users = postgres
   ;stats_users = monitoring userid
   auth_type = trust
   ; put these files somewhere sensible
   auth_file = users.txt
   logfile = pgbouncer.log
   pidfile = pgbouncer.pid
   ; required for 9.0
   ignore_startup_parameters = application_name
   ```

```
    server_reset_query = DISCARD ALL;
    ; default values
    pool_mode = session
    default_pool_size = 20
    log_pooler_errors = 0
```

2. Create a `users.txt` file. This must exist, and must contain at least the minimum users mentioned in `admin_users` and `stats_users`. For example:

   "postgres"   ""

   pgbouncer also supports md5 authentication. To use that effectively, you need to copy the encrypted passwords from the database server.

   You may wish to create the `users.txt` file by directly copying the details from the server. That can be done using the following psql script:

   ```
   postgres=> \o users.txt
   postgres=> \t
   postgres=> SELECT <»›||rolname||›» «›||rolpassword||›»›
   postgres-> FROM pg_authid;
   postgres=> \q
   ```

3. Launch pgbouncer:

   ```
   pgbouncer -d pgbouncer.ini
   ```

4. Test the connection—it should respond `reload`:

   ```
   psql -p 6543 -U postgres pgbouncer -c "reload"
   ```

Also, check that pgbouncer's `max_client_conn` parameter does not exceed `max_connections` parameter on PostgreSQL.

How it works...

pgbouncer is a great piece of software. It's feature set is very carefully defined to ensure that it is simple, robust, and very fast. pgbouncer is not multi-threaded, so it runs in a single process, and thus on a single CPU. It is very efficient, though very large data transfers will tie up more time and reduce concurrency, so make those data dumps using a direct connection.

pgbouncer doesn't support SSL connections. If it did, then all of the encryption/decryption would need to take place in the single process, which would make that solution perform poorly. If you need secure communications, then you should use *stunnel*.

pgbouncer provides connection pooling. If you set:

```
    pool_mode = transaction
```

then pgbouncer will also provide connection concentration. This allows hundreds or thousands of incoming connections to be managed while only a few server connections are made.

As new connections/transactions/statements arrive, the pool will increase in size up to the defined user maximums. Those connections will stay around for at most server_idle_timeout before the pool releases those connections.

pgbouncer also releases sessions every `server_lifetime`. This allows the server to free backends in rotation to avoid issues with very long-lived session connections.

There's more...

It's possible to connect to pgbouncer itself to issue commands. This can be done interactively as if you were entering psql, or it can be done using single commands or scripts.

To shut down the server, we can just type `SHUTDOWN`, or enter a single command as follows:

```
psql -p 6543 pgbouncer -c "SHUTDOWN"
```

You can also use the command `RELOAD` to make the server reload (that means reread) the parameter files.

If you are using `pool_mode = transaction` or `pool_mode = statement`, then you can use the `PAUSE` command. This allows the current transaction to complete before holding further work on that session. This allows you to perform DDL more easily or restart the server.

pbouncer also allows you to use SUSPEND mode. This waits for all server-side buffers to flush.

`PAUSE` or `SUSPEND` should eventually be followed by `RESUME` when the work is done.

In addition to the pgbouncer control commands, there are also a selection of `SHOW` commands:

Show command	Result set
SHOW STATS	Traffic stats. Total and avg requests, query duration, bytes sent/received.
SHOW SERVERS	One row per connection to database server
SHOW CLIENTS	One row per connection from client
SHOW POOLS	One user per pool of users
SHOW LISTS	Gives a good summary of resource totals
SHOW USERS	Lists uses in `user.txt`
SHOW DATABASES	Lists databases in `pgbouncer.ini`
SHOW CONFIG	Lists configuration parameters
SHOW FDS	Show file descriptors
SHOW SOCKETS	Show file sockets
SHOW VERSION	pgbouncer version

5
Tables & Data

In this chapter, we will cover the following:

- ▶ Choosing good names for database objects
- ▶ Handling objects with quoted names
- ▶ Enforcing same name, same definition for columns
- ▶ Identifying and removing duplicate rows
- ▶ Preventing duplicate rows
- ▶ Finding a unique key for a set of data
- ▶ Generating test data
- ▶ Randomly sampling data
- ▶ Loading data from a spreadsheet
- ▶ Loading data from flat files

Introduction

This chapter covers a range of general recipes for your tables and working with the data they contain. Many of the recipes contain general advice, though with specific PostgreSQL examples.

Some system administrators I've met work only on the external aspects of the database server. What's actually in the database is someone else's problem.

Look after your data, and your database will look after you. Keep your data clean, and your queries will run faster, cause less application errors, and you'll gain many friends in the business. Getting called in the middle of the night to fix data problems just isn't cool.

Choosing good names for database objects

The easiest way to help other people understand a database is to make sure that all the objects have a meaningful name.

What makes a meaningful name?

How to do it...

▸ The name follows the existing standards and practices in place. Inventing new standards isn't helpful; enforcing existing ones is.

▸ The name clearly describes the role or table contents.

▸ For major tables use short, powerful names.

▸ For lookup tables, name them after the table to which they are linked, such as account_status.

▸ For associative or linked tables, use all of the names of the major tables to which they relate, such as customer_account.

▸ Make sure that the name is clearly distinct from other similar names.

▸ Use consistent abbreviations.

▸ Use underscores. Case is not preserved by default, so using camelCase names, such as customerAccount, as used in Java will just leave them unreadable. See recipe on handling objects with quoted names..

▸ Use consistent plurals, or not.

▸ Use suffixes to identify the content type/domain of object. PostgreSQL already uses suffixes for automatically generated objects.

▸ Think ahead. Don't pick names that refer to the current role or location of an object. So don't name a table "London" because it exists on a server in London. That server might get moved to L.A.

▸ Think ahead. Don't pick names that imply that this is the only one of its kind, such as a table named TEST, or a table named BACKUP_DATA.

▸ Avoid using acronyms in place of long table names. For example, money_allocation_ decision is much better than MAD. This is especially important when PostgreSQL translates the names to lower case, so the fact that it is an acronym may not be clear.

▸ The tablename is commonly used as the root for other objects that are created, so don't add the suffix "table" or similar ideas.

There's More

The standard names for indexes in PostgreSQL are:

```
{tablename}_{columnname(s)}_{suffix}
```

where the suffix is one of the following:

- ▶ pkey for a Primary Key constraint
- ▶ key for a Unique constraint
- ▶ excl for an Exclusion constraint
- ▶ idx for any other kind of index

Standard suffix for sequences is

- ▶ seq for all sequences

Tables can have multiple triggers fired on each event. Triggers are executed in alphabetical order, so trigger names should have some kind of action name to differentiate them and to allow the order to be specified. It might seem a good idea to put INSERT, UPDATE, or DELETE in the trigger name, though that can get confusing if you have triggers that work on both UPDATE and DELETE, and may end up as a mess.

A useful naming convention for triggers is:

{tablename}_{actionname}_{after|before}__trig

If you do find yourself with strange and/or irregular object names, it will be a good idea to use the RENAME subcommands to get things tidy again. Examples are:

```
ALTER INDEX badly_named_index RENAME TO tablename_status_idx;
```

Handling objects with quoted names

PostgreSQL object names can contain spaces and mixed case characters if we enclose the tablenames in double quotes. This can cause some difficulties, so this recipe is designed to help you if you get stuck with this kind of problem.

Case sensitivity issues can often be a problem for people more used to working with other database systems, such as MySQL, or for people who are facing the challenge of migrating code away from MySQL.

Getting ready

First, let's create a table that uses a quoted name with mixed case, such as the following:

```
CREATE TABLE "MyCust"
AS
SELECT * FROM cust;
```

How to do it...

If we try to access these tables without the proper case we get the following error:

```
postgres=# SELECT count(*) FROM mycust;
ERROR:  relation "mycust" does not exist
LINE 1: SELECT * FROM mycust;
```

So we write it in the correct case:

```
postgres=# SELECT count(*) FROM MyCust;
ERROR:  relation "mycust" does not exist
LINE 1: SELECT * FROM mycust;
```

which still fails, and in fact gives the same error.

If you want to access a table that was created with quoted names, then you must use quoted names, such as the following:

```
postgres=# SELECT count(*) FROM "MyCust";
 count
-------
     5
(1 row)
```

The usage rule is that if you create your tables using quoted names, then you need to write your SQL using quoted names. Alternatively, if your SQL uses quoted names, then you will probably have to create the tables using quoted names as well.

How it works...

PostgreSQL folds all names to lowercase when used within an SQL statement, which means that:

```
SELECT * FROM mycust;
```

is exactly the same as:

```
SELECT * FROM MYCUST;
```

and is also exactly the same as

```
SELECT * FROM MyCust;
```

though is not the same thing as

```
SELECT * FROM "MyCust";
```

There's more...

If you are extracting values from a table that is being used to create object names, then you may need to use a handy function named `quote_ident()`. This function puts double quotes around a value if PostgreSQL would require that for an object name, such as

```
postgres=# select quote_ident('MyCust');
 quote_ident
-------------
 "MyCust"
(1 row)
postgres=# select quote_ident('mycust');
 quote_ident
-------------
 mycust
(1 row)
```

`quote_ident()` may be especially useful if you are creating a table based on a variable name in a PL/pgSQL function, such as.

```
EXECUTE 'CREATE TEMP TABLE ' || quote_ident(tablename) ||
               '(col1            INTEGER);'
```

Enforcing same name, same column definition

Sensibly designed databases have smooth, easy to understand definitions. This allows all users to understand the meaning of data in each table. It is an important way of removing data quality issues.

Getting ready

If you want to run the queries in this recipe as a test, then use the following examples. Alternatively, you can just check for problems in your own database:

```
CREATE SCHEMA S1;
CREATE SCHEMA S2;
CREATE TABLE S1.X
(col1 INTEGER
,col2 TEXT);
CREATE TABLE S2.X
(col1 INTEGER
,col3 NUMERIC);
```

How to do it...

Columns

We can identify columns that are defined in different ways in different tables using a query against the catalog. We use an Information Schema query, as follows:

```
SELECT
 table_schema
,table_name
,column_name
,data_type
   ||coalesce(' ' || text(character_maximum_length), '')
   ||coalesce(' ' || text(numeric_precision), '')
   ||coalesce(',' || text(numeric_scale), '')
   as data_type
FROM information_schema.columns
WHERE column_name IN
(SELECT
 column_name
FROM
(SELECT
  column_name
 ,data_type
 ,character_maximum_length
 ,numeric_precision
 ,numeric_scale
 FROM information_schema.columns
 WHERE table_schema = 'public'
 GROUP BY
  column_name
 ,data_type
 ,character_maximum_length
 ,numeric_precision
 ,numeric_scale
) derived
```

```
GROUP BY column_name
HAVING count(*) > 1
)
AND table_schema NOT IN ('information_schema', 'pg_catalog')
ORDER BY column_name
;
```

gives output, such as the following:

```
table_schema | table_name | column_name |   data_type
-------------+------------+-------------+---------------
s2           | x          | col1        | integer 32,0
s1           | x          | col1        | smallint 16,0
(2 rows)
```

Tables

Comparing two tables is more complex, as there are so many ways that a table might be similar and yet a little different. The following query looks for all tables of the same name (and hence in different schemas) that have different definitions:

```
SELECT
 table_schema
,table_name
,column_name
,data_type
FROM information_schema.columns
WHERE table_name IN
(SELECT
   table_name
 FROM
 (SELECT
    table_schema
   ,table_name
   ,string_agg(' '||column_name||' '||data_type)
   FROM information_schema.columns
   GROUP BY
    table_schema
   ,table_name
 ) def
 GROUP BY
  table_name
 HAVING
  count(*) > 1
)
ORDER BY
```

```
    table_name
  ,table_schema
  ,column_name;
```

This has output, such as the following:

```
  table_schema | table_name | column_name | data_type
  -------------+------------+-------------+-----------
    s1         | x          | col1        | smallint
    s1         | x          | col2        | text
    s2         | x          | col1        | integer
    s2         | x          | col3        | numeric
  (4 rows)
```

How it works...

The definitions of tables are held within PostgreSQL, and can be accessed using the Information Schema catalog views.

There might be valid reasons why the definitions differ. We've excluded PostgreSQL's own internal tables, because there are similar names between the two catalogs: PostgreSQL's implementation of the SQL Standard Information Schema and PostgreSQL's own internal `pg_catalog` schema.

Those queries are fairly complex. In fact, there is even more complexity we could add to those queries to compare all sorts of other things like DEFAULT values or constraints. The basic idea can be extended in various directions from.

There's more...

We can compare the definitions of any two tables using the following function:

```
CREATE OR REPLACE FUNCTION diff_table_definition
(t1_schemaname text
,t1_tablename text
,t2_schemaname text
,t2_tablename text)
RETURNS TABLE
(t1_column_name text
,t1_data_type text
,t2_column_name text
,t2_data_type text
)
LANGUAGE SQL
as
```

```
$$
SELECT
 t1.column_name
,t1.data_type
,t2.column_name
,t2.data_type
FROM
  (SELECT column_name, data_type
   FROM information_schema.columns
   WHERE table_schema = $1
     AND table_name = $2
  ) t1
  FULL OUTER JOIN
  (SELECT column_name, data_type
   FROM information_schema.columns
   WHERE table_schema = $3
     AND table_name = $4
  ) t2
  ON (t1.column_name = t2.column_name)
WHERE t1.column_name IS NULL OR t2.column_name IS NULL
;
$$;
```

Identifying and removing duplicates

Relational databases work on the idea that items of data can be uniquely identified. However hard we try, there will always be bad data arriving from somewhere. Following is how to diagnose that, and clean up the mess.

Getting ready

Let's start by looking at our example table `cust`

```
postgres=# SELECT * FROM cust;
 customerid | firstname | lastname | age
------------+-----------+----------+-----
          1 | Philip    | Marlowe  |  38
          2 | Richard   | Hannay   |  42
          3 | Holly     | Martins  |  25
          4 | Harry     | Palmer   |  36
          4 | Mark      | Hall     |  47
(5 rows)
```

that has a duplicate value in `customerid`.

Before you delete duplicate data, remember that sometimes it isn't the data that is wrong, it is your understanding of it. In those cases, it may be that you haven't properly normalized your database model, and that you need to include additional tables to account for the shape of the data. You might also find that duplicate rows are caused by having decided to exclude a column somewhere earlier in a data load process. Check twice, delete once.

How to do it...

First, identify the duplicates using a query, such as the following:

```
SELECT *
FROM cust
WHERE customerid IN
  (SELECT customerid
   FROM cust
   GROUP BY customerid
   HAVING count(*) > 1);
```

The results can be used to identify the bad data manually, and resolve the problem by carrying out the following steps:

- Merge the two rows to give the best picture of the data, if required. This might use values from one row to update the row you decide to keep, such as:

```
UPDATE cust
SET age = 47
WHERE customerid = 4
AND lastname = 'Palmer';
```

- DELETE the remaining undesirable rows:

```
DELETE FROM cust
WHERE customerid = 4
AND lastname = 'Hall';
```

In some cases, the data rows might be completely identical, as in the table new_cust, which looks like the following:

```
postgres=# SELECT * FROM new_cust;
 customerid
------------
          1
          2
          3
          4
          4
(5 rows)
```

In the preceding case, we can't tell the data apart at all, so we can remove duplicate rows without any manual process. SQL is a set-based language, so picking just one row out of a set is slightly harder than most people want it to be. Use a query block like the following to delete all the exactly duplicate rows, leaving just one row from each set of duplicates:

```
BEGIN;
LOCK TABLE new_cust IN ROW EXCLUSIVE MODE;
DELETE FROM  new_cust
WHERE ctid NOT IN
    (SELECT min(ctid)
     FROM new_cust
     WHERE customer_id IN (4)  --specify exact duplicate ids

     GROUP BY customerid);
COMMIT;
```

and then follow that with

```
VACUUM new_cust;
```

to clean up the table after the deletions.

How it works...

The first query works by grouping together the rows on the unique column and counting rows. Anything with more than one row must be caused by duplicate values. If we're looking for duplicates of more than one column (or even all columns) then we have to use an SQL of the following form:

```
SELECT *
FROM mytable
WHERE  (col1, col2, … ,colN) IN
(SELECT col1, col2, … ,colN
 FROM mytable
 GROUP BY  col1, col2, … ,colN
 HAVING count(*) > 1);
```

with (col1, col2, ... , colN) as the list of columns of the key.

Note that this type of query will need to sort the complete table on all of the key columns. That will require sort space equal to the size of the table, so you'd better think first before running that SQL on very large tables. You'll probably benefit from a large work_mem setting for this query, probably 128 MB or more.

The DELETE query that we showed only works with PostgreSQL, because it uses the ctid value which is the internal identifier of each row in the table. If you wanted to run that query against more than one column, as we did earlier in the chapter, you'd need to extend the query like the following:

```
DELETE FROM mytable
WHERE ctid NOT IN
    (SELECT min(ctid)
     FROM has_duplicates
     -- need WHERE clause to filter only exact duplicates

     GROUP BY col1, col2, …, colN);
```

The preceding query works by grouping together all the rows with similar values and then finding the row with the lowest `ctid` value. Lowest will mean nearer to the start of the table, so duplicates will be removed from the far end of the table. When we run VACUUM, we may find that the table gets smaller, because we have removed rows from the far end.

The BEGIN and COMMIT commands wrap the LOCK and DELETE commands into a single transaction. The LOCK command applies a sufficiently high level of lock against the table to prevent UPDATES and DELETES from being executed against the table while we remove duplicates.

There's more...

Locking the table against changes for long periods may not be possible while we remove duplicate rows. That gives some fairly hard problems with large tables. In that case, we need to do things slightly differently:

▶ Identify the rows to be deleted, and save them into a side table

▶ Build an index on the main table to speed access to rows

▶ Write a program that reads the rows from the side table in a loop, performing a series of smaller transactions.

▶ Start a new transaction

▶ Read a set of rows from the side table that match

▶ Select for update those rows from the main table, relying on the index to make those accesses happen quickly

▶ Delete the appropriate rows

▶ Commit, and then loop again

The aforementioned program can't be written as a database function, as we can't have multiple transactions in a function. We need multiple transactions to ensure we hold locks on each row for the shortest possible duration.

Preventing duplicate rows

Preventing duplicate rows is one of the most important aspects of data quality for any database. PostgreSQL offers some useful features in this area, extending beyond most relational databases.

Getting ready

Identify the set of columns that you wish to make unique. Does this apply to all rows, or just a subset of rows?

Let's start with our example table:

```
postgres=# SELECT * FROM newcust;
 customerid
------------
          1
          2
          3
          4
(4 rows)
```

How to do it...

To prevent duplicate rows, we need to create a unique index that the database server can use to enforce uniqueness of a particular set of columns.

We can do this in the following three similar ways for basic data types:

1. Create a Primary Key constraint on the set of columns. We are allowed only one of these per table. The values of the data rows must not be NULL, as we force the columns to be NOT NULL if they aren't already.

    ```
    ALTER TABLE newcust ADD PRIMARY KEY(customerid);
    ```

    which creates a new index named newcust_pkey

2. Create a UNIQUE constraint on the set of columns. We can use these instead of/as well as, a PRIMARY KEY. There is no limit on the number of these per table. NULLs are allowed in the columns.

    ```
    ALTER TABLE newcust ADD UNIQUE(customerid);
    ```

    which creates a new index named newcust_customerid_key

3. Create a UNIQUE INDEX on the set of columns.

    ```
    CREATE UNIQUE INDEX ON newcust (customerid);
    ```

    which creates a new index named newcust_customerid_idx

All of these techniques exclude duplicates, just with slightly different syntaxes. All of them create an index, though only the first two create a formal "constraint". Each of those techniques can be used when we have a primary key or unique constraint that uses multiple columns.

The last method is important, because it allows you to specify a WHERE clause on the index. This can be useful if you know that the column values are unique only in certain circumstances. The resulting index is then known as a partial index.

If our data looked like the following:

```
postgres=# select * from partial_unique;
 customerid | status | close_date
------------+--------+------------
          1 | OPEN   |
          2 | OPEN   |
          3 | OPEN   |
          3 | CLOSED | 2010-03-22
(4 rows)
```

then we could put a partial index on the table to enforce uniqueness of customerids only for status = 'OPEN', for example:

```
CREATE UNIQUE INDEX ON partial_unique (customerid)
  WHERE status = 'OPEN';
```

If your uniqueness constraint needs to be enforced across more complex datatypes, then there is a more advanced syntax you may need to use. A few examples will help here.

Let's start with the simplest example: Create a table of boxes and put sample data in it. This may be the first time you've seen PostgreSQL's datatype syntax, so bear with me.

```
postgres=# CREATE TABLE boxes (name text, position box);
CREATE TABLE
postgres=# INSERT INTO boxes VALUES
                      ('First', box '((0,0), (1,1))');
INSERT 0 1
postgres=# INSERT INTO boxes VALUES
                      ('Second', box '((2,0), (2,1))');
INSERT 0 1
postgres=# SELECT * FROM boxes;
  name  |   position
--------+-------------
 First  | (1,1),(0,0)
 Second | (2,1),(2,0)
(2 rows)
```

We can see two boxes that neither touch nor overlap, based upon their (x, y) coordinates.

To enforce uniqueness here, we want to create a constraint that will throw out any attempt to add a position that overlaps with any existing box. The overlap operator for the box datatype is defined to be &&, so we use the following syntax to add the constraint:

```
postgres=# ALTER TABLE boxes ADD EXCLUDE USING gist
                      (position WITH &&);
NOTICE:  ALTER TABLE / ADD EXCLUDE will create implicit index "boxes_
position_exclusion" for table "boxes"
ALTER TABLE
```

which creates a new index named `boxes_position_excl`.

We can use the same syntax even with the basic datatypes. So a fourth way of performing our first example would be as follows:

```
ALTER TABLE newcust ADD EXCLUDE (customerid WITH =);
```

which creates a new index named `newcust_customerid_excl`.

How it works...

Uniqueness is always enforced by an index.

Each index is defined with a datatype operator. When a new row is inserted or the set of column values are updated, we use the operator to search for existing values that conflict with the new data.

So, to enforce uniqueness, we need an index and a search operator defined on the datatypes of the columns. When we define normal `UNIQUE` constraints, we simply assume we mean the equality operator ("=") for the datatype. The `EXCLUDE` syntax offers a richer syntax to allow us to express the same problem with different datatypes and operators.

There's more...

Unique constraints can be marked as "deferrable". However, there are a number of restrictions on this that make this feature not very usable in PostgreSQL 9.0. The restrictions are as follows:

 ► You must define a constraint as `DEFERRABLE` on the `CREATE TABLE`. You cannot define this on a `CREATE TABLE AS SELECT`, nor can these be added later with an `ALTER TABLE` command.

 ► You cannot mix deferrable unique constraints with Foreign Keys. You will get an error message if you try to add a Foreign Key that refers to a unique constraint that is deferrable.

It's likely that those restrictions will be lifted in later releases.

Duplicate indexes

Note that PostgreSQL allows you to have multiple indexes with exactly the same definition. This is useful in some contexts, but can also be annoying if you accidentally create multiple indexes. You can also have constraints defined using each of the aforementioned different ways. Each of these ways enforce essentially the same constraint. Take care.

Uniqueness without indexes

It's possible to have uniqueness in a set of columns without creating an index. That might be useful if all we want is to ensure uniqueness rather than allow index lookups.

To do that, you can:

 ▸ Use a serial datatype

 ▸ Manually alter the default to be the `nextval()` of a sequence

Each of these will provide a unique value for use as a row's key. The uniqueness is not enforced, nor will there be a unique constraint defined. So, there is still a possibility that someone might reset the sequence to an earlier value, which would eventually cause duplicate values.

You might also wish to have *mostly* unique data, such as using the `timeofday()` function to provide ascending times to microsecond resolution.

Real World Example: IP address range allocation

The problem is assigning ranges of IP addresses while at the same time ensuring that we don't allocate (or potentially allocate) the same addresses to different people or purposes. This is easy to do if we keep track of each individual IP address, though much harder to do if we want to deal solely with ranges of IP addresses.

Initially, you may think of designing the database as follows:

```
CREATE TABLE iprange
(iprange_start inet
,iprange_stop inet
,owner text);
INSERT INTO iprange VALUES
    ('192.168.0.1','192.168.0.16', 'Simon');
INSERT INTO iprange VALUES
    ('192.168.0.17','192.168.0.24', 'Greg');
INSERT INTO iprange VALUES
    ('192.168.0.32','192.168.0.64', 'Hannu');
```

However, you realize that there is no way to create a unique constraint that enforces the constraint. You could create an after trigger that checks existing values, but it's going to be messy.

Download and install the ip4r datatype module for PostgreSQL, so we can get access to a good datatype for solving this type of problem. Download the ip4r module from the following website:

```
http://pgfoundry.org/projects/ip4r/
```

and then create a table like the following, and populate it with the same data in a slightly different form:

```
CREATE TABLE iprange2
(iprange ip4r
,owner text);
INSERT INTO iprange2 VALUES
    ('192.168.0.1-192.168.0.16', 'Simon');
INSERT INTO iprange2 VALUES
    ('192.168.0.17-192.168.0.24', 'Greg');
INSERT INTO iprange2 VALUES
    ('192.168.0.32-192.168.0.64', 'Hannu');
```

You can now create a unique exclusion constraint on the table using the following command:

```
ALTER TABLE iprange2
ADD EXCLUDE USING GIST (iprange WITH &&);
```

Real World Example: Range of time

In many databases there will be historical data tables with data that has a START_DATE and an END_DATE, or similar. Another external module for PostgreSQL supports this, with a datatype named a "period".

A period is a pair of TIMESTAMPTZ values that allow you to define the start and end timestamptz (date/time). Take a look at the following website:

```
http://temporal.projects.postgresql.org/
```

Real World Example: Prefix ranges

Another common problem is assigning credit card numbers or telephone numbers. For example, with credit card numbers, we may need to perform additional checking for certain financial institutions.

The prefix range datatype has been specifically designed to address this class of problem. Again, this is available as a PostgreSQL plugin at the following URL:

```
http://github.com/dimitri/prefix
```

Finding a unique key for a set of data

Sometimes it can be difficult to find a unique set of key columns that describe the data.

Getting ready

Let's start with a small table, where the answer is fairly obvious.

```
postgres=# select * from ord;
 orderid | customerid |  amt
---------+------------+--------
   10677 |          2 |   5.50
    5019 |          3 | 277.44
    9748 |          3 |  77.17
(3 rows)
```

How to do it...

First of all, there's no need to do this through a brute-force approach. Checking all of the permutations of columns to see which is unique might take you a long time.

Let's start by using PostgreSQL's own optimizer statistics. Run the following command on our table to get a fresh sample of statistics:

```
postgres=# analyze ord;
ANALYZE
```

This runs quickly, so not long to wait.

Now we can examine the relevant columns of the statistics.

```
postgres=# SELECT attname, n_distinct
                  FROM pg_stats
                  WHERE schemaname = 'public'
                    AND tablename = 'ord';

   attname   | n_distinct
-------------+------------
 orderid     |         -1
 customerid  |  -0.666667
 amt         |         -1
(3 rows)
```

The preceding example was chosen because we have two potential answers. If the value of n_distinct is -1, then the column is thought to be unique within the sample of rows examined.

We would then need to use our judgment to decide whether one or both of those columns are unique by chance, or as part of the design of the database that created them.

It's possible that there is no single column that uniquely identifies the rows. Multiple column keys are fairly common. If none of the columns were unique, then we would start to look for unique keys that are combinations of the most unique columns. The following query shows a frequency distribution for the table: a value occurs twice in one case, and another value occurs only once.

```
postgres=# SELECT count as num_of_values, count(*)
                    FROM (SELECT customerid, count(*)
                            FROM ord
                            GROUP BY customerid) s
                GROUP BY count
                ORDER BY count(*);
 num_of_values | count
---------------+-------
            2 |     1
            1 |     1
(2 rows)
```

and we can change the query to include multiple columns, like the following:

```
SELECT count as num_of_values, count(*)
FROM (SELECT    column1, column2.... columnN
            ,count(*)
            FROM ord
            GROUP BY column1, column2.... columnN
        ) s
GROUP BY count
ORDER BY count(*);
```

This query will result in just one row, once we find a set of columns that is unique. As we get closer to finding the key, we will see that the distribution gets tighter and tighter.

How it works...

Finding a unique key is possible for a program, though in most cases, a human can do this much faster by looking at things like column names, foreign keys, or business understanding to reduce the number of searches required by the brute-force approach.

ANALYZE works by taking a sample of the table data, and then performing a statistical analysis of the results. The n_distinct value is the estimate of the "number of distinct values" for the column.

Generating test data

DBAs frequently need to generate test data for a variety of reasons, whether it's to set up a test database or just to generate a test case for an SQL performance issue.

How to do it...

To create a table of test data we need the following:

- ▸ Some rows
- ▸ Some columns
- ▸ Some order

Rows

To generate a lot of rows of data, we use something named a "set returning function". You can write your own, though PostgreSQL includes a couple of very useful ones.

You can generate a sequence of rows using a query, like the following:

```
postgres=# SELECT * FROM generate_series(1,5);
 generate_series
-----------------
               1
               2
               3
               4
               5
(5 rows)
```

or you can generate a list of dates, like the following:

```
postgres=# SELECT date(generate_series(now(), now() + '1 week', '1
day'));
    date
-----------
 2010-03-30
 2010-03-31
 2010-04-01
 2010-04-02
 2010-04-03
 2010-04-04
 2010-04-05
 2010-04-06
(8 rows)
```

Either of those functions can be used to generate both rows and reasonable Primary Key values for them.

Columns

Now, we want to generate a value for each column in the test table. We can break that down into a series of functions, using the following examples as a guide:

Random integer

```
(random()*(2*10^9))::integer
```

Random bigint

```
(random()*(9*10^18))::bigint
```

Random numeric data

```
(random()*100.)::numeric(4,2);
```

Random length string, up to a maximum length

```
repeat('1',(random()*40)::integer)
```

Random length substring

```
substr('abcdefghijklmnopqrstuvwxyz',1, (random()*26)::integer)
```

Random string from a list of strings

```
(ARRAY['one','two','three'])[1+random()*3]
```

ORDER

We can put both together to generate our table:

```
postgres=# SELECT generate_series(1,10) as key
                     ,(random()*100.)::numeric(4,2)
                     ,repeat('1',(random()*25)::integer);

 key | numeric |          repeat
-----+---------+-------------------------
   1 |   83.05 | 1111
   2 |    5.28 | 11111111111111
   3 |   41.85 | 111111111111111111111111
   4 |   41.70 | 1111111111111111
   5 |   53.31 | 1
   6 |   10.09 | 11111111111111111
   7 |   68.08 | 111
   8 |   19.42 | 11111111111111111
   9 |   87.03 | 11111111111111111111111
  10 |   70.64 | 1111111111111111
(10 rows)
```

or even using a random ordering

```
postgres=# SELECT generate_series(1,10) as key
                     , (random()*100.)::numeric(4,2)
                     , repeat('1', (random()*25)::integer)
                     ORDER BY random();
 key | numeric |           repeat
-----+---------+-------------------------
   6 |   70.31 | 111111111111111111111111
   4 |    2.37 | 11111111111111111111
   1 |   76.99 | 1111111111111
   8 |   35.90 | 111111111111
   3 |   59.21 | 111111111
   2 |   88.86 | 11111111
   7 |   67.32 | 111111
   9 |   15.66 | 111111
   5 |   79.90 | 11111
  10 |   25.09 | 1
(10 rows)
```

How it works...

Set returning functions literally return a set of rows. That allows them to be used in either the FROM clause, as if they were a table, or in the SELECT clause. The generate_series() set of functions return either dates or integers, depending upon the datatypes of the input parameters you use.

The :: operator is used to cast between datatypes.

The "random string from a list of strings" example uses PostgreSQL arrays. You can create an array using the ARRAY constructor syntax, and then use an integer to reference one element in the array. In our case, we used a random subscript.

There's more...

There are also some commercial tools to generate application-specific test data for PostgreSQL. Both of the tools listed here are under $250 per copy. Not too much money, so OK to mention in an open source software book!

http://www.sqlmanager.net/products/postgresql/datagenerator

http://www.datanamic.com/datagenerator/index.html

Key features for any data generator would be as follows:

- ▶ Ability to generate data in the right format for custom data types
- ▶ Ability to add data to multiple tables, while respecting Foreign Key constraints between tables
- ▶ Ability to add data in non-uniform distributions

See also

The tools and tricks shown here are cool and clever, though there are some problems hiding here as well. Real data has so many strange things in it that it can be very hard to simulate. One of the most difficult things is generating data that follows realistic distributions. For example, if we had to generate data for people's heights, then we'd want to generate data to follow a normal distribution. If we were generating customer bank balances we'd want to use a Zipf distribution, or for number of reported insurance claims, perhaps a Poisson distribution (or perhaps not). Replicating the real quirks in data can take some time.

You can use existing data to generate test databases using sampling. That's the subject of our next recipe.

Randomly sampling data

DBAs may be asked to set up a test server, and populate it with test data. Often, that server will be old hardware, possibly with smaller disk sizes. So, the subject of data sampling raises its head.

The purpose of sampling is to reduce the size of the data set and improve the speed of later analysis. Some statisticians are so used to the idea of sampling that they may not even question whether its use is valid, or cause further complications.

How to do it...

First, you should realize that there isn't a simple tool to slice off a sample of your database. It would be neat if there were, but there isn't. You'll need to read all of this to understand why.

We first need to consider some SQL to derive a sample. Random sampling is actually very simple, because we can use the SQL function `random()` within the `WHERE` clause. For example:

```
postgres=# SELECT count(*) FROM mybigtable;
  count
 -------
  10000
(1 row)
postgres=# SELECT count(*) FROM mybigtable
                   WHERE random() < 0.01;
  count
```

```
    -------
        95
    (1 row)
    postgres=# SELECT count(*) FROM mybigtable
                          WHERE random() < 0.01;
      count
    -------
       106
    (1 row)
```

The clause WHERE random() < 0.01 will generate a random number between 0.0 and 1.0 for each row, and then see if the number is less than 0.01. In other words, this WHERE clause will generate a 1% random sample of rows in the table. You can use a similar clause to vary the percentage to be anything you choose. Easy.

Now we need to get the sampled data out of the database, which is tricky for a few reasons. First, there is no option to specify a WHERE clause for pg_dump. Second, if you create a view that contains the WHERE clause, pg_dump only dumps the view definition, not the view itself.

You can use pg_dump to dump all databases apart from a set of tables, so you can produce a sampled dump like the following:

```
pg_dump --exclude-table=MyBigTable > db.dmp
pg_dump --table=MyBigTable –schema-only > mybigtable.schema
psql -c '\copy (SELECT * FROM MyBigTable
                WHERE random() < 0.01) to mybigtable.dat'
```

and then reload onto a separate database using

```
psql -f db.dmp
psql -f mybigtable.schema
psql -c '\copy mybigtable from mybigtable.dat'
```

Overall, my advice is to avoid sampling if you can. Otherwise, at least minimize it to a few very large tables. This avoids both the mathematical issues surrounding sample design, and the difficulty of extracting the data.

How it works...

The extract mechanism shows off the capabilities of the PostgreSQL command-line tools, psql and pg_dump, as pg_dump allows you to include or exclude files and to dump the whole table, or just its schema, whereas Psql allows you to dump out the result of an arbitrary query to a file.

I haven't discussed how random the random() function is. This isn't the right place for such details; if you prefer another mechanism, you can find an external random number generator, and call out to it from SQL using a C language function.

The sampling method shown earlier is a simple random sampling technique that has an "equal probability of selection" (EPS) design.

EPS samples are considered useful because the variance of the sample attributes is similar to the variance of the original data set. Though, bear in mind that this is only useful if you are considering variances.

Simple random sampling can make the eventual sample biased towards more frequently occurring data. For example, if you have 1% sample of data on which some kinds of data occur only 0.001% of the time, you may end up with a data set that doesn't have any of that outlying data.

What you might wish to do is to pre-cluster your data, and take different samples from each group, to ensure that you have a sampled data set that includes many more outlying attributes. A simple method might be to:

- Include 1% of all normal data
- Include 25% of outlying data

Note that if you do this, then it is no longer an "EPS" sample design.

See also

There are no doubt statisticians who will be in apoplexy after reading this. You're welcome to use the facilities of the SQL language to create a more accurate sample. Please, just make sure that you know what you're doing and/or check out some good statistical literature, websites, or textbooks.

Loading data from a spreadsheet

Spreadsheets are the most obvious starting place for most data stores. Studies within a range of businesses consistently show that more than 50% of smaller data stores are held in spreadsheets or small desktop databases. Loading data from these sources is a frequent and important task for many DBAs.

Getting ready

Spreadsheets combine data, presentation, and programs all in one file. That's perfect for power users wanting to work quickly. Like other relational databases, PostgreSQL is mainly concerned with the lowest level of data, so extracting just the data can present some challenges.

We can easily handle spreadsheet data if that spreadsheet's layout follows a very specific form, as follows:

- ▶ Each spreadsheet column becomes one column in one table.
- ▶ Each row of the spreadsheet becomes one row in one table.
- ▶ Data is only in one worksheet of the spreadsheet.
- ▶ Optionally, the first row is a list of column descriptions/titles.

This is a very simple layout and more often there will be other things in the spreadsheet, such as titles, comments, constants for use in formulas, summary lines, macros, images, and so on. If you're in this position, the best thing to do is to create a new worksheet within the spreadsheet in the pristine form described earlier, and then set up cross-worksheet references to bring in the data. An example of a cross-worksheet reference would be "=Sheet2.A1". You'll need a separate worksheet for each set of data that will become one table on PostgreSQL. You can load multiple worksheets into one table though.

Some spreadsheet users will say that this is all unnecessary, and is evidence of the problems of databases. The real spreadsheet gurus do actually advocate this type of layout: data in one worksheet, calculation and presentation in other worksheets. So it is actually best practice to design spreadsheets in this way; however, we must work with the world the way it is.

How to do it...

If your spreadsheet data is neatly laid out in a single worksheet as shown in the following screenshot, then you can do **File | Save As** and then select **CSV** as the file type to be saved.

This will export the current worksheet into a file like the following:

```
"Key","Value"
1,"c"
2,"d"
```

We can then load it into an existing PostgreSQL table, using the psql command

```
postgres=# \COPY sample FROM sample.csv CSV HEADER
postgres=# SELECT * FROM sample;
 key | value
-----+-------
   1 | c
   2 | d
```

Or from the command line this would be, as follows:

```
psql -c '\COPY sample FROM sample.csv CSV HEADER'
```

Note that the file can include a full file path if the data is in a different directory. The `psql \COPY` command transfers data from the client system where you run the command through to the database server, so the file is on the client.

If you are submitting SQL through another type of connection, then you would use the following SQL statement:

```
COPY sample FROM '/mydatafiledirectory/sample.csv' CSV HEADER;
```

Note that the preceding SQL statement runs on the database server, and can only be executed by a superuser. So you would need to transfer the data yourself to the server, and then load. The COPY statement shown in the preceding SQL statement uses an absolute path to identify data files, which is required.

The COPY (or `\COPY`) command does not create the table for you; that must be done beforehand. Note also that the `HEADER` option does nothing but ignore the first line of the input file, so the names of the columns from the `.csv` file don't need to match the Postgres table. If it hasn't occurred to you yet, this is also a problem. If you say HEADER and the file does not have a header line, then all it does is ignore the first data row. Unfortunately, there's no way for PostgreSQL to tell whether the first line of the file is truly headers or not. Be careful.

There isn't a standard tool to load data directly from the spreadsheet to the database. It's fairly simple to write a spreadsheet macro to automate the aforementioned tasks, but not a topic for this book.

How it works...

The `\COPY` command executes a `COPY` SQL statement, so the two methods described earlier are very similar. There's more to be said about `COPY`, so we'll cover that in the next recipe.

See also

There are many data extract and loading tools available out there, some cheap, some expensive. Remember that the hardest part of loading data from any spreadsheet is separating out the data from all the other things they contain. I've not yet seen a tool that can help with that.

Loading data from flat files

Loading data into your database is one of the most important tasks. You need to do this accurately and quickly. Here's how.

Getting ready

You'll need a copy of **pgloader** that is available at the following website:

```
http://pgloader.projects.postgresql.org/
```

How to do it...

PostgreSQL includes a command named COPY that provides the basic data load/unload mechanism. COPY doesn't do enough when loading data, so let's skip the basic command and go straight to pgloader.

To load data we need to understand our requirements, so let's break this down into a step-by-step process, as follows:

- ▶ Identify data files and where they are located. Make sure pgloader is installed at the location of the files.

- ▶ Identify the table into which we are loading, and ensure that we have permissions to load, and check the available space.

- ▶ Work out the file type (fixed, text, or CSV), and check the encoding.

- ▶ Specify the mapping between columns in the file and columns on the table being loaded. Make sure you know which columns in the file are not needed—pgloader allows you to include only the columns you want. Identify any columns in the table for which we don't have data. Do we need them to have a DEFAULT value on the table, or does pgloader need to generate values for those columns through functions or constants?

- ▶ Specify any transformations that need to take place. The most common issue is date formats, though possibly there may be other issues.

- ▶ Write the pgloader script and test it using --dry-run. Then, try loading just a few records using --count.

- ▶ Consider whether you need a log file to record whether the load has succeeded or failed, and whether that needs automating. Also, consider what will happen to rejected rows, and where you want the rejected log file to be placed, in case it overflows.

- ▶ Lastly, consider what settings we need for performance options. This is definitely last, as fiddling with things earlier can lead to confusion when you're still making the load work correctly.

Yes, I always recommend that you use a script to execute pgloader. It makes it much easier to iterate towards something that works. Loads never work first time, except in the movies.

Let's look at a typical example: `cookbook_pgloader.conf`

```
[pgsql]
host = 192.168.0.5
base = pgloader
user = dim
log_file            = /tmp/pgloader.log
log_min_messages    = DEBUG
client_min_messages = WARNING
lc_messages         = C
client_encoding = 'utf-8'
copy_every        = 10000
null          = ""
empty_string = "\ "
max_parallel_sections = 4
[load]
table           = load_example
filename        = simple/simple.data
format      = csv
datestyle   = dmy
field_sep   = |
trailing_sep = True
columns         = a:1, b:3, c:2
reject_log   = /tmp/simple.rej.log
reject_data  = /tmp/simple.rej
section_threads = 4
```

We can use the load script like the following:

```
pgloader --summary --vacuum --config cookbook_pgloader.conf
```

How it works...

pgloader copes gracefully with errors. `copy` loads all rows in a single transaction, so only a single error is enough to abort the load. pgloader breaks down an input file into reasonably sized chunks, and loads them piece-by-piece. If some rows cause errors, then pgloader will iteratively check them so that it can skip those bad rows.

pgloader is written in Python, and allows connection to PostgreSQL through the standard Python client interface. Yes, pgloader is less efficient than loading data files using a COPY command, but running a COPY has many more restrictions: the file has to already be in the right place on the server, has to be in the right format, and must be unlikely to throw errors on load. pgloader has additional overhead, but it also has the ability to load data using multiple parallel threads, so it can be faster to use as well. pgloader's ability to call out to reformat functions written in Python is often essential in most cases; straight COPY is just too simple.

pgloader also allows loading from fixed-width files, which COPY cannot.

There's more...

If you need to reload the table from fresh completely, then specify `--truncate` on the command line of pgloader.

After loading, if we had load errors, then there will be some junk loaded into the PostgreSQL tables. Not junk you can see, or that gives any semantic errors, but think of it more like fragmentation. You should think about whether you need to run with `--vacuum` as an additional option, though this will make the load take possibly much longer.

We need to be careful to avoid loading data twice. The only easy way of doing that is to make sure there is at least one unique index defined on every table that you load. The load should then fail very quickly.

String handling can often be difficult, because of the presence of formatting or non-printable characters. The default setting for PostgreSQL is to have a parameter named `standard_conforming_strings` set off, which means that backslashes will be assumed to be escape characters. Put another way, by default the string '\n' means linefeed, that can cause data to appear truncated. You'll need to turn `standard_conforming_strings = on`, or you'll need to specify an escape character in the load-parameter file.

If you are re-loading data that has been unloaded from PostgreSQL, then you may want to use the `pg_restore` utility instead.. The `pg_restore` utility has an option to reload data in parallel, -j number_of_threads, though this is only possible if the dump was produced using the `custom pg_dump` format. Refer to the recipes in the *Backup* chapter for more details. This can be useful for reloading dumps, though it lacks almost all of the other pgloader features discussed here.

See also

You may wish to send an e-mail to Dimitri Fontaine, the current author and maintainer of most of pgloader. He always loves to receive e-mails from users.

6
Security

In this chapter, we will cover the following:

- ▶ Revoking user access to a table
- ▶ Granting user access to a table
- ▶ Creating a new user
- ▶ Temporarily preventing a user from connecting
- ▶ Removing a user without dropping their data
- ▶ Checking whether all users have a secure password
- ▶ Giving limited superuser powers to specific users
- ▶ Auditing DDL changes
- ▶ Auditing data changes
- ▶ Integrating with LDAP
- ▶ Connecting using SSL
- ▶ Encrypting sensitive data

Introduction

Databases are mostly used for keeping data, which has several restrictions on how it is used. Some records or tables can only be seen by certain users, and even for those tables which are visible to everyone, there can be restrictions on who can use the data, insert new data or change the existing data. All this is managed by a privilege system, where users are granted different privileges for different tables or other database objects, such as schemas or functions.

It is a good practice to not "grant" these roles directly to users, but to use an intermediate ROLE for collecting a set of privileges. Then, this role is granted to users who fit this role. For example, a role "clerk" may have rights to both insert data and update existing data in table `user_account`, but may have rights only to insert data in `audit_log` table.

Another aspect of database security is making sure that only the right people can access the database, and that one can't see what other users are doing (unless you are administrator or auditor,) that users can or cannot grant forward the roles granted to them.

Part of security is also making sure that database servers are in physically secure locations, and that procedures to access these servers are secure. However, this is not a general guide to securing your database, server machine, or network, which is too large a topic to be covered here.

If you are serious about security, then read some of the available books and articles on security, or hire a security consultant. Database security is just a small piece in the overall security puzzle.

Typical user role

The minimal production database setup contains at least two types of users, namely, administrators and end-users, where administrators can do everything (are superusers), and end-users can only do very little, usually just modify the data in a few tables, and read from a few more.

It is not a good idea to let ordinary users create or change database object definitions, meaning that they should not have the CREATE privilege on any schema, including PUBLIC.

There can be other roles for end-users, such as analysts, who can only select from a single table or view, or execute a few functions.

Alternatively, there can also be a manager role, which can grant and revoke roles for other users, but is not supposed to do anything else.

Revoking user access to a table

This recipe answers the question "How do I make sure that the user X cannot access the table Y?"

Getting ready

The current user must either be a superuser, the owner of the table, or must have a GRANT option for the table.

Also, you can't revoke rights from a user who is a superuser.

How to do it...

To revoke all rights to table `mysecrettable` from user `userwhoshouldnotseeit`, one must run the following SQL command:

```
REVOKE ALL ON mysecrettable FROM userwhoshoudnotseeit;
```

However, because the table is usually also accessible to all users through role `PUBLIC`, the following must also be run:

```
REVOKE ALL ON mysecrettable FROM PUBLIC;
```

How it works...

By default all users have a set of rights (`SELECT`, `INSERT`, `UPDATE`, `DELETE`, `TRUNCATE`, `REFERENCES`, and `TRIGGER`) to all newly created tables through the special role `PUBLIC`.

To make sure that some user no longer can access a table, the right(s) to that table must be revoked from both `PUBLIC` and that specific user.

There's more...

`GRANT` option and `CASCADE`

`REVOKE ... SCHEMA`

Best practices

For production systems, it is usually a good idea to include `GRANT` and `REVOKE` statements in the database creation script always, so you can be sure that only the right set of users has access to the table. If it is done manually, it is easy to forget. Also, this way, we are sure that the same roles are used on development and testing environments, so there are no surprises at deployment time.

Sample extract from database creation script is as follows:

```
CREATE TABLE table1(
...
);
REVOKE ALL ON table1 FROM GROUP PUBLIC;
GRANT SELECT ON  table1 TO GROUP webreaders;
GRANT SELECT, INSERT, UPDATE, DELETE ON  table1 TO editors;
GRANT ALL ON table1 TO  admins;
```

Default search path

It is always a good practice to use a fully qualified name when revoking or granting rights, as you may otherwise inadvertently be working with the wrong table.

To see effective database path, run the following:

```
pguser=# show search_path ;
  search_path
----------------
 "$user",public
(1 row)
```

To see which table would be affected if you omit the schema name, run the following in psql:

```
pguser=# \d x
      Table "public.x"
 Column | Type | Modifiers
--------+------+-----------
```

The table name `public.x` in the response contains the full name including the schema.

Granting user access to a table

A user needs to have access to a table in order to perform any action on it. Although the default behavior of PostgreSQL database is to give full access to all users through role PUBLIC, a security-conscious database setup revokes rights from PUBLIC after table creation.

Getting ready

Make sure that you have appropriate "roles" defined, and that privileges are "revoked" from role PUBLIC.

How to do it...

Grant access to schema containing the table to:

```
GRANT ALL ON someschema TO somerole;
GRANT SELECT, INSERT, UPDATE, DELETE ON  someschema.sometable TO
somegroup;
GRANT somerole TO someuser, otheruser;
```

How it works...

This sequence of commands first grants full access in schema to a role, gives viewing (SELECT) and modifying (INSERT, UPDATE, DELETE) rights to the role, and then grants membership in this role to two database users.

There's more...

There is no requirement in PostgreSQL to have some privileges in order to have others. That is, you may well have "write-only" tables, where you are allowed to insert but you can't select. This can be used for implementing a mail queue like functionality, where several users post messages to one user, but can't see what other users have posted.

Alternatively, you can write a record, but you can't change or delete it. This is useful for auditing log type tables, where all changes are recorded, and with which are not tampered.

Access to schema is also needed

In order to access any table, the user first needs access to the schema containing the table:

```
GRANT USAGE ON SCHEMA someschema TO someuser;
```

Granting access to a table through a group role

It is often desirable to give groups of users similar permissions to a group of database objects. To do this, you first assign all the permissions to a proxy role (also known as a permission group), and then assign the group to selected users, as follows:

```
CREATE GROUP webreaders;
GRANT SELECT ON pages TO webreaders;
GRANT INSERT ON viewlog TO webreaders;
GRANT webreaders TO tim, bob;
```

Now, both tim and bob have the SELECT privilege on table pages, and INSERT on table viewlog. You can also add privileges to the group role after assigning it to users. So after:

```
GRANT INSERT, UPDATE, DELETE ON comments TO webreaders;
```

both bob and tim have all these privileges on table comments.

Granting access to all objects in schema

Before Version 9.0 of PostgreSQL, there was no easy way to manipulate privileges to more than one object at a time, except listing them all in the GRANT or REVOKE command.

Version 9.0 added a capability to GRANT or REVOKE privileges on all objects of a certain kind in a specific schema:

```
GRANT SELECT ON ALL TABLES IN SCHEMA staging TO bob;
```

You still need to grant the privileges on the schema itself in a separate grant statement.

Creating a new user

In this recipe we show two ways of creating a new database user, one from the command line, and one using SQL commands.

Getting ready

To create new users, you must either be a superuser or have the createrole or createuser privilege.

How to do it...

From command line, you run the creatuser command, and answer a few questions:

```
pguser@hvost:~$ createuser bob
Shall the new role be a superuser? (y/n) n
Shall the new role be allowed to create databases? (y/n) y
Shall the new role be allowed to create more new roles? (y/n) n
pguser@hvost:~$ createuser tim
Shall the new role be a superuser? (y/n) y
```

How it works...

The program createuser is just a shallow wrapper around executing SQL against the database cluster. It connects to database "postgres", asks a question, and then executes SQL commands for user creation. To create the same users through SQL, you run CREATE USER SQL command as follows:

```
CREATE ROLE bob WITH NOSUPERUSER INHERIT NOCREATEROLE CREATEDB LOGIN;
CREATE ROLE tim WITH SUPERUSER;
```

There's more...

Checking roles of a user

```
pguser=# \du tim
            List of roles
  Role name | Attributes  | Member of
 -----------+-------------+-----------
   tim       | Superuser   | {}
            : Create role
            : Create DB
pguser=# \du bob
            List of roles
  Role name | Attributes  | Member of
 -----------+------------ +-----------
   bob       | Create DB   | {}
```

CREATE USER and CREATE GROUP

Starting from Version 8.x, the commands CREATE USER and CREATE GROUP are actually variations of CREATE ROLE.

CREATE USER u; is equivalent to CREATE ROLE u LOGIN; and CREATE GROUP g; is equivalent to CREATE ROLE g NOLOGIN;

Temporarily preventing a user from connecting

Sometimes you need to temporarily revoke user's connection rights without actually deleting the user or changing the user's password.

This recipe presents ways to do this.

Getting ready

To modify other users, you must either be a superuser or have the CREATEROLE privilege (in the latter case only non-superuser roles can be altered).

How to do it...

To temporarily prevent the user from logging in, run the following:

```
pguser=# alter user bob nologin;
ALTER ROLE
```

To let the user connect again, run the following:

```
pguser=# alter user bob login;
ALTER ROLE
```

How it works...

This sets a flag in the system catalog telling PostgreSQL not to let the user to log in. It does not kick out already connected users.

Limiting number of concurrent connections by a user

The same result can be achieved by setting `connection limit` for that user to `0`:

```
pguser=# alter user bob connection limit 0;
ALTER ROLE
```

To allow bob 10 concurrent connections, run the following:

```
pguser=# alter user bob connection limit 10;
ALTER ROLE
```

To allow an unlimited number of connections by this user, run the following:

```
pguser=# alter user bob connection limit -1;
ALTER ROLE
```

Forcing NOLOGIN users to disconnect

In order to make sure that all users whose login privilege has been revoked are disconnected right away, run the following SQL statement as a superuser:

```
SELECT pg_terminate_backend(procpid)
  FROM from pg_stat_activity a
    JOIN pg_roles r ON a.usename = r.rolname AND not rolcanlogin;
```

On older versions of postgresql, where `pg_terminate_backend()` function does not exist, you can get the same effect from shell by running the following as user postgres on the database server:

```
postgres@hvost:~$ psql -t -c "\
 select 'kill ' || procpid from pg_stat_activity a \
 join pg_roles r on a.usename = r.rolname and not rolcanlogin;"\
  | bash
```

This incantation constructs proper `kill` commands from a query, and then feeds them to the shell for execution.

Removing a user without dropping their data

When trying to drop a user who owns some tables or other database objects, you get the following error and the user is not dropped:

```
testdb=# drop user bob;
ERROR:  role "bob" cannot be dropped because some objects depend on it
DETAIL:  owner of table bobstable
owner of sequence bobstable_id_seq
```

This recipe presents solutions to this problem.

Getting ready

To modify users, you must either be a superuser or have the CREATEROLE privilege.

How to do it...

The easiest solution to this problem is to not drop the user at all, but just use the trick from a previous recipe to disallow the user from connecting:

```
pguser=# alter user bob nologin;
ALTER ROLE
```

This has the added benefit of having the original owner of the table available later, if needed, for auditing or debugging purposes ("why is this table here? Who created it?")

How it works...

This turns the user into a role with no login.

You can assign the rights of the "deleted" user to a new user

Use the following code:

```
pguser=# grant bob bobs_replacement;
GRANT
```

Assigning ownerships to other users

If you really need to get rid of a user, you have to assign all ownerships to another user, then run the following query, which is a PostgreSQL extension to SQL standard:

```
REASSIGN OWNED BY bob TO  bobs_replacement;
```

It does exactly what its says—assigns ownership of all database objects currently owned by role bob to role bobs_replacement;

However, you need to have privileges on both the old and new role to do that and you need to do it in all databases where bob owns any objects, as the REASSIGN OWNED works only on the current database.

Reassigning ownership in older databases

REASSIGN OWNED was added to PostgreSQL in Version 8.2. If you need to change ownership in older databases, then this can be done with Unix command-line utilities magic.

First extract the ownership assignments from schema dump:

```
dbuser:~$ pg_dump -s mydatabase | grep -i "alter.*owner to bob"
ALTER FUNCTION public.somefunction() OWNER TO bob;
ALTER TABLE public.directory OWNER TO bob;
ALTER TABLE public.directory_seq OWNER TO bob;
ALTER TABLE public.document_id_seq OWNER TO bob;
ALTER TABLE public.documents OWNER TO bob;
```

Then just replace Bob in this output with new users name and feed the commands back to database:

```
dbuser:~$ pg_dump -s mydb | grep -i "owner to bob" > tmp.sql
dbuser:~$ sed -e 's/TO bob/TO bobs_replacement/' < tmp.sql | psql
mydb
```

Of course it is a good idea to look at the changed data first.

```
dbuser:~$ pg_dump -s mydb | grep -i "owner to bob" > tmp.sql
dbuser:~$ sed -e 's/TO bob/TO bobs_replacement/' < tmp.sql >tmp2.sql
dbuser:~$ less tmp2.sql
dbuser:~$ psql  mydb < tmp2.sql
```

Again, this works on one database at a time, so you have to repeat it in all databases that have objects owned by the role you want to delete.

Checking all users have a secure password

PostgreSQL has no built-in facilities to make sure that you are using strong passwords.

The best you can do is to make sure that all users' passwords are encrypted, and that your pg_hba file does not allow logins with a plain password. That is, always use MD5 as login method for users.

For client applications connecting from trusted private networks, either real or virtual (VPN), you may use host based access. That is, if you know that the machine on which the application is running is also not used by some non-trusted individuals. For remote access over public networks, it may be a better idea to use SSL client certificates.

Getting ready

To see which users have unencrypted passwords, use the following query:

```
test2=# select usename,passwd from pg_shadow where passwd not like
'md5%' or length(passwd) <> 35;
 usename   |    passwd
-----------+--------------
 tim       | weakpassword
 asterisk  | md5chicken
(2 rows)
```

To see users with encrypted passwords, use the following:

```
test2=# select usename,passwd from pg_shadow where passwd like 'md5%'
and length(passwd) = 35;
 usename   |                passwd
-----------+-------------------------------------
 bob2      | md518cf038878cd04fa207e7f5602013a36
(1 row)
```

How to do it...

Having the passwords encrypted in the database is just half of the equation.

The bigger problem is making sure that the users actually use passwords that are hard to guess. That is passwords like "password", 'secret', or 'test' are out, and also, most common words are not good passwords.

If you don't trust your users to select strong passwords, you can write a wrapper application that checks the password strength and have them use that when changing passwords. There exists a contrib module for doing so for a limited set of cases (password sent from client to server in plaintext). Visit the following website for more information:

```
http://developer.postgresql.org/pgdocs/postgres/passwordcheck.html
```

Giving limited superuser powers to specific users

First, the superuser role has some privileges, which can also be granted to non-superuser roles separately.

To give the role Bob the ability to create new databases, run the following:

```
ALTER ROLE BOB WITH CREATEDB;
```

To give the role bob the ability to create new users, run the following:

```
ALTER ROLE BOB WITH CREATEUSER;
```

However, it is also possible to give ordinary users more fine-grained and controlled access to some action reserved for superusers by using SECURITY DEFINER functions. The same trick can also be used for passing on partial privileges between different users.

Getting ready

First, you must have access to the database as a superuser in order to delegate some powers. Here, we assume the use of the default superuser named postgres.

We will demonstrate two cases of making some superuser-only functionality available to select an ordinary user.

The database must have support for embedded language PL/pgSQL installed. Starting from PostgreSQL 9.0 the recommended default behavior is to have pl/pgSQL installed in newly created database, but this can be changed by package creators or site administrators. If it is not, run the following as PostgreSQL superuser:

```
test2=# CREATE LANGUAGE plpgsql;
CREATE LANGUAGE
```

How to do it...

One thing that a superuser can do, and ordinary users cannot, is telling postgres to copy table data from file:

```
pguser@hvost:~$ psql -U postgres
 test2
...
test2=# create table lines(line text);
CREATE TABLE
test2=# copy lines from '/home/bob/names.txt';
```

```
COPY 37
test2=# SET SESSION AUTHORIZATION bob;
SET
test2=> copy lines from '/home/bob/names.txt';
ERROR:  must be superuser to COPY to or from a file
HINT:  Anyone can COPY to stdout or from stdin. psql's \copy command
also works for anyone.
```

To let user Bob copy directly from file, the superuser can write a special wrapper function for Bob, as follows:

```
create or replace function copy_from(tablename text, filepath text)
returns void
security definer
as
$$
 declare
 begin
     execute 'copy ' || tablename || ' from ''' || filepath || '''';
 end;
$$ language plpgsql;
```

It is usually a good idea to restrict usage of such a function to the intended user only:

```
revoke all on function copy_from( text,  text) from public;
grant execute on function copy_from( text,  text) to bob;
```

You may also want to check that Bob imports files only from his home directory.

How it works...

When a function defined with `security definer` is called, then postgres changes the sessions rights to those of the user who defined the function while that function is executed.

So when Bob executes function copy_from(tablename, filepath), he is effectively promoted to superuser for the time the function is running.

This behavior is similar to `setuid` in unix systems, where you can have a program to be run by anybody (with execute access) as the owner of that program. It also carries similar risks.

There's more...

There are other operations that are reserved for PostgreSQL superusers, such as setting some parameters.

Writing a debugging_info function for developers

Several of the parameters controlling logging are reserved to be used by only superusers.

If you want to let some of your developers set logging on, and if you can write a function for them to do just that:

```
create or replace function debugging_info_on()
returns void
security definer
as
$$
  begin
    set client_min_messages to 'DEBUG1';
    set log_min_messages to 'DEBUG1';
    set log_error_verbosity to 'VERBOSE';
    set log_min_duration_statement to 0;
  end;
$$ language plpgsql;
revoke all on function debugging_info_on() from public;
grant execute on function debugging_info_on() to bob;
```

You may also want to have a function to return to the default logging state by assigning DEFAULT to all the variables:

```
create or replace function debugging_info_reset()
returns void
security definer
as
$$
  begin
    set client_min_messages to DEFAULT;
    set log_min_messages to DEFAULT;
    set log_error_verbosity to DEFAULT;
    set log_min_duration_statement to DEFAULT;
  end;
$$ language plpgsql;
```

No need to fiddle with GRANTs and REVOKEs here, as setting it back to default does not pose a security risk. Instead of SET xxx to DEFAULT, you can also use a shorter version of the same command, namely, RESET xxx.

Alternatively, you may just end your session, as the parameters are valid only for the current session.

Auditing DDL changes

This recipe shows how one can collect **DDL** (**Data Definition Language**) from database logs in order to audit changes to the database structure.

Getting ready

Edit your `postgresql.conf` file, and set the following:

```
log_statement = 'ddl'
```

Setting it to 'mod' or 'all' is also ok for this. Don't forget to reload the configuration:

```
/etc/init-d/postgresql reload
```

How to do it...

Now find all occurrences of CREATE, ALTER, and DROP commands in the log.

```
postgres@hvost:~$ egrep -i "create|alter|drop" \ /var/log/postgresql/
postgresql-8.4-main.log
```

If log rotation is in effect, you may need to grep all logs also.

In case the log is too old, and you have not saved the older logs in some other place, you are out of luck.

The default settings in `postgresql.conf` file for log rotation are as follows:

```
log_filename = 'postgresql-%Y-%m-%d_%H%M%S.log'
```

```
log_rotation_age = 1d
```

```
log_rotation_size = 10MB
```

Make sure to check those if you think you may need logs that are older than seven days.

How it works...

The "Getting ready" part instructs postgreSQL to log all DDL commands in PostgreSQL's main log.

The *How to do it...* part extracts just the DDL queries from the logfile.

Was the change committed

It is possible to have some statements recorded in the log file, but not visible in the database structure. Most DDL commands in PostgreSQL can be ROLLBACKed, so what is in the log, is just a list of commands executed by postgresql, not what was actually committed. The log file is not transactional, and also keeps commands that were rolled back.

Who made the change

To be able to know the database user who made the DDL changes, you have to make sure that this info is logged as well.

In order to do so, you may have to change the `log_line_prefix` parameter to include the `%u` format string.

A recommended minimal `log_line_prefix` format string for auditing DDL is '%t %u %d', which tells postgresql to log timestamp, database user, and database name at the start of every log line.

Can't I find out this information from the database

If you don't have logging enabled, or don't have all the logs, then you can get only very limited information on who changed the database schema and when from system tables, and even that is not reliable.

What you can can get is the "owner" of the database object (table, sequence, function, and so on) but this may have been changed by "ALTER TABLE ... SET OWNER to yyyy".

You may be able to guess the approximate time of object creation or of the latest modification by looking up the transaction id in `xmin` system column in `pg_class` and `pg_attrib` system tables. And then, try to find close `xmin` from some table which has automatic insert date logging, maybe having `DEFAULT CURRENT_TIMESTAMP` defined for some column.

Auditing data changes

This recipe provides different ways to collect changes to data contained in the tables for auditing purposes.

Determine the following:

▶ Do you need to audit all changes or only some?

▶ What information about the changes do you need to collect: just the fact of change?

- New value of a field or tuple, is old value also needed here?

- Is it enough to record the user doing the change, or is the IP address and other connection information also needed?

- How secure (tamper-proof) must the auditing info be? For example, does it need to be kept separately, away from the database being audited?

Based on answers to the aforementioned questions, you can start selecting the right auditing method from the ones presented next.

How to do it...

Collecting data changes from server log

- Set `log_statement` = `'mod'` or to `'all'` in the server log

- Collect all `INSERT`, `UPDATE`, `DELETE`, and `TRUNCATE` commands from log

- Alternatively, just set up a way to store the logs on either the database server or copy them to another host

Collecting changes using triggers

- Write trigger function to collect new (and if needed also old) values from tuples and save them to auditing table(s)

- Add such triggers to tables for which changes need to be tracked

- Sample (modified from "A PL/pgSQL Trigger Procedure For Auditing" sample in postgreSQL manual)

```
CREATE TABLE emp (
    empname          text NOT NULL,
    salary           integer
);
CREATE TABLE emp_audit(
    operation        text      NOT NULL,
    stamp            timestamp NOT NULL,
    userid           text      NOT NULL,
    empname          text      NOT NULL,
    salary integer
);
CREATE OR REPLACE FUNCTION process_emp_audit() RETURNS TRIGGER AS
$emp_audit$
    BEGIN
        IF (TG_OP = 'DELETE') THEN
            INSERT INTO emp_audit SELECT 'DEL', now(), user,
OLD.*;
        ELSIF (TG_OP = 'UPDATE') THEN
```

```
                -- save old and new values
                    INSERT INTO emp_audit SELECT 'OLD', now(), user,
OLD.*;
                    INSERT INTO emp_audit SELECT 'NEW', now(), user,
NEW.*;
            ELSIF (TG_OP = 'INSERT') THEN
                    INSERT INTO emp_audit SELECT 'INS', now(), user,
NEW.*;
            ELSEIF (TG_OP = 'TRUNCATE') THEN
                    INSERT INTO emp_audit SELECT 'TRUNCATE', now(), user,
'-', -1;
            END IF;
            RETURN NULL; -- result is ignored bacause this is an AFTER
trigger
    END;
$emp_audit$ LANGUAGE plpgsql;
CREATE TRIGGER emp_audit
AFTER INSERT OR UPDATE OR DELETE ON emp
    FOR EACH ROW EXECUTE PROCEDURE process_emp_audit();
CREATE TRIGGER emp_audit_truncate
AFTER TRUNCATE ON emp
    FOR EACH STATEMENT EXECUTE PROCEDURE process_emp_audit();
```

Collecting changes using triggers and saving them to another database using dblink or plproxy

For security-critical systems, having the audit logs on the same machine with the rest of the data may not be enough. In that case, you may need to implement remote-change logging functionality. One way to do it is using pl/proxy to send change logs to a remote database.

The following is a sample how to log to the preceding example to a remote database auditdb:

► Create the emp_audit log table in the remote auditing database

► Create a function log_emp_audit() in the remote database as follows:

```
CREATE FUNCTION log_emp_audit(
  operation text, userid text, empname text, salary integer
) RETURNS VOID AS
$$

INSERT INTO emp_audit VALUES($1, now(), $2, $3, $4)
$$ LANGUAGE SQL;
```

► Create a proxy function for log_emp_audit() in the local audited database

(You need to have the pl/proxy language installed in the database for this)

```
CREATE OR REPLACE FUNCTION log_emp_audit(
  operation text, userid text, empname text, salary integer
```

```
) RETURNS VOID AS $$
 CONNECT 'dbname=auditdb';
$$ LANGUAGE plproxy;
```

▸ Create trigger functions that use the proxy function to save the data to an external database:

```
CREATE OR REPLACE FUNCTION do_emp_audit() RETURNS TRIGGER AS
$$
    BEGIN
        IF (TG_OP = 'DELETE') THEN
            PERFORM log_emp_audit('DEL', user, OLD.empname, OLD.
salary);
        ELSIF (TG_OP = 'UPDATE') THEN
            -- save old and new values
            PERFORM log_emp_audit('OLD', user, OLD.empname, OLD.
salary);
            PERFORM log_emp_audit('NEW', user, NEW.empname, NEW.
salary);
        ELSIF (TG_OP = 'INSERT') THEN
            PERFORM log_emp_audit('INS', user, NEW.empname, NEW.
salary);
        END IF;
        RETURN NULL; -- result is ignored since this is an AFTER
trigger
    END;
$$ LANGUAGE plpgsql;
```

▸ Add the triggers to the emp table:

```
CREATE TRIGGER emp_remote_audit
AFTER INSERT OR UPDATE OR DELETE ON emp
    FOR EACH ROW EXECUTE PROCEDURE do_emp_audit();
```

Ensure that the audit database is secure. This includes checking that the only thing the audit_logger user can do is call the log_emp_audit() function.

More info on pl/proxy can be found at the following website:

```
http://plproxy.projects.postgresql.org/doc/tutorial.html
```

Integrating with LDAP

This recipe shows how to set up your PostgreSQL system so that it uses **LDAP** (**lightweight Directory Access Protocol**) for authentication.

Getting ready

Ensure that the usernames in database and your LDAP server match, as this method works for user authentication checks for users already defined in the database.

How to do it...

In PostgreSQL's authentication file, `pg_hba.conf`, define some of address ranges to use LDAP as an authentication method, and configure the LDAP server for this addess range.

```
host    all         all         10.10.0.1/16        ldap \
    ldapserver=ldap.our.net ldapprefix="cn=" ldapsuffix=", dc=our,
dc=net"
```

How it works...

This setup makes postgresql server check passwords from the configured LDAP server.

User rights are not queried from LDAP server, but have to be defined inside the database, using ALTER USER, GRANT, and REVOKE commands.

There's more...

Setting up the client to use LDAP

If you are using the `pg_service.conf` file for defining your database access parameters, you may define some of those to be queried from LDAP server, by including line similar to the following in your `pg_service.conf` file:

```
ldap://ldap.mycompany.com/dc=mycompany,dc=com?uniqueMember?one?(cn=my
database)
```

See also

For server setup, visit the following website:

`http://www.postgresql.org/docs/8.4/static/auth-methods.html#AUTH-LDAP`

For client setup, visit the following website:

`http://www.postgresql.org/docs/8.4/static/libpq-ldap.html`

Connecting using SSL

Here we demonstrate how to enable PostgreSQL to use SSL for protecting database connections by encrypting all data passed over that connection. Using SSL makes it much harder to sniff the database traffic including usernames, passwords, and sensitive data that are passed between client and database by someone listening to a network somewhere between them. An alternative to using SSL is running the connection over a **VPN** (**Virtual private Network**).

Using SSL makes the data transfer on the encrypted connection a little slower, so you may not want to use it if you are sure your network is safe. The performance impact can be quite large if you are doing lots of short connections, as setting up a SSL connection is quite CPU-heavy. In this case, you may want to run a local spooling solution, such as **PgBouncer**, to which you connect without encryption, and make the SSL-protected connection using stunnel as described in PgBouncer FAQ at the following website:

```
http://pgbouncer.projects.postgresql.org/doc/faq.html
```

Getting ready

Get or generate an SSL server key and certificate pair for the server, and store these into the data directory of current database instance as files `server.key` and `server.crt`.

It may already be done for you on some platforms. For example, on Ubuntu, postgres is set up to support SSL connections by default.

How to do it...

Set `ssl = on` in `postgresql.conf`, and restart the database.

How it works...

If `ssl = on` is set, then postgresql listens to both plain and SSL connections on the same port (5432 by default), and determines the type of connection from the first byte of a new connection.

Then, it proceeds to set up an SSL connection, if an incoming request asks for it.

There's more...

You can leave the choice of whether or not to use SSL to the client, or you can force SSL usage from the server's side.

To let the client choose, use lines such as the following:

```
host database   user   IP-address   IP-mask   auth-method
```

To let in only clients using SSL, use `hostssl` instead of `host`.

The following fragment of `pg_hba.conf` enables non-SSL connections from local subnet (192.168.1.0/24), but requires SSL for access from everybody accessing the database from other networks.

```
host      all      all      192.168.54.1/32      md5
hostssl   all      all      0.0.0.0/0            md5
```

Getting SSL key and certificate

For web servers, you usually get your SSL certificate from a recognized **Certificate Authority** (**CA**), as most browsers complain if the certificate is not issued by a known CA, and make the user jump through hoops if it wants to connect to a server with a certificate issued by an unknown CA.

For your database, it is usually sufficient to generate the certificate yourself using `openssL`. The following commands generate a self-signed certificate for your server:

```
openssl genrsa 1024 > server.key
openssl req -new -x509 -key server.key -out server.crt
```

 Read more on x509 keys and certificates in openSSL's *HowTo* pages at the following website:
`http://www.openssl.org/docs/HOWTO/`

Setting up a client to use SSL

Client behavior is controlled by an environment variable, **PGSSLMODE**, that can have the following values, as defined in the official PostgreSQL documents:

SSL mode	Eavesdropping protection	MITM protection	Statement
disabled	No	No	I don't care about security, and I don't want to pay the overhead of encryption.
allow	Maybe	No	I don't care about security, but I will pay the overhead of encryption if the server insists on it.
prefer	Maybe	No	I don't care about encryption, but I wish to pay the overhead of encryption if the server supports it.
require	Yes	No	I want my data to be encrypted, and I accept the overhead. I trust that the network will make sure I always connect to the server that I want.
verify-ca	Yes	Depends on CA-policy	I want my data encrypted, and I accept the overhead. I want to be sure that I connect to a server that I trust.

SSL mode	Eavesdropping protection	MITM protection	Statement
verify-full	Yes	Yes	I want my data encrypted, and I accept the overhead. I want to be sure that I connect to a server I trust, and that it's the one I specify.

The MITM in the preceding table means Man-In-The-Middle attack, that is, someone posing as your server, but actually just observing and forwarding the traffic.

Checking server authenticity

The last two SSL modes allow you to be reasonably sure that you are actually talking to your server, by checking the SSL certificate presented by the server.

See also

To understand more about SSL in general, and OpenSSL library used by PostgreSQL in particular, visit `http://www.openssl.org`, or get a good book about SSL.

There was also a nice presentacion named "Encrypted PostgreSQL" explaining these issues at pgcon2009. The slides are available at the following website:

`http://www.pgcon.org/2009/schedule/events/120.en.html`

Encrypting sensitive data

This recipe shows how to encrypt data using the **pgcrypto** package.

Getting ready

Make sure you (or your database server) are in a country where encryption is not illegal—it still is in some countries.

Make sure pgcrypto is installed on your database host. On Ubuntu, it comes in package **postgresql-contrib**.

Install it into the database in which you want to use it:

`psql mydb < /usr/share/postgresql/8.4/contrib/pgcrypto.sql`

You also need to have GPG keys set up:

```
pguser@laptop:~$ gpg --gen-key
```

Answer some questions here, select key type "DSA and Elgamal", and enter an empty password.

Now export the keys:

```
pguser@laptop:~$ gpg -a --export "PostgreSQL User (test key for PG
Cookbook) <pguser@somewhere.net>" > public.key
pguser@laptop:~$ gpg -a --export-secret-keys " PostgreSQL User (test
key for PG Cookbook) <pguser@somewhere.net>" > secret.key
```

Make sure only you and postgres database users have access to the secret key.

```
pguser@laptop:~$ sudo chgrp postgres secret.key
pguser@laptop:~$ chmod 440 secret.key
pguser@laptop:~$ ls -l *.key
-rw-r--r-- 1 pguser pguser    1718 2010-03-26 13:53 public.key
-r--r----- 1 pguser postgres 1818 2010-03-26 13:54 secret.key
```

How to do it...

Encrypting

To ensure that the secret keys are never visible in database logs, write a wrapper function for getting the keys from the file. You need to do it in a trusted embedded language, such as pl/pythonu, as only trusted languages can access file system. You need to be postgresql superuser in order to create functions in trusted languages.

```
create or replace function get_my_public_key() returns text as $$
return open('/home/pguser/public.key').read()
$$
language plpythonu;
revoke all on function get_my_public_key() from public;
create or replace function get_my_secret_key() returns text as $$
return open('/home/pguser/secret.key').read()
$$
language plpythonu;
revoke all on function get_my_secret_key() from public;
```

If you don't want other database users to actually see the keys, you also need to write wrapper functions for encryption and decryption, and then give access to these wrapper functions to end users.

The encryption function is as follows:

```
create or replace function encrypt_using_my_public_key(
    cleartext text,
    ciphertext out bytea
)
AS $$
DECLARE
```

```
    pubkey_bin bytea;
BEGIN
    -- text version of public key needs to be passed through function
dearmor() to get to raw key
    pubkey_bin := dearmor(get_my_public_key());
    ciphertext := pgp_pub_encrypt(cleartext, pubkey_bin);
END;
$$ language plpgsql security definer;
revoke all on function encrypt_using_my_public_key(text) from public;
grant execute on function encrypt_using_my_public_key(text) to bob;
```

And the decryption function is as follows:

```
create or replace function decrypt_using_my_secret_key(
    ciphertext bytea,
    cleartext out text
)
AS $$
DECLARE
    secret_key_bin bytea;
BEGIN
    -- text version of secret key needs to be passed through function
dearmor() to get to raw binary key
    secret_key_bin := dearmor(get_my_secret_key());
    cleartext := pgp_pub_decrypt(ciphertext, secret_key_bin);
END;
$$ language plpgsql security definer;
revoke all on function decrypt_using_my_secret_key(bytea) from public;
grant execute on function decrypt_using_my_secret_key(bytea) to bob;
```

And now, test the encryption:

```
test2=# select encrypt_using_my_public_key('X marks the spot!');
```

returns a byte result that looks something like the following:

```
encrypt_using_my_public_key | \301\301N\003\22
3o\215\2125\203\252;\020\007\376-z\233\211H...
```

To see that it actually works both ways:

```
test2=# select decrypt_using_my_secret_key(encrypt_using_my_public_
key('X marks the spot!'));
 decrypt_using_my_secret_key
-----------------------------
 X marks the spot!
(1 row)
```

Yes, we got back our initial string.

How it works...

What we have done here is:

- hidden the keys from non-superuser database users
- provided wrappers for authorized users to still use the encryption and decryption functionality

To ensure that your sensitive data is not stolen while in transit between client and database, make sure you connect to PostgreSQL server using an SSL-encrypted connection, or connect from localhost.

You also have to trust your server administrators and other users with superuser privileges to be sure your encrypted data is safe.

There's more...

For really sensitive data

For some data, you don't want to risk having the decryption password on the same machine as the encrypted data.

In those cases, you either use public/private key cryptography and do only the encryption part on the database server. This also means that you only have the encryption key on the database host, and not the key needed for decryption. Alternatively, you can deploy a separate, extra secure encryption server in your server infrastructure that provides just the encrypting/decrypting functionality as a remote call.

For really, really really, sensitive data

For even more sensitive data, you may never want the data to leave the client computer unencrypted. Hence, you need to encrypt the data before sending it to the database. In that case, PostgreSQL receives already encrypted data, and never sees the unencrypted version. This also means that the only useful indexes you can have are for use in "WHERE encrypted_ column = encrypted_data" and for ensuring uniqueness. Even the "WHERE =" can be used only if the encryption algorithm always produces the same ciphertext for the same plaintext, which weakens the strength of encryption.

Two versions of pg_crypto

Pgcrypto is usually compiled to use openssl library (http://www.openssl.org). If for some reason, you don't have openssl or just don't want to use it, it is possible to compile a version of pg_crypto without it, with a smaller number of supported encryption algorithms, and slightly reduced performance.

See also

PgCrypto page in postgreSQL online documentation at the following website:

```
http://www.postgresql.org/docs/9.0/static/pgcrypto.html
```

The OpenSSL web page at the following website:

```
http://www.openssl.org/
```

The GNU Privacy Handbook at the following website:

```
http://www.gnupg.org/gph/en/manual.html
```

7
Database Administration

In this chapter, we will cover the following:

- ▶ Writing a script that either all succeeds or all fails
- ▶ Writing a psql script that exits on first error
- ▶ Performing actions on many tables
- ▶ Adding/removing columns on tables
- ▶ Changing data type of a column
- ▶ Adding/removing schemas
- ▶ Moving objects between schemas
- ▶ Adding/removing tablespaces
- ▶ Moving objects between tablespaces
- ▶ Accessing objects in other PostgreSQL databases
- ▶ Making views updateable

Introduction

The *Tables & Data* chapter spent time looking at the contents of tables and various complexities. Now, we turn our attention to larger administration tasks that we will need to perform from time-to-time such as creating, moving things around, storing things neatly, and removing them when they're no longer required.

The most sensible way to perform major administrative tasks is to write a script to do what you think is required. If you're unsure, you can always run the script on a system test server, and then run it again on the production server once you're happy. Manically typing commands against production database servers isn't wise. Worse, using an admin tool can lead to serious issues, if that tool doesn't show you the SQL you're about to execute. If you haven't dropped your first live table yet, don't worry; you will. Perhaps you might want to read the chapter on *Backups* first, eh? Back it up using scripts.

Scripts are great because you can automate common tasks. No need to sit there with a mouse, working your way through a hundred changes.

If you're drawn to the discussion about Command line vs. GUI, then my thoughts and reasons are completely orthogonal to that. I want to encourage you to avoid errors and save time by repetitive and automatic execution of small administration programs or scripts. If it were safe or easy to do the equivalent of mouse movements in a script, then that would be an option; but it's definitely not. The only viable way to write a repeatable script is by writing text SQL commands.

Which scripting tool is a more interesting debate. We talk about psql here because, if you've got PostgreSQL, then you've got psql. So, we're on solid ground to provide examples that way.

On to the recipes! First, we start by looking at some scripting techniques that are valuable with PostgreSQL. This will make you more accurate, more repeatable, and free up time for other cool things.

Writing a script that either all succeeds or all fails

Database administration often involves applying a coordinated set of changes to the database. One of PostgreSQL's great strengths is the transaction system, where almost all actions can be executed inside a transaction. This allows us to build a script that will either all succeed or all fail, which can be critically important on a production system.

Transactions definitely apply to **DDL (Data Definition Language)**, which refers to the set of SQL commands used to define, modify, and delete database objects. The term DDL goes back many years, though it persists because that subset is a useful short name for the commands that most administrators need to execute: CREATE, ALTER, DROP, and so on.

How to do it...

The basic way to ensure that we get all commands successful or none at all is to literally wrap your script into a transaction like the following:

```
BEGIN;
command 1;
command 2;
```

```
command 3;
COMMIT;
```

Writing a transaction control command involves editing the script, which you may not want or even have access to do. There are also other ways.

From psql, you can do this more simply just by using the command line options `-1` or `--single -transaction` as follows:

```
bash $ psql -1 -f myscript.sql
bash $ psql --single-transaction -f myscript.sql
```

The `-1` is short, though I recommend using `--single-transaction`, as it's much clearer which option is being selected.

How it works...

The whole script will fail if at any point, one of the commands gives an error or higher message. Almost all of the SQL for defining objects (DDL) allows a way to avoid throwing errors.

Typically, commands that begin with the keyword `DROP` have an option `IF EXISTS`. This allows you to execute the `DROP`, whether or not the object already exists; so by the end of the command that object will not exist.

```
DROP VIEW IF EXISTS cust_view;
```

Also, commands that begin with the keyword `CREATE`, mostly have the optional suffix `OR REPLACE`. This allows the `CREATE` to overwrite the definition if one already exists, or add the new object if it didn't exist yet, such as the following:

```
CREATE OR REPLACE VIEW cust_view AS
SELECT * FROM cust;
```

If both `DROP IF EXISTS` and `CREATE OR REPLACE` options exist, then you might think you would just use `CREATE OR REPLACE`. If you change the output definition of a function or a view, then using `OR REPLACE` is not sufficient. In that case, you must use `DROP` and recreate, as follows:

```
postgres=# CREATE OR REPLACE VIEW cust_view AS
SELECT col as title1 FROM cust;
CREATE VIEW
postgres=# CREATE OR REPLACE VIEW cust_view
AS SELECT col as title2 FROM cust;
ERROR:  cannot change name of view column "title1" to "title2"
```

Note also that `CREATE INDEX` does not have an `OR REPLACE` option. If you run it twice, you'll get two indexes on your table, unless you specifically name the index. There is a `DROP INDEX IF EXISTS`, but it may take a long time to drop and recreate an index.

Please note the return messages in the following few commands:

```
postgres=# BEGIN;
BEGIN
postgres=# BEGIN;
WARNING:  there is already a transaction in progress
BEGIN
postgres=# COMMIT;
COMMIT
postgres=# COMMIT;
WARNING:  there is no transaction in progress
COMMIT
```

PostgreSQL takes the first or *outermost* BEGIN but also the first, which in this case is the *innermost* COMMIT. So, if you have used transaction-control commands in your script, then wrapping them again in a higher level script or command can cause problems.

> Warning : PostgreSQL accepts, but does not act on nested transactional control commands. The commands after the first commit will be assumed to be transactions in their own right and will persist, should the script fail. Be careful.

There's more...

The following commands cannot be included in a script that uses transactions in the way described:

- ▶ CREATE DATABASE / DROP DATABASE
- ▶ CREATE TABLESPACE / DROP TABLESPACE
- ▶ CREATE INDEX CONCURRENTLY
- ▶ VACUUM

None of those actions need to be run manually on a regular basis within complex programs, so shouldn't be a problem for you.

Writing a psql script that exits on first error

The default mode for the psql script tool is to continue processing when it finds an error. That sounds dumb, though it exists for historical compatibility only. There are some easy and mostly permanent ways around that, so let's look at them.

Getting ready

Let's start with a trivial script, with a command we know will fail as follows:

```
$ $EDITOR test.sql
mistake1;
mistake2;
mistake3;
```

Execute the following script using psql to see what the results look like:

```
$ psql -f test.sql
psql:test.sql:1: ERROR:   syntax error at or near "mistake1"
LINE 1: mistake1;
        ^

psql:test.sql:2: ERROR:   syntax error at or near "mistake2"
LINE 1: mistake2;
        ^

psql:test.sql:3: ERROR:   syntax error at or near "mistake3"
LINE 1: mistake3;
        ^
```

How to do it...

To exit the script on first error, we can do the following:

```
$ psql -f test.sql -v ON_ERROR_STOP=on
psql:test.sql:1: ERROR:   syntax error at or near "mistake1"

LINE 1: mistake1;
        ^
```

Or, edit the file `test.sql` with an initial line, like the following:

```
$ $EDITOR test.sql
\set ON_ERROR_STOP
mistake1;
mistake2;
mistake3;
```

Note that this will *not* work because we have missed the crucial ON:

```
$ psql -f test.sql -v ON_ERROR_STOP
```

How it works...

ON_ERROR_STOP is a psql special variable that controls the behavior of psql as it executes in script mode. When this variable is set, an SQL error will generate an OS return code 3, whereas other OS-related errors will return code 1.

There's more...

You can place some psql commands in a profile that will get executed when you run psql. Adding ON_ERROR_STOP into your profile will ensure that this setting is applied to all psql sessions:

```
$ $EDITOR ~/.psqlrc
\set ON_ERROR_STOP
```

You can forcibly override this, and request psql to execute without a profile by using -X, which is probably the safest thing to do for batch execution of scripts.

Performing actions on many tables

As a database administrator, you will often need to apply multiple commands as part of the same overall task. That is one of the following:

- ▸ Many different actions on multiple tables
- ▸ Same action, multiple tables
- ▸ Same action, multiple tables, in parallel
- ▸ Different actions, one on each table, in parallel

The first is the general case where you need to make a set of coordinated changes. The solution is "write a script" as we've already discussed. We can also call this static scripting, because you write the script manually, and then execute it.

The second type of task can be achieved very simply with dynamic scripts, where we write a script that writes a script. That technique is the main topic of this recipe.

Performing actions in parallel sounds really cool, and it would be useful if it was easy. In some ways it is, though trying to run multiple tasks concurrently and trap and understand all the errors is much harder. And if you're thinking it won't matter if you don't check for errors, think again. If you run tasks in parallel, then you cannot run them inside the same transaction; so you definitely need error checking.

Don't worry; running parallel is usually much easier than that, and we'll explain how after a few basics.

Getting ready

Let's just create a basic schema to run some examples on the following:

```
postgres=# create schema test;
CREATE SCHEMA
postgres=# create table test.a (col1 INTEGER);
CREATE TABLE
postgres=# create table test.b (col1 INTEGER);
CREATE TABLE
postgres=# create table test.c (col1 INTEGER);
CREATE TABLE
```

How to do it...

Our task is to run an SQL statement using this form, with X as the tablename, against each of our three test tables:

```
ALTER TABLE   X
ADD COLUMN last_update_timestamp TIMESTAMP WITH TIME ZONE;
```

Our starting point is a script that lists the tables we want to perform tasks against, something like the following:

```
postgres=# SELECT relname
   FROM pg_class c
   JOIN pg_namespace n
   ON c.relnamespace = n.oid
   WHERE n.nspname = 'test';
 relname
---------
 a
 b
 c
(3 rows)
```

We then use the preceding SQL to generate the text for an SQL script, substituting the schema name and tablename into the SQL text. We then output to a script file named `multi.sql` as follows:

```
postgres=# \t on
postgres=# \o multi.sql
postgres=# SELECT 'ALTER TABLE '|| n.nspname
   || '.' || c.relname ||
 ' ADD COLUMN last_update_timestamp TIMESTAMP WITH TIME ZONE;'
FROM pg_class c
```

```
JOIN pg_namespace n
ON c.relnamespace = n.oid
WHERE n.nspname = 'test';
```

Once we've generated the script, we can just check if it all looks correct:

```
postgres=# \! cat multi.sql
 ALTER TABLE test.a ADD COLUMN last_update_timestamp TIMESTAMP WITH
TIME ZONE;
 ALTER TABLE test.b ADD COLUMN last_update_timestamp TIMESTAMP WITH
TIME ZONE;
 ALTER TABLE test.c ADD COLUMN last_update_timestamp TIMESTAMP WITH
TIME ZONE;
```

and then run the script and watch the results (success!).

```
postgres=# \i multi.sql
ALTER TABLE
ALTER TABLE
ALTER TABLE
```

How it works...

Overall, this is just an example of dynamic scripting, and has been used by DBAs for many decades, even before PostgreSQL was born.

It can go wrong in various ways, especially if you generate SQL text with syntax errors. Just fix that, and carry on.

The \t command means "tuples only", so \t on will ensure there are no headers, command tags, or row counts following results.

The \o command redirects output to a file.

\! runs operating system commands, so \! cat will show the file contents on *nix systems.

The \i command redirects input from a file, or in simpler terms, will execute the named file. Running the script in this way will probably ignore earlier recipes, so I still recommend following those earlier guidelines.

Dynamic scripting might also be named a quick-and-dirty approach. The previous scripts didn't filter out views and other objects in the test schema, so you'd need to add that yourself, or not, as required.

There is another way of doing this, as well.

```
DO $$
DECLARE c record;
BEGIN
    FOR c IN SELECT t.*, n.nspname
    FROM pg_class c JOIN pg_namespace n
    ON c.relnamespace = n.oid
    WHERE n.nspname = 'test' /* ; not needed */
    LOOP
    EXECUTE 'ALTER TABLE '|| quote_ident(n.nspname) ||
            '.' || quote_ident(c.relname) ||
            ' ADD COLUMN last_update_timestamp ' ||
            'TIMESTAMP WITH TIME ZONE;'
    END LOOP;
END $$;
```

Using this is not my preference because it executes the SQL directly and doesn't allow you to keep the script afterwards.

There's more...

Earlier I said I'd explain how to run multiple tasks in parallel. Some practical approaches are possible, with a little discussion.

Making tasks run in parallel can be thought of as subdividing the main task so that we run x2, x4, x8, and such other subscripts, rather than one large script.

First, you should note that error checking gets worse the more parallel tasks you spawn, whereas performance improves most for the first few subdivisions. Also, we're often constrained by CPU, RAM, or I/O resources for intensive tasks. That means that splitting a main task into two to four parallel subtasks isn't practical without some kind of tool to help us manage this.

There are two approaches here, depending on the two types of the task, as follows:

- ▶ Task consists of many smaller tasks, all roughly the same size
- ▶ Task consists of many smaller tasks, where the execution times vary according to the size/complexity of the database object

If we have lots of smaller tasks, then we can just run out scripts multiple times using a simple round-robin split of tasks, so that each subscript runs half of the subtasks.

- ▶ Script 1: Add WHERE c.oid % 2 = 0
- ▶ Script 2: Add WHERE c.oid % 2 = 1

The task we were performing as an example was to add a column onto many tables. In the previous example, we were adding the column with no specified default; so the new column will have a NULL value, and, as a result, with ALTER TABLE it will run very quickly, even on large tables. If we change the ALTER TABLE statement so that we specify a default, then the SQL will need to re-write the whole table. So, the run time will vary according to table size (approximately, though also by number and type of indexes).

Now that our subtasks vary in runtime according to size, we need to be more careful splitting up the subtasks, so that we end up with multiple scripts that will run for about the same time.

If we already know that we have just a few big tables, it's easy to just split those out manually into their own scripts.

If the database has many large tables, then we can sort SQL statements by size and then distribute them using round-robin distribution into multiple subscripts that will have approximately similar runtime. The following two SQL statements are an example of this technique:

```
\t on
\o script0.sql
SELECT sql FROM (
SELECT 'ALTER TABLE '|| n.nspname || '.' || c.relname ||
' ADD COLUMN last_update_timestamp TIMESTAMP WITH TIME ZONE   DEFAULT
now();' as sql
,row_number() OVER (ORDER BY pg_relation_size(c.oid))
FROM pg_class c
 JOIN pg_namespace n
 ON c.relnamespace = n.oid
WHERE n.nspname = 'test'
ORDER BY 2 DESC) as s
WHERE row_number % 2 = 0;
\o script1.sql
SELECT sql FROM (
SELECT 'ALTER TABLE '|| n.nspname || '.' || c.relname ||
' ADD COLUMN last_update_timestamp TIMESTAMP WITH TIME ZONE DEFAULT
now();' as sql
,row_number() OVER (ORDER BY pg_relation_size(c.oid))
FROM pg_class c
 JOIN pg_namespace n
 ON c.relnamespace = n.oid
WHERE n.nspname = 'test'
ORDER BY 2 DESC) as s
WHERE row_number % 2 = 1;
```

Then, execute the jobs in parallel, like the following:

```
$ psql -f script0.sql &
$ psql -f script1.sql &
```

Note how we use the window function `row_number()` to sort the data by size, then we split the data into pieces using the following:

```
WHERE row_number % N = i;
```

N is the total number of scripts we're producing, and i is the number of the current script. The numbering starts at zero because we are using modulo arithmetic to distribute the subtasks.

Using pg_batch to run tasks in parallel

There is a tool for running tasks in parallel, available at the following URL:

```
http://reorg.projects.postgresql.org/pg_batch.html
```

`pg_batch` runs tasks in the order it finds them, and splits them up blindly across multiple parallel sessions. That means that you'll need to write a script to pre-order the items that need to be executed, so that the tasks are distributed evenly across sessions, so you'll end up writing something that looks exactly like the preceding scripts anyway.

Adding/Removing the columns of a table

As designs change, we may want to add or remove columns from our data tables. These are common operations in development, though they need more careful planning on a running production database server, as these operations take full locks and may run for long periods.

How to do it...

You can add a new column to a table using the following:

```
ALTER TABLE mytable
ADD COLUMN last_update_timestamp TIMESTAMP WITHOUT TIME ZONE;
```

Or drop the same column using the following command:

```
ALTER TABLE mytable
DROP COLUMN last_update_timestamp;
```

You can combine multiple operations when using ALTER TABLE, which then applies the changes in sequence. This allows you to do a useful trick, which is to add a column unconditionally, using IF EXISTS, such as the following:

```
ALTER TABLE mytable
DROP COLUMN IF EXISTS last_update_timestamp,
ADD COLUMN last_update_timestamp TIMESTAMP WITHOUT TIME ZONE;
```

Note that this will have almost the same effect as:

```
UPDATE mytable SET last_update_timestamp = NULL;
```

Though the ALTER TABLE runs much faster. That's very cool if you want to do an update, though not much fun if you want to keep the column data already there.

How it works...

ALTER TABLE, to add or drop a column, takes a full table lock (at AccessExclusiveLock level); so that it can prevent all other actions on the table. So, we want it to be as fast as possible.

DROP COLUMN doesn't actually remove the column from each row of the table, it just marks the column as dropped. This makes DROP COLUMN a very fast operation.

ADD COLUMN is also very fast if we are adding a nullable column with a null default value. If we use a NOT NULL constraint, or we specify an explicit default value, then we need to rewrite every row of the table, which can be quite slow.

ALTER TABLE allows us to execute many column operations at once, as shown in the main recipe. ALTER TABLE is optimized, so that we include all column operations into a single pass of the table, greatly improving speed for complex sets of changes, for example:

```
ALTER TABLE mytable
ADD COLUMN last_update_userid INTEGER,
ADD COLUMN last_update_comment TEXT;
```

If we rewrite the table, then the dropped columns are removed. If not, they may stay there for some time. Subsequent INSERT and UPDATE operations will insert a null value for the dropped column(s). Updates will reduce the size of stored rows if they were not already null. So in theory, you just have to wait, and the database will eventually reclaim the space. In practice, this only works if all of the rows in the table are updated within a given period of time. Many tables contain historical data, and so space would not be reclaimed at all without additional actions.

The PostgreSQL manual recommends changing the data type of a column to the same type, which forces rewriting every row. I don't recommend this because it will completely lock the table for a long period, at least on larger databases. My recommendation is to not drop the column at all, if you can avoid it, when you're in production. Just keep a track of the changes you would make if you get time, if ever. If you're looking at alternatives, then VACUUM will not rewrite the table, though a VACUUM FULL will. Though be careful there also, because that also holds a full table lock.

There's more...

Indexes that depend upon a dropped column are automatically dropped as well. All other objects that depend upon the column(s) will cause the ALTER TABLE to be rejected. You can override that, and drop everything in sight by using the CASCADE option, as follows:

```
ALTER TABLE x
DROP COLUMN  last_update_timestamp
CASCADE;
```

Changing datatype of a column

Changing column datatypes is not an everyday task, thankfully. But when we do have to do it, we need to know all the details so that we can perform the conversion on a production system without error.

Getting ready

Let's start with a simple example table as follows:

```
postgres=# select * from birthday;
 name  |   dob
-------+--------
 simon | 690926

(1 row)
```

It is created using the following:

```
CREATE TABLE birthday
( name           TEXT
, dob            INTEGER);
```

How to do it...

Let's say we want to change the dob column to another data type. Let's try with a simple example first, which is as follows:

```
postgres=# ALTER TABLE birthday
postgres-# ALTER COLUMN dob SET DATA TYPE text;
ALTER TABLE
```

This works fine. Let's just put that back to integer, so that we can try moving to something more complex, such as a date datatype, like the following:

```
postgres=# ALTER TABLE birthday
postgres-# ALTER COLUMN dob SET DATA TYPE integer;
ERROR:  column "dob" cannot be cast to type integer
```

Oh! What went wrong? Let's try using an explicit conversion with the USING clause as follows:

```
postgres=# ALTER TABLE birthday
            ALTER COLUMN dob SET DATA TYPE integer
            USING dob::integer;
ALTER TABLE
```

It works as expected. Now let's try moving to a DATE type:

```
postgres=# ALTER TABLE birthday
ALTER COLUMN dob SET DATA TYPE date
USING  date(to_date(dob::text, 'YYMMDD') -
    (case when dob/10000 < 15 then interval '0'
     else interval '100 years' end);
```

It then gives what we were hoping to see:

```
postgres=# select * from birthday;
 name  |     dob
-------+------------
 simon | 26/09/1969
(1 row)
```

With PostgreSQL you can also set or drop default expressions, whether or not the NOT NULL constraints are applied.

```
ALTER TABLE foo
ALTER COLUMN col DROP DEFAULT expression;
ALTER TABLE foo
ALTER COLUMN col SET DEFAULT 'expression';
ALTER TABLE foo
ALTER COLUMN col SET NOT NULL;
ALTER TABLE foo
ALTER COLUMN col DROP NOT NULL;
```

How it works...

Moving from the integer to the date type used a complex USING expression. Let's break that down step-by-step so that we can see why, as follows:

```
postgres=# ALTER TABLE birthday
ALTER COLUMN dob SET DATA TYPE date
USING  date(to_date(dob::text, 'YYMMDD') -
    (case when dob/10000 <=15 then interval '0'
     else interval '100 years' end);
```

First, we can't move directly from integer to date, we need to first convert to text and then onto date. dob::text means "cast to text".

Once we have text, we use to_date() function to move into a date.

That's not enough. Our starting data was `690926`, which we presume is a date in the form 'YYMMDD'. When PostgreSQL converts to a date, it assumes that two-digit year 69 is in the current century. So, it outputs 2069 rather than 1969. So, the `case` statement is added to reduce any year more than 15 to be a date in the previous century, by explicitly subtracting an interval of 100 years.

I recommend very strongly that you test this conversion by performing a `SELECT` first. Converting datatypes, especially to/from dates always causes some problems, so don't try to do this quickly. Always take a backup of the data first.

There's more...

The `USING` clause can also be used to handle complex expressions involving other columns. This could be used for data transformations, which might be useful for DBAs in some circumstances, such as migrating to a new database design on a production database server. Let's put everything together into an example, look at a full working example. For example, if you wished to transform the following table:

```
postgres=# select * from cust;
 customerid | firstname | lastname | age
------------+-----------+----------+-----
          1 | Philip    | Marlowe  |  38
          2 | Richard   | Hannay   |  42
          3 | Holly     | Martins  |  25
          4 | Harry     | Palmer   |  36
(4 rows)
```

Into a table design like the following:

```
postgres=# select * from cust;
 customerid |     custname     | age
------------+------------------+-----
          1 | Philip Marlowe   |  38
          2 | Richard Hannay   |  42
          3 | Holly Martins    |  25
          4 | Harry Palmer     |  36
(4 rows)
```

You might decide to do it using the following four simple steps.

```
ALTER TABLE cust ADD COLUMN custname text not null default '';
UPDATE cust SET custname = firstname || ' ' || lastname;
ALTER TABLE cust DROP COLUMN firstname;
ALTER TABLE cust DROP COLUMN lastname;
```

You can also use the SQL commands directly or make them use a tool like **pgAdmin3**. Following those steps could cause problems, as the changes aren't within a transaction that other users can see the changes when they are only half finished. So, it would be better to do this in a single transaction, using BEGIN and COMMIT. Also, those four changes require us to make two passes of the table. However, we can perform the whole transformation in one pass of the table by using multiple clauses on the ALTER TABLE command. So instead, do the following:

```
BEGIN;
ALTER TABLE cust
   ALTER COLUMN firstname SET DATA TYPE text
    USING firstname || ' ' || lastname,
   ALTER COLUMN firstname SET NOT NULL,
   DROP COLUMN lastname;
ALTER TABLE cust RENAME firstname TO custname;
COMMIT;
```

This is a great example of why I personally prefer to use scripts to make such changes on large production databases rather than making the changes directly using a GUI.

Adding/Removing schemas

Separating groups of objects is a good way of improving administration efficiency. We need to know how to create new schemas and remove schemas that are no longer required.

How to do it...

To add a new schema, issue the following command:

```
CREATE SCHEMA sharedschema;
```

If you want that schema to be owned by a particular user, then you can add the following option:

```
CREATE SCHEMA sharedschema AUTHORIZATION scarlett;
```

Or, if you want to create a new schema which has the same name as an existing user, so that the user becomes the owner, then try the following:

```
CREATE SCHEMA AUTHORIZATION scarlett;
```

In many database systems, the schema name is the same as the owning user. PostgreSQL allows schemas owned by one user to have objects owned by another user within them. That can be especially confusing when you have a schema of the same name as the owning user. To avoid this you should have two types of schema: schemas named the same as the owning user should be limited to just objects owned by that user. Other general schemas can have shared ownership.

There are no additional options on the CREATE SCHEMA command.

To remove a schema named str, we can issue the following command:

```
DROP SCHEMA str;
```

Note that there isn't a *CREATE OR REPLACE SCHEMA* command, so when you want to create a schema whether or not it already exists you can do the following:

```
DROP SCHEMA IF EXISTS newschema;
CREATE SCHEMA newschema;
```

The DROP SCHEMA won't work unless the schema is empty and unless you use the nuclear option:

```
DROP SCHEMA IF EXISTS newschema CASCADE;
```

The nuclear option kills all known germs, and all of your database objects also.

There's more...

In the SQL Standard, you can also create a schema and the objects it contains all in one SQL statement. PostgreSQL accepts this syntax if you need it, as follows:

```
CREATE SCHEMA foo
    CREATE TABLE account
    (id              INTEGER NOT NULL PRIMARY KEY
    ,balance       NUMERIC(50,2))
    CREATE VIEW accountsample AS
    SELECT *
    FROM account
    WHERE random() < 0.1;
```

Though mostly, I find it limiting. This syntax exists to allow creating more than one object at the same time. That can be achieved more easily by using PostgreSQL's ability to allow transactional DDL, which is discussed in an earlier recipe.

Schema-level privileges

Privileges can be for objects in a schema using the GRANT command, as follows:

```
GRANT SELECT ON ALL TABLES IN SCHEMA sharedschema TO PUBLIC;
```

Though this will only affect tables that already exist, tables created in the future will inherit privileges defined by the ALTER DEFAULT PRIVILEGES command, for example:

```
ALTER DEFAULT PRIVILEGES IN SCHEMA sharedschema
GRANT SELECT ON TABLES TO PUBLIC;
```

Moving objects between schemas

Once you've created schemas for administration purposes, you'll want to move existing objects to keep things tidy.

How to do it...

To move one table from its current schema to a new schema, use the following:

```
ALTER TABLE cust
SET SCHEMA anotherschema;
```

If you want to move all objects, you might consider just renaming the schema itself using the following query:

```
ALTER SCHEMA existingschema RENAME TO anotherschema;
```

This only works if another schema with that name does not already exist.

Otherwise, you'll need to run `ALTER TABLE` for each table you would like to move. You can use the recipe for performing the same action on many tables to achieve that.

Views, sequences, functions, aggregates, and domains can also be moved by `ALTER` commands with `SET SCHEMA` options.

How it works...

When you move a table to a new schema, all of the indexes, triggers, and rules defined on those tables will also be moved to the new schema. If you've used a `SERIAL` data type, and an implicit sequence has been created, then that also moves to the new schema. Schemas are a purely an administrative concept, and do not affect the location of the table's data files. Tablespaces don't work this way, as we will see in later recipes.

Databases, users/roles, languages, conversions don't exist in a schema. Schemas exist in a particular database. = Schemas don't exist within schemas; they are not arranged in a tree or hierarchy.

There's more...

Text search objects exist in a specific schema though there are no commands to move them to a new schema. Similarly, operator(s), operator class(es), and operator family(s) exist in a schema, though there are no commands to move them to new schemas. Also *casts* don't exist in a schema, though the data types and functions they reference don't. These things are not typically something we want to move around anyway; this is just a note in case you're wondering how things work.

Adding/Removing tablespaces

Tablespaces allow us to store PostgreSQL data across different devices. We might want to do that for performance, administrative ease, or your database might just have run out of disk space.

Getting ready

Before we can create a useful tablespace, we need to prepare the underlying devices in production-ready form.

Think carefully about the speed, volume, and robustness of the disks you are about to use. Make sure they are configured correctly. Those decisions will affect your life for the next few months and years.

Disk performance is a subtle issue that most people think can be decided in a few seconds. We recommend you read the *Performance* section of this book, as well as additional books on this topic.

Once you've done all that, then you can create a directory for our tablespace.
The directory must:

- Be empty
- Be owned by the PostgreSQL owning userid
- Be specified with an absolute path name

On Linux/Unix systems, you shouldn't use a mount point directly. Create a subdirectory and use that instead. That simplifies ownership and avoids some filesystem-specific issues, such as having lost+found directories.

It also needs to follow sensible naming conventions, so we clearly identify which tablespace goes with which server. Do not be tempted to use something simple, such as data, because it will make later administration more difficult. Be especially careful that test or development servers do not and cannot get confused with production systems.

How to do it...

Once you've created your directory, adding the tablespace is simple, as follows:

```
CREATE TABLESPACE new_tablespace
LOCATION '/usr/local/pgsql/new_tablespace';
```

And, the command to remove the tablespace is also simple, which is:

```
DROP TABLESPACE new_tablespace;
```

A tablespace can only be dropped when it is empty, so how do you know when a tablespace is empty?

Tablespaces can contain both permanent and temporary objects.

Permanent data objects are tables, indexes, and toast objects. We don't need to worry too much about toast objects, because they are created and always live in the same tablespace as their main table, plus, you cannot manipulate their privileges or ownership.

Indexes can exist in separate tablespaces, as a performance option, though that requires explicit specification on the CREATE INDEX statement. The default is to create indexes in the same tablespace as the table to which they belong.

Temporary objects may also exist in a tablespace. These exist when users have explicitly created temporary tables or there may be implicitly created data files when large queries overflow their work_mem settings. These files are created according to the setting of the temp_tablespaces parameter. That might cause an issue, because you can't tell for certain what the setting of temp_tablespaces is for each user. The users can change their setting of temp_tablespaces away from the default value specified in the postgresql.conf.

We can identify the tablespace of each user object using the following query:

```
SELECT          spcname
                ,relname
                ,CASE WHEN relistemp THEN 'temp ' ELSE '' END ||
                CASE
                        WHEN relkind = 'r' THEN  'table'
                        WHEN relkind = 'v' THEN  'view'
                        WHEN relkind = 'S' THEN  'sequence'
                        WHEN relkind = 'c' THEN  'type'
                ELSE 'index' END                        as objtype
FROM            pg_class c join pg_tablespace ts
ON              (CASE WHEN c.reltablespace = 0 THEN
                        (SELECT dattablespace FROM pg_database
                          WHERE datname = current_database())
                ELSE c.reltablespace END) = ts.oid
WHERE           relname NOT LIKE 'pg_toast%'
AND             relnamespace NOT IN (SELECT oid FROM pg_namespace WHERE
nspname IN ('pg_catalog', 'information_schema'))
;
```

```
      spcname       |  relname  |  objtype
--------------------+-----------+------------
 new_tablespace     | x         | table
 new_tablespace     | y         | table
 new_tablespace     | z         | temp table
 new_tablespace     | y_val_idx | index
```

You may also want to look at columns `spcowner`, `relowner`, `relacl`, and `spcacl` to determine who owns what, and what they're allowed to do. The `relacl` and `spcacl` columns refer to the "access control list" that details the privileges available on those objects. The `spcowner` and `relowner` columns record the owners of the tablespace and tables/indexes, respectively.

How it works...

A tablespace is just a directory where we store PostgreSQL data files. We use symbolic links from the data directory to the tablespace.

We exclude toast tables because they are always in the same tablespace as their parent tables, though remember toast tables are always in a separate schema. You can exclude toast tables using the `relkind` column, but that would still include the indexes on the toast tables. Toast tables and toast indexes both start with `pg_toast`, so we can exclude those easily from our queries.

The preceding query needs to be complex, because `pg_class` entry for an object will show `reltablespace = 0` when an object is created in the database's default tablespace. So, if you directly join `pg_class` and `pg_tablespace`, you end up losing rows.

Note that we can see a temporary object exists and which tablespace in which it is created, even though we cannot refer to a temp object in another user's session.

There's more...

Some further notes on best practices follows.

A tablespace can contain objects from multiple databases, so it's possible to be in a position where there are no objects visible in the current database. The tablespace just refuses to go away, giving the following error:

```
ERROR:  tablespace "old_tablespace" is not empty
```

You are strongly advised to make a separate tablespace for each database, to avoid confusion. This can be especially confusing if you have the same schema names and table names in the separate databases.

How to avoid this? If you just created a new tablespace directory, you might want to create subdirectories within that for each database that needs space, and then make the subdirectories into tablespaces instead.

You may also wish to consider giving each tablespace a specific owner, using the following query:

```
ALTER TABLESPACE new_tablespace OWNER TO eliza;
```

if that helps smooth administration.

You may also wish to set `default_tablespaces` for a user, so that tables are automatically created there by issuing the following query:

```
ALTER USER eliza SET default_tablespace = 'new_tablespace';
```

Putting pg_xlog on a separate device

You may seek advice about putting the `pg_xlog` directory onto a separate device for performance reasons. This sounds very similar to tablespaces, though there is no explicit command to do this once you have a running database. Please look for the recipe in the *Performance* chapter.

Tablespace-level tuning

As each tablespace has different I/O characteristics, we may wish to alter the planner cost parameters for each tablespace. These can be set with the following command:

```
ALTER TABLESPACE new_tablespace SET
(seq_page_cost = 0.05, random_page_cost = 0.1);
```

Settings are roughly appropriate for an SSD drive, which assumes that the drive is faster than an HDD by x10 for random reads, and x20 for sequential reads.

The values given need more discussion than we have time for here.

Moving objects between tablespaces

Moving data around between tablespaces may sometimes be required.

Getting ready

First, create your tablespaces. Once the old and new tablespaces exist, we can issue the commands to move them.

How to do it...

Tablespaces can contain both permanent and temporary objects.

Permanent data objects are tables, indexes, and toast objects. We don't need to worry too much about toast objects, because they are created and always live in the same tablespace as their main table. So if you alter the tablespace of a table, it's toast objects will move also.

```
ALTER TABLE mytable SET TABLESPACE new_tablespace;
```

Indexes can exist in separate tablespaces, and moving a table leaves the indexes where they are. Don't forget to run `ALTER INDEX` commands as well, one for each index, as follows:

```
ALTER INDEX mytable_val_idx SET TABLESPACE new_tablespace;
```

Temporary objects cannot be explicitly moved, so we take that to mean you want to "ensure they are created somewhere else in the future". To do that you need to:

- Edit `temp_tablespaces`
- Reload the server to allow new configuration settings to take effect

There is no single command to do this that will work for all users.

How it works...

If you want to move a table and its indexes all in one pass, you can issue all the commands in a single transaction as follows:

```
BEGIN;
ALTER TABLE mytable SET TABLESPACE new_tablespace;
ALTER INDEX mytable_val1_idx SET TABLESPACE new_tablespace;
ALTER INDEX mytable_val2_idx SET TABLESPACE new_tablespace;
COMMIT;
```

Moving tablespaces means bulk-copying data. Copying happens sequentially block-by-block, and that performs well, but there's no way to avoid the fact that the bigger the table, the longer it will take.

Performance will be optimized if archiving or streaming replication is not active, as no WAL will be written in that case.

You should be aware that the table is fully locked (AccessExclusiveLock) while the copy takes place, so this can cause an effective outage for your application. Be *very* careful.

If you want to ensure that objects are created in the right place next time you create one, then you can use the following:

```
SET default_tablespace = 'new_tablespace';
```

You can run this automatically for all users that connect to a database using the following query:

```
ALTER DATABASE mydb SET default_tablespace = 'new_tablespace';
```

Take care that you do not run the next command by mistake though:

```
ALTER DATABASE mydb SET TABLESPACE new_tablespace;
```

As this literally moves all objects that do not have an explicitly defined tablespace into `new_` `tablespace`. For a large database, this will take a very long time, and your database will be completely locked while it runs. Not cool, if you do it by accident.

There's more...

If you just discovered that indexes don't get moved when you move a table, then you may want to check to see if any indexes are in different tablespaces from their parent tables. Run the following to check:

```
SELECT      i.relname as indexname
            ,tsi.spcname
            ,t.relname as tablename
            ,tst.spcname
FROM        (((pg_class t                /* tables */
            JOIN pg_tablespace tst
            ON      t.reltablespace = tst.oid)
            JOIN pg_index pgi
            ON pgi.indrelid = t.oid)
            JOIN pg_class i        /* indexes */
            ON      pgi.indexrelid = i.oid)
            JOIN pg_tablespace tsi
            ON      i.reltablespace = tsi.oid
WHERE       i.relname NOT LIKE 'pg_toast%'
AND         i.reltablespace != t.reltablespace
;
```

If we have one table with an index in a separate tablespace, we might see this as psql definition:

```
postgres=# \d y
      Table "public.y"
 Column | Type | Modifiers
--------+------+-----------
 val    | text |
Indexes:
    "y_val_idx" btree (val), tablespace "new_tablespace"
Tablespace: "new_tablespace2"
```

Running the query presented previously, gives the following:

```
   relname   |      spcname      | relname |     spcname
-------------+-------------------+---------+----------------
 y_val_idx   | new_tablespace    | y       | new_tablespace2
(1 row)
```

Accessing objects in other PostgreSQL databases

Sometimes we want to access data in other PostgreSQL databases. Reasons might be as follows:

▶ You have more than one database server, and you need to extract data from one and load it into the other, such as reference data.

▶ You want to access data that is in a different database on the same database server which had been split up for administrative purposes.

▶ You want to perform some changes that you do not wish to rollback in the event of an error or transaction abort—known as function side-effects or autonomous transactions.

You might also be considering this because you are exploring scale out, sharding or load-balancing approaches. If so, please read the last part of this recipe *See Also,* and then skip to the chapter on *Replication*.

Getting ready

Install dblink, which is a contrib module for PostgreSQL.

Next, we create some access definitions. This can be done in various ways, but these commands are SQL Standard (SQL/MED), so it seems useful to follow them:

```
postgres=# CREATE FOREIGN DATA WRAPPER postgresql
VALIDATOR postgresql_fdw_validator;
CREATE FOREIGN DATA WRAPPER
postgres=# CREATE SERVER otherdb
FOREIGN DATA WRAPPER postgresql
OPTIONS (host 'foo', dbname 'otherdb', port '5432');
CREATE SERVER
postgres=# CREATE USER MAPPING FOR PUBLIC
SERVER otherdb;
CREATE USER MAPPING
```

You need only create one FOREIGN DATA WRAPPER, though you need to create one SERVER for each PostgreSQL destination database to which you may wish to connect to. This is just the connection definition, not the connection itself.

Creating a public user mapping with no options seems strange, though it will mean that we use the libpq default behavior. This will mean that we will connect the remote database using the value of PGUSER, or if not set, use the operating system user.

How to do it...

Connect using an unnamed connection as follows:

```
SELECT dblink_connect('otherdb');
 dblink_connect
----------------
 OK
(1 row)
```

Disconnect from the unnamed connection by running the following:

```
SELECT dblink_disconnect();
 dblink_connect
----------------
 OK
(1 row)
```

EXECUTE COMMAND

To execute the following command:

```
postgres=# INSERT INTO audit_log VALUES (current_user, now());
INSERT 0 1
```

Run it on the unnamed remote connection as follows:

```
postgres=# SELECT dblink_exec('INSERT INTO audit_log VALUES'||
    ' (current_user, now())', true);
 dblink_exec
-------------
 INSERT 0 1
(1 row)
```

Notice that the remote command returns the command tag and number of rows processed as the return value of the function. The second option means "fail on error". If you look closely, there's also a subtle error—when the INSERT was executed locally, we use this server's value of current_user, though when we execute remotely, we use the remote server's value of current_user, which might differ, depending upon the user mapping defined previously.

EXECUTE QUERY

To execute the following query:

```
SELECT generate_series(1,3)
```

on the unnamed remote connection as follows:

```
SELECT *
FROM dblink('SELECT generate_series(1,3)')
  AS link(col1 integer);
 col1
 ------
    1
    2
    3
(3 rows)
```

Note that we need to specify the output columns and column types. If `dblink()` is unable to determine the result specification of the query, it will execute when we parse the query, so we must explicitly define the output that we expect when the query executes.

How it works...

dblink establishes a persistent connection with the other database. The dblink functions track the details of that connection, so you don't need to worry about doing so yourself. You should be aware that this is an external "resource", and so the generic programming problem of "resource leaks" becomes possible; if you forget about your connection and forget to disconnect it, you may experience problems later. The remote connections will be terminated should your session disconnect.

Note that the remote connection persists even across transaction failures and other errors, so there is no need to reconnect.

`dblink()` executes the remote query, and will assemble the result set in memory before the local reply begins to be sent. That means that very large queries might fail through lack of memory, and everybody else will notice also. This isn't a problem; this is simply not designed to handle bulk data flows. Look at the recipe about data loading instead, if that's what you want to do.

Running slightly larger queries can be achieved using cursors. These allow us to bring the answer set back in smaller chunks. Conceptually, we need to open the cursor, loop while fetching rows until we are done, and then close the cursor. Some example code for that is as follows:

```
postgres=# SELECT dblink_open('example',
                        'SELECT generate_series(1,3)', true);
 dblink_open
 -------------
 OK
(1 row)
```

```
postgres=# SELECT *
                        FROM dblink_fetch('example', 10, true)
                        AS link (col1 integer);
 col1
------
    1
    2
    3
(3 rows)
```

Notice that we didn't need to define the cursor when we opened it, though we do need to define the results from the cursor when we fetch from it, just as we did with a normal query. Fetch 10 rows at a time.

```
postgres=# SELECT *
                        FROM dblink_fetch('example', 10, true)
                        AS link (col1 integer);
 col1
------
(0 rows)
postgres=# SELECT dblink_close('example');
 dblink_close
--------------
 OK
(1 row)
```

dblink also allows you to use more than one connection. Using just one connection is generally not good for modular programming. For more complex situations, it's a good practice to assume that the connection you want is not the same one that another part of the program might need. dblink allows named connections, so you don't need to hope that the default connection is still the right one. There is also a function named dblink_get_connections() that will allow you to see what connections you have active.

There's more...

Remote data sources look like they can be treated as tables, though in practice this doesn't work in all the ways you might hope and expect.

There is no federated query optimizer. If we join a local and a remote table, then data from the remote database is simply pulled through, even if it would have been quicker to send through data, and then pull back matching rows.

The local WHERE clause is not sent to the remote database, so a query like the following would perform poorly:

```
SELECT *
FROM dblink('otherdb',
    'SELECT * FROM bigtable') AS link ( … )
WHERE filtercolumn > 100;
```

We would need to explicitly add the WHERE clause onto the remote query, like the following:

```
SELECT *
FROM dblink('otherdb',
    'SELECT * FROM bigtable' ||
    ' WHERE filtercolumn > 100') AS link ( … );
```

which means that, in general, setting up views of remote data isn't very helpful, as it encourages users to think that the table location doesn't matter, whereas from a performance perspective, it definitely does. This isn't really any different from other federated or remote access database products.

There are also a few performance considerations that you may wish to consider. The first is that when the remote query executes, the current session waits for it to complete. You can also execute queries without waiting for them to return using the following functions:

- ▸ dblink_send_query()
- ▸ dblink_is_busy()
- ▸ dblink_get_result()

If you are concerned about the overhead of connection time, then you may want to consider using a session pool. This will reserve a number of database connections that will allow you to reduce apparent connection time. Look at the connection-pool recipes in the *Server Control* chapter.

See also

Another, sometimes easier way of accessing other databases is with a tool named **PL/Proxy**. PL/Proxy allows you to create a local database function that is a proxy for a remote database function. PL/Proxy only works for functions, and some people regard that as a restriction, and that is why I explained dblink for the main part of this recipe.

Creating a local proxy function is simple:

```
CREATE FUNCTION my_task(VOID)
RETURNS SETOF text AS $$
    CONNECT 'dbname=myremoteserver';
    SELECT my_task();
$$ LANGUAGE plproxy;
```

You need a local function, but you don't need to call a remote function; you can use SQL statements directly. The following example shows a parameterized function:

```
CREATE FUNCTION get_cust_email(p_username text)
RETURNS SETOF text AS $$
    CONNECT 'dbname=myremoteserver';
    SELECT email FROM users WHERE username = p_username;
$$ LANGUAGE plproxy;
```

PL/Proxy is specifically designed to allow more complex architectures for sharding and load balancing. The RUN ON command allows us to specify the remote database dynamically on which we will run the SQL statement. So the preceding example becomes like the following:

```
CREATE FUNCTION get_cust_email(p_username text)
RETURNS SETOF text AS $$
    CLUSTER 'mycluster';
    RUN ON hashtext(p_username);
    SELECT email FROM users WHERE username = p_username;
$$ LANGUAGE plproxy;
```

You'll likely need to read the chapter on *Replication* also before you begin designing application architectures using these concepts.

Making views updateable

PostgreSQL supports the SQL Standard command CREATE VIEW, though the views it creates are not automatically updateable. This could change in later releases, but at 9.0, that difficulty still exists for the administrator to overcome. We discuss those issues here.

Getting ready

First, you need to consider that only simple views can be made to receive inserts, updates, and deletes easily. The SQL Standard differentiates between views that are "simple updateable" and more complex views that could not be expected to be updateable.

So before we proceed, we need to check the understanding of what is a simply updateable view and what is not. Starting from the cust table as follows:

```
postgres=# SELECT * FROM cust;
 customerid | firstname | lastname | age
------------+-----------+----------+-----
          1 | Philip    | Marlowe  |  38
          2 | Richard   | Hannay   |  42
          3 | Holly     | Martins  |  25
          4 | Harry     | Palmer   |  36
          4 | Mark      | Hall     |  47
(5 rows)
```

We create a very simple view on top of it like the following:

```
CREATE VIEW cust_view AS
SELECT customerid
    ,firstname
    ,lastname
    ,age
FROM cust;
```

Each row in our view corresponds to one row in a single-source table and each column is referred to directly without a function call. So we expect to be able to make inserts, updates, and deletes pass through our view into the base table.

The following examples are all views where inserts, updates, and deletes cannot easily be made to flow to the base table.

If we had views that look like the following:

```
CREATE VIEW cust_avg AS
SELECT avg(age)
FROM cust;
CREATE VIEW cust_above_avg_age AS
SELECT customerid
        ,substr(firstname, 1, 20) as fname
        ,substr(lastname, 1, 20) as lname
        ,age -
        (SELECT avg(age)::integer
         FROM cust) as years_above_avg
FROM cust
WHERE age >
    (SELECT avg(age)
     FROM cust);
CREATE VIEW  potential_spammers AS
SELECT customerid
FROM cust
ORDER BY spam_score(firstname, lastname) DESC
LIMIT 100;
```

So, before we proceed to the steps to allow any/all of inserts, updates, or deletes to flow from views to base tables, we need to be clear about whether that makes sense conceptually.

How to do it...

PostgreSQL provides a facility to create query rewrite rules. These are in some ways similar to Oracle's instead-of triggers; though no other database has an exactly similar concept to PostgreSQL rules.

Let's start from a very simple view that might exist purely for administrative purposes, as follows:

```
CREATE VIEW cust_view AS
SELECT customerid
    ,firstname
    ,lastname
    ,age
FROM cust;
```

At first, if we try to INSERT into our view, we get the following error:

```
postgres=# INSERT INTO cust_view
postgres-# VALUES (5, 'simon', 'riggs', 133);
ERROR:  cannot insert into a view
HINT:  You need an unconditional ON INSERT DO INSTEAD rule.
```

So let's try one of those as follows:

```
CREATE RULE cust_view_insert AS
ON insert TO cust_view
DO INSTEAD
INSERT INTO cust
VALUES (new.customerid, new.firstname, new.lastname, new.age);
```

And now retry our INSERT as follows:

```
postgres=# INSERT INTO cust_view
postgres-# VALUES (5, 'simon', 'riggs', 133);
INSERT 0 1
```

This now works. Let's add rules for UPDATE and DELETE also, by running the following query:

```
CREATE RULE cust_view_update AS
ON  update TO cust_view
DO INSTEAD
UPDATE cust SET
 firstname = new.firstname
,lastname = new.lastname
,age = new.age
WHERE customerid = old.customerid;
CREATE RULE cust_view_delete AS
ON  delete TO cust_view
DO INSTEAD
DELETE FROM cust
WHERE customerid = old.customerid;
```

How it works...

We've just scratched the surface of what you can achieve with rules, though personally I find them too complex for widespread use.

You can do a lot of things with rules though, you need to make sure that everything you do makes sense and has a practical purpose. There are some other important things that I should mention about rules before you dive in and start using them everywhere.

Rules are applied by PostgreSQL after the SQL has been received by the server and parsed for syntax errors, but before the planner tries to optimize the SQL statement.

In the rules in the preceding recipe, we reference the values of the *old* or the *new* row, just as we do within trigger functions. Similarly, there are only new values in an INSERT and only old values in a DELETE.

One of the big downsides of using rules is that you cannot bulk load data into the table using the COPY command. We cannot transform a stream of inserts into a single COPY command, nor can we do a COPY against the view. Bulk loading requires direct access to the table.

If we have a view like the following:

```
CREATE VIEW cust_minor AS
SELECT customerid
    ,firstname
    ,lastname
    ,age
FROM cust
WHERE age < 18;
```

then we have some more difficulties. If we wish to update this view, then you might read the manual, and see we can use a conditional rule by adding a WHERE clause to match the WHERE clause in the view as follows:

```
CREATE RULE cust_minor_update AS
ON  update TO cust_minor
WHERE new.age < 18
DO INSTEAD
UPDATE cust SET
  firstname = new.firstname
,lastname = new.lastname
,age = new.age
WHERE customerid = old.customerid;
```

This fails however, so we need to add two rules, one as an unconditional rule that does nothing (literally) and needs to exist for internal reasons, and one that does the work we want.

```
CREATE RULE cust_minor_update_dummy AS
ON   update TO cust_minor
DO INSTEAD NOTHING;
CREATE RULE cust_minor_update_conditional AS
ON   update TO cust_minor
WHERE new.age < 18
DO INSTEAD
UPDATE cust SET
  firstname = new.firstname
,lastname = new.lastname
,age = new.age
WHERE customerid = old.customerid;
```

There's more...

It should be noted that some, or even perhaps many, DBAs find *rules* to be a serious annoyance. Here's one more reason why. Let's try doing our main example a different way using triggers. We'd like to make this view updateable as follows:

```
CREATE VIEW cust_view AS
SELECT customerid
    ,firstname
    ,lastname
    ,age
FROM cust;
```

We can't create triggers on views, so let's try to create a table instead as follows:

```
CREATE TABLE cust_view AS SELECT * FROM cust WHERE 1 = 0;
```

We emulate the view by first creating a select rule on the dummy table, and then try to create triggers on the table for the `INSERT`, `UPDATE`, and `DELETE` actions. The rule only works if the table is completely empty, and if the rule is named `_RETURN`.

```
postgres # CREATE RULE "_RETURN" AS
            ON SELECT TO cust_view
            DO INSTEAD
            SELECT * FROM cust;
CREATE RULE
postgres # CREATE TRIGGER cust_view_modify_after_trig
            AFTER INSERT OR UPDATE OR DELETE ON cust
            FOR EACH ROW
            EXECUTE PROCEDURE cust_view_modify_trig_proc();
ERROR:  "cust_view" is not a table
```

Huh? So what is it if it's not a table?

```
postgres # DROP TABLE cust_view;
ERROR:  "cust_view" is not a table
HINT:  Use DROP VIEW to remove a view
postgres # DROP VIEW cust_view;
DROP VIEW
```

Wow! That works! Yes, we created a table, then added a rule to it, and it *turned the table into a view*. So, now we realize that we can't put triggers on a view, and we can't put a `SELECT` rule on a table without it becoming a view. So, this route won't work at all. It is probably best just to accept that if you want to load data into a table, then you have to refer to the table directly, rather than use a view. PostgreSQL 9.1 will support INSTEAD OF triggers on views, providing a full solution to updateable views that follows the SQL Standard.

8
Monitoring and Diagnosis

In this chapter, we will cover the following:

- ▶ Is the user connected?
- ▶ What are they running?
- ▶ Are they active or blocked?
- ▶ Who is blocking them?
- ▶ Killing a specific session
- ▶ Resolving an in-doubt prepared transaction
- ▶ Is anybody using a specific table?
- ▶ When did anybody last use it?
- ▶ How much disk space is used by temporary data?
- ▶ Why are my queries slowing down?
- ▶ Investigating and reporting a bug
- ▶ Producing a daily summary of logfile errors

Introduction

In this chapter, you find recipes for some common monitoring and diagnosis actions you want to do inside your database. They are meant to answer specific questions that you often face when using PostgreSQL.

Monitoring is important

Databases are not isolated entities. They live on computer hardware using CPUs, RAM, and disk subsystems. Users access the database using networks. Depending on the setup, the databases themselves may need network resources to function, either by performing some authentication checks when users log in, or using disks that are mounted over the network (not generally recommended), or doing remote function calls to other databases.

This means that monitoring only the database is not enough. As a minimum, one should also monitor everything directly involved in using the database, such as the following:

- Is the database host available? Does it accept connections?
- How much of the network bandwidth is in use? Have there been network interruptions and dropped connections?
- Is there enough RAM available for most common tasks? How much is left?
- Is there enough disk space available? When will it run out of disk space?
- Is the disk subsystem keeping up? How much more load can it take?
- Can the CPU keep up with load? How much of spare idle cycles do the CPUs have?
- Are other network services the database access depends on (if any) available? For example, if you use Kerberos for authentication you have to monitor it as well.
- How many context switches are happening when the database is running?

And, for most of these things, you are interested in history, that is, how things have evolved? Was everything mostly the same yesterday? Last week? When did the disk usage start changing rapidly?

For any larger installation, you probably already have something in place for monitoring the health of your hosts and network.

The two aspects of monitoring are collecting historical data to see how things have evolved and getting alerts when things go seriously wrong. **RRDtool (Round Robin Database Tool)** based tools, such as **Cacti** or **Munin**, are quite popular for collecting the historical information on all aspects of the servers, and presenting this information in an easy-to-follow graphical form. Seeing several statistics on the same timescale can really help when trying to figure out why the system is behaving the way it is.

Another aspect of monitoring is getting alerts when something goes really wrong and needs (immediate) attention.

For alerting, one of the most widely-used tools is the **Nagios**.

And then, of course, there is **SNMP (Simple Network Management Protocol)**, which is supported by a wide array of commercial monitoring solutions. Basic support for monitoring PostgreSQL through SNMP is found in pgsnmpd, available at the following URL:

```
http://pgsnmpd.projects.postgresql.org/
```

Providing PostgreSQL information to monitoring tools

The historical monitoring information is best to use when all of it is available from the same place and at the same timescale. Most monitoring systems have a plugin architecture, so adding new kinds of data inputs to them means installing a plugin. Sometimes, you may need to write or develop this plugin, but writing a plugin for something, such as Cacti is easy; you just have to write a script that outputs monitored values in simple text format.

Some useful things to get into graphs are number of connections, disk usage, number of queries, number of WAL files, most numbers from `pg_stat_user_tables` and `pg_stat_user_indexes`, and so on.

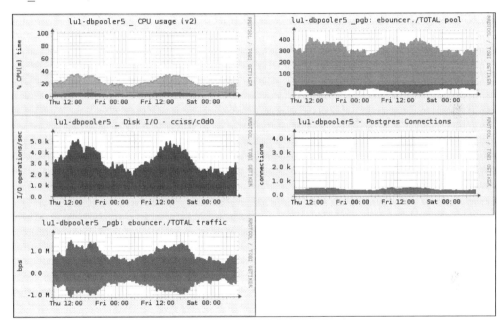

The preceding Cacti screenshot includes data for CPU, disk and network usage, pgbouncer connection pooler, and number of postgresql client connections. As you can see, they are nicely correlated.

One *Swiss Army* knife script, which can be used from both Cacti and Nagios, is `check_postgres`, available at `http://bucardo.org/check_postgres/check_postgres.pl.html`. It has ready-made reporting actions for a large array of things worth monitoring in PostgreSQL. Another similar effort for Nagios is available at the following URL:

`http://pgfoundry.org/projects/nagiosplugins/`

For Munin, there are some PostgreSQL plugins available at the Munin plugin repository at the following URL:

`http://exchange.munin-monitoring.org/plugins/search?keyword=postgres`

Where to find more information about generic monitoring tools

Setting up the tools themselves is a larger topic, and outside the scope of this book. In fact, each of these tools have more than one book written about them. The basic setup information and the tools themselves can be found at the following URLs:

- ▶ RRDtool (http://www.mrtg.org/rrdtool/)
- ▶ Cacti (http://www.cacti.net/)
- ▶ Munin (http://munin-monitoring.org/)
- ▶ Nagios (http://www.nagios.org/)

Realtime view using pgAdmin

You can also use pgAdmin to get a quick view of what is going on in the database. To do this, connect to the database, and then select menu item **Tools | Server Status**. This will open a window similar to the following screenshot, showing locks and running transactions:

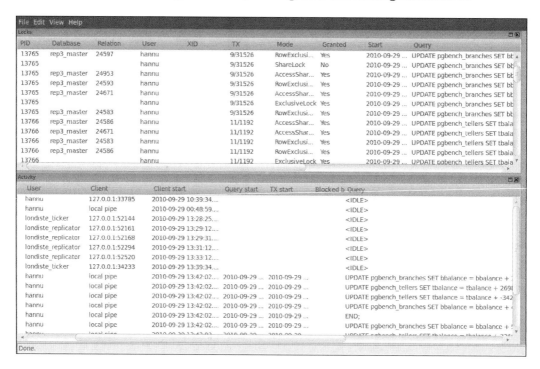

Is the user connected?

Here we show how to learn if a certain database user is currently connected to database.

Getting ready

Make sure that you are logged in as a superuser.

How to do it...

Issue the following query to see if the user bob is connected:

```
SELECT datname FROM pg_stat_activity WHERE usename = 'bob';
```

If this query returns any rows, then database user bob is connected to database. The returned value is the name of the database to which the user is connected.

How it works...

PostgreSQL system view pg_stat_activity keeps a track of all running PostgreSQL backends, including what queries are running, who is connected and when they were connected, and when the current transaction and current query were started.

There's more...

There is more information in the pg_stat_activity view than just username. For example, lets hel the user who asks.

What if I want to know "is that computer connected?"

Often, several different processes may connect as the same database user. In that case, you actually want to know if there is a connection from a specific connection.

You still can get this information from pg_stat_activity view, as it includes the connected client's IP addresses and ports. The port is only needed in case you have more than one connection from the same client computer and need to do further digging to see which process there connects to which database. Run the following:

```
SELECT datname,usename,client_addr,client_port FROM pg_stat_activity ;
```

The client_addr and client_port help you look up the exact computer, and even the process on that computer that has connected to this database.

What are they running?

Here we show how to check what query is currently running.

Getting ready

Make sure that you are logged in as a superuser or as the same database user you want to check.

Make sure that the parameter `track_activities` = on is set.

This can be done either in the `postgresql.conf` file or by the superuser using the following SQL statement:

```
SET track_activities = on
```

How to do it...

To see what all connected users are running now, just run the following:

```
SELECT datname,usename,current_query FROM pg_stat_activity ;
```

On systems with a lot of users, you may notice that the majority of backends are running a weird query `<IDLE>`. This denotes the state, where no query is actually running, and PostgreSQL is waiting for new commands from the user.

To see information for only active queries, exclude the idle ones by running the following:

```
SELECT datname,usename,current_query
FROM pg_stat_activity
WHERE current_query != '<IDLE>' ;
```

How it works...

When `track_activities` = on is set, then PostgreSQL collects data about all running queries. Users with sufficient right can then view this data using system view `pg_stat_activities`.

The view `pg_stat_activities` uses a system function named `pg_stat_get_activity` (procpid int) that you can use directly to watch for activity of a specific backend by supplying the process ID as an argument. Giving `NULL` as argument returns information for all backends.

There's more...

Sometimes you don't care about getting all queries currently running, but are just interested in seeing some of these. Or you may not like to connect to database just to see what is running.

How to catch queries which only run for a few milliseconds

As most queries on modern **OLTP (Online Transaction Processing)** systems take only a few milliseconds to run, it is often hard to catch those when simply probing the `pg_stat_activity` table.

To see them actually executing you'd have to slow them down. We don't want to do that!

In PostgreSQL 9.0, there is a contrib module called pg_stat_statements that captures query execution statistics in real time. See the documentation at the following URL:

`http://www.postgresql.org/docs/9.0/interactive/pgstatstatements.html`

In both cases, you can script the queries and use `select pg_sleep(5)` to get the `<wait>` happen automatically. You can get subsecond waits by using floating numbers, such as `pg_sleep(0.5)` for a half second delay.

To collect the queries you just forced to be logged you can start tail `-f /var/log/postgresql/postgresql-9.0-main.log > account_queries.log` in one window, then run the preceding lock trick in another and then just use Ctrl-C to kill the tail `-f` process.

Now you have a much smaller log in account_queries.log.

How to watch longest queries

Another thing of interest for which you may want to look is long-running queries. To get a list of running queries ordered by how long they have been executing, use the following:

```
select
    current_timestamp - query_start as runtime,
    datname,
    usename,
    current_query
  from pg_stat_activity
  where current_query != '<IDLE>'
  order by 1 desc;
```

This will return currently running queries ordered by how long they have been running, with the longest ones in front (the first field: `order by 1 desc`). On busy systems, you may want to limit the set of queries returned to only the first few ones (add `LIMIT 10` to the end), or only to queries which have been running over a certain time (for queries which have been running over one minute add 'current_timestamp – query_start 1' min to the WHERE clause).

Watching queries from ps

If you want, you can also make the queries being run show up in process titles, by setting the following:

```
update_process_title = on
```

Although `ps` or `top` output is not the best place for watching the database queries; it may make sense in some circumstances.

See also

The page in PostgreSQL's online documentation, which covers related settings, is available at the following URL:

```
http://www.postgresql.org/docs/9.0/interactive/runtime-config-
statistics.html
```

Are they active or blocked?

Here we show how to find out if a query is actually running, or is it waiting for some other query.

Getting ready

Again, log in as a superuser.

How to do it...

Run the following query:

```
SELECT datname,usename,current_query
FROM pg_stat_activity
WHERE waiting = true;
```

You get a list of queries which are waiting on other backends.

How it works...

The system view `pg_stat_activity` has a boolean field `waiting`, which selects `pg_terminate_backend(procpid)` from `pg_stat_activity`, where `current_query` = `<IDLE>` in transaction, and `current_timestamp - query_start > '1 min'`; indicates that a certain backend is waiting on a system lock.

The preceding query uses it to filter out only queries which are waiting.

There's more...

Some more explanations about the preceding may be appropriate here.

No need for "= true"

As the column waiting is already boolean, you can safely omit the `= true` part from the query and simply write the following:

```
SELECT datname,usename,current_query
FROM pg_stat_activity
WHERE waiting;
```

This catches only queries waiting on locks

The `pg_stat_activity.waiting` field shows only if the query is waiting on a PostgreSQL internal lock.

Although this is the main cause of waiting when using pure SQL, it is possible to write something in any of the PostgreSQL's embedded languages, which can wait on other system resources, such as waiting for an http response, a file write to complete, or just waiting on timer.

An example:

Write a simple function in PL/PythonU (the **U** version means untrusted; that is, only superusers can create functions in this language):

```
create or replace function wait(seconds float)
returns void as $$
import time;
time.sleep(seconds)
$$
language plpythonu;
```

When you run the following function:

```
db=# select wait(10);
<it "stops" for 10 seconds here>
 wait
------
(1 row)
```

it will show up with as not waiting in the `pg_stat_activity` view, even though the query is in fact "blocked" on timer.

Who is blocking them?

Once you have found out that some query is blocked, you need to know who or what is blocking them.

Getting ready

Same as others, just use any superuser account to run the queries.

How to do it...

Run the following query:

```
SELECT
    w.current_query as waiting_query,
    w.procpid as w_pid,
    w.usename as w_user,
    l.current_query as locking_query,
    l.procpid as l_pid,
    l.usename as l_user,
    t.schemaname || '.' || t.relname as tablename
from pg_stat_activity w
join pg_locks l1 on w.procpid = l1.pid and not l1.granted
join pg_locks l2 on l1.relation = l2.relation and l2.granted
join pg_stat_activity l on  l2.pid = l.procpid
join pg_stat_user_tables t on l1.relation = t.relid
where w.waiting;
```

It returns process ID, user, and current query about both blocked and blocking backends, and also the schema and table name of the table that causes the blocking.

How it works...

This query first selects all waiting queries (where w.waiting), then gets the locks on which this query is waiting (join pg_locks l1 on w.procpid = l1.pid and not l1.granted), then looks up the lock which is granted on the same table (join pg_locks l2 on l1.relation = l2.relation and l2.granted), and finally looks up a row in pg_stat_activity corresponding to the granted lock. It also resolves the relation identifier (relid) of the table to its full name using system view pg_stat_user_tables.

Killing a specific session

Sometimes the only way to let the system as a whole continue is by terminating some offending database sessions.

Getting ready

Again, this is a superuser-only capability, so log in as a superuser.

How to do it...

Once you have figured out the backend you need to kill, use the function named

`pg_terminate_backend(processid)` to actually kill it.

How it works...

When a backend executes the `pg_terminate_backend(processid)` function, it sends a signal **SIGQUIT** to the backend given as an argument, after checking that the process identified by the argument `processid` actually is a PostgreSQL backend.

The backend receiving this signal stops whatever it is doing, and terminates it in a controlled way.

The client using that backend loses the connection to database. Depending on how it is written, it may silently reconnect or it may show an error to the user.

There's more...

Killing the session may not always be what you really want, so consider other options as well.

Try to cancel the query first

You may want to try a milder version `pg_cancel_backend(processid)` first.

The difference between these two is that `pg_cancel_backend()` just cancels the current query, whereas `pg_terminate_backend()` really kills the backend.

If the backend won't terminate

If `pg_terminate_backend(processid)` won't kill the backend, and you really need to reset the database state to make it continue processing requests, then you have yet another option—sending `SIGKILL` to the offending backend.

This can be done only from the command line, as root or user postgres on the same host the database is running by executing the following:

```
kill -9 <backendpid>
```

which kills that backend immediately without giving it a chance to clean up, therefore forcing the postmaster to also kill all other backends and to restart the whole cluster.

Therefore, it actually does not matter which of the PostgreSQL backends you kill.

But beware that in case you have set the parameter `synchronous_commit` to `off`, you may end up losing some supposedly *committed* transactions if you `kill -9` a backend.

So `kill -9` is the last resort thing to be done, only if nothing else helps, and not on a regular basis.

Use statement timeout to clean up queries which take too long

Often you know that you don't have any use for queries running more than *x* times. Maybe your web frontend just refuses to wait for more than 10 seconds for a query to complete and returns some default answer to users if it takes longer, abandoning the query.

In such a case, it is a good idea to set `statement_timeout = 15 sec` either in `postgresql.conf` or as a per user or per database setting, so that queries running too long don't consume precious resources and make others' queries fail as well.

The queries terminated by statement timeout show up in log as follows:

```
hannu=# set statement_timeout = '3 s';
SET
hannu=# select wait(10);
ERROR:  canceling statement due to statement timeout
```

They used to show up as a more confusing "query canceled due to user request" on the older version of PostgreSQL.

Killing "Idle in transaction" queries

Sometimes, people start a transaction, run some queries, and then just leave without ending the transaction. This can leave some system resources in a state where some housekeeping processes can't be run or they may even have done something more serious, such as locking a table, thereby causing immediate *denial of service* for other users needing that table.

You can use the following query to kill all backends that have an open transaction but have been doing nothing for the last 10 minutes:

```
select pg_terminate_backend(procpid)
  from pg_stat_activity
where current_query = '<IDLE> in transaction'
   and current_timestamp - query_start > '10 min';
```

You can even schedule this to be running every minute while you are trying to find the specific PHP frontend, which keeps leaving open transactions behind, or you have a lazy administration leaving psql connection open, or a flaky network that drops clients without the server noticing it.

You can also kill the backend from command line

Another possibility to terminate a backend is by using a Unix/Linux command named `kill N`, which sends the signal to process N on the system where it is running. You have to be either the root user or the user running the database backends (usually postgres) to be able to send signals to processes.

Resolving an in-doubt prepared transaction

When using 2PC (two phase commit), you may end up in a situation where you kind of have something locked, but cannot find a backend that holds the locks.

For example:

```
db=# select t.schemaname || '.' || t.relname as tablename,
db-# l.pid, l.granted
db-# from pg_locks l join pg_stat_user_tables t
db-# on l.relation = t.relid;
 tablename |  pid  | granted
-----------+-------+---------
    db.x   |       | t
    db.x   | 27289 | f
(2 rows)
```

has a lock on table `db.x`, which has no process associated with it.

Getting ready

Look at the recipe on Removing old prepared transactions in Chapter 9 Regular Maintenance

Is anybody using a specific table?

This one helps you when you are in doubt if some obscure table is used any more, or is it just leftover from old times that just takes up space.

Getting ready

Make sure that you are a superuser, or at least have full rights on the table in question.

How to do it...

To see if a table is currently in active use, that is, if anyone is using it while you watch, run the following:

```
create temp table tmp_stat_user_tables as select * from pg_stat_user_
tables;
```

Then wait a little, and see what is changed.

```
select * from pg_stat_user_tables n
  join tmp_stat_user_tables t
    on n.relid=t.relid
    and (n.seq_scan,n.idx_scan,n.n_tup_ins,n.n_tup_upd,n.n_tup_del) <>
(t.seq_scan,t.idx_scan,t.n_tup_ins,t.n_tup_upd,t.n_tup_del);
```

How it works...

The table `pg_stat_user_tables` is a view that shows current statistics for table usage.

To see if a table is used, you check for changes in its usage counts.

The previous query selects all tables where any of the usage counts for selector data manipulation have changed.

There's more...

The quick and dirty way

If you are sure that you have no use for the cumulative statistics gathered by PostgreSQL, you can just reset all table statistics by doing

```
select pg_stat_reset()
```

This sets all statistics to 0, and you can detect table use by just looking for tables where any usage count is not 0

Of course, you can make a backup copy of statistics table first, as follows:

```
create table backup_stat_user_tables as
select current_timestamp as snaptime, *
from  pg_stat_user_tables;
```

Collecting daily usage statistics

It is often useful to have historical usage statistics of tables available when trying to solve performance problems or just understanding the usage patterns.

For this purpose, you can collect the usage data in a regular manner daily or even more often using either cron or a PostgreSQL-specific scheduler like `pg_agent`.

The following query adds a timestamped snapshot of current usage statistics to the table created earlier:

```
insert into backup_stat_user_tables
select current_timestamp as snaptime, *
from  pg_stat_user_tables;
```

When did anybody last use it?

Once you find out that a table is not used currently, the next question is "when was it last used?"

Getting ready

Get access to the database as a superuser or to the database host computer as user postgres.

How to do it...

PostgreSQL does not have any built-in last-used information about tables, so you have to use other means to figure it out.

If you have set up a cronjob to collect usage statistics, as described in the previous chapter, then it is relatively easy to find out the last change date using an SQL query.

Else, you have basically two possibilities, neither of which gives you absolutely reliable answers.

You can either look at actual timestamps of the files in which the data is stored, or you can use the `xmin` and `xmax` system columns to find out the latest transaction ID that has changed the table data.

Looking at file dates

To find out the file name(s) in which the table data is stored, you have to do the following:

Here is a sample PL/PythonU function that lists main file statistics for files used to store a table. You need to have PL/PythonU installed in your database for this to work. If you don't have it, use the following:

```
CREATE LANGUAGE plpythonu;
```

to install the language in the database. This assumes you have the support for PL/PythonU available on the database host.

First, we create a return type for the function, and then the function itself as follows:

```
CREATE TYPE fileinfo AS (
  filename text,
  filesize bigint,
  ctime abstime,
  mtime abstime,
  atime abstime
  );
CREATE OR REPLACE FUNCTION table_file_info(schemaname text, tablename
text)
RETURNS SETOF fileinfo
AS $$
import datetime, glob, os
db_info = plpy.execute("""
select datname as database_name,
       current_setting('data_directory') || '/base/' || db.oid as
data_directory
  from pg_database db
 where datname = current_database()
""")
#return db_info[0]['data_directory']
table_info_plan = plpy.prepare("""
select nspname as schemaname,
       relname as tablename,
       relfilenode as filename
  from pg_class c
  join pg_namespace ns on c.relnamespace=ns.oid
 where nspname = $1
   and relname = $2;
""", ['text', 'text'])
table_info = plpy.execute(table_info_plan, [schemaname, tablename])
filemask = '%s/%s*' % (db_info[0]['data_directory'], table_info[0]
['filename'])
res = []
for filename in glob.glob(filemask):
    fstat = os.stat(filename)
    res.append((
      filename,
      fstat.st_size,
      datetime.datetime.fromtimestamp(fstat.st_ctime).isoformat(),
      datetime.datetime.fromtimestamp(fstat.st_mtime).isoformat(),
      datetime.datetime.fromtimestamp(fstat.st_atime).isoformat()
    ))
return res
$$ LANGUAGE plpythonu;
```

Now, you can see the latest modification and access times for a table using the following query:

```
select
    max(mtime) as latest_mod,
    max(atime) as latest_read
from table_file_info(<schemaname>, <tablename>);
```

How it works...

The function `table_file_info(schemaname, tablename)` returns creation, modification, and access times for files used by PostgreSQL to store the table data.

The last query uses this data to get the latest time any of these files were modified or read by PostgreSQL. This is not a very reliable way to get information about the latest *use* of any table, but it gives you a rough upper-limit estimate about when it was last modified or read.

If you have shell access to the database host, then you can carry out the preceding steps by hand, say in case you can't or don't want to install PL/PythonU for some reason.

You can also get the information using built-in functions `pg_ls_dir(dirname text)` and `pg_stat_file(filename text)`. For example, the following query:

```
select pg_ls_dir, (select modification from pg_stat_file(pg_ls_dir))
as modtime from pg_ls_dir('.');
```

lists all files and directories in PostgreSQL data directory.

There's more...

There may be last-use information in future version of PostgreSQL

There has been some discussion recently about adding last-used data to the information PostgreSQL keeps about tables, so it is entirely possible that answering the question "When did anybody last use this table?" will be much easier in the next version of PostgreSQL.

How much disk space is used by temporary data?

In addition to ordinary stable tables, you can also create temporary tables.

Also, PostgreSQL may use temporary files for query processing if it can't fit all the needed data to memory.

So, how do you find out how much data is used by temporary tables and files?

Getting ready

Same as previous—you can do this using any untrusted embedded language, or directly on the database host. You have to use an untrusted language, because trusted ones run in a sandbox, which prohibits them from accessing the host file system directly.

How to do it...

First, check if your database defines special tablespaces for temporary files as follows:

```
select current_setting('temp_tablespaces');
```

When temp_tablespaces has one or more tablespaces

If it does, then your task is easy, because all temporary files, both for temporary table and those used for query processing, are inside the directories for these tablespaces—just look up the corresponding directories from pg_tablespaces as follows:

```
select spcname,spclocation from pg_tablespace;
```

Then, a simple du command shows you the space used by temporary files.

A sample session is as follows:

```
db=# select current_setting('temp_tablespaces');
 current_setting
-----------------
 temp1, temp2
(1 row)
db=#
db=# select spcname,spclocation from pg_tablespace where spcname in
('temp1', 'temp2');
 spcname |   spclocation
---------+----------------
 temp1   | /test/pg_tmp1
 temp2   | /test/pg_tmp2
(2 rows)
db=# \q
user@host:~$
sudo du -s /test/pg_tmp1 /test/pg_tmp2
102136 /test/pg_tmp1
35144  /test/pg_tmp2
```

Because the amount of temporary disk space used can vary a lot on an active system, you may want to repeat the last du -s command several times to get a better picture of how the disk usage changes.

When temp_tablespaces is empty

If the `temp_tablespaces` setting is empty, then the temporary tables are stored in the same directory as ordinary tables, and temp files used for query processing are stored in the `pgsql_tmp` directory inside the main database directory.

Look up the clusters home directory as follows:

```
select current_setting('data_directory') || '/base/pgsql_tmp'
```

The size of this directory gives the total size of current temporary files for query processing.

The total size of temporary files used by this database can be found by running the following query:

```
select sum(pg_total_relation_size(relid))
  from pg_stat_all_tables
where schemaname like 'pg_%temp%';
```

How it works...

Because all the temporary tables and other temporary on-disk data are stored in files, you use PostgreSQL's internal tables to find the location of these files, and then determine the total size of these files.

There's more...

While the preceding information about temporary tables is correct, it is not the wholes story.

Finding out if temporary file is in use any more

Because temporary files are not carefully preserved as ordinary tables (this is actually one of the benefits of temporary tables, as less bookkeeping makes them faster) it may sometimes happen that a system crash can leave around some temporary files, which can, in worst cases, take up a significant amount of disk space.

As a rule, you can clean up such files by shutting down the PostgreSQL server, and then deleting all files from the `pgsql_temp` directory.

Logging temporary file usage

If you set `log_temp_files = 0` or a larger value, then the creation of all temporary files that are larger than this value in kilobytes are logged to standard PostgreSQL log.

Why are my queries slowing down?

Queries that used to run in tens of milliseconds suddenly take several seconds.

A summary query for a report that used to run in a few seconds takes half an hour to complete.

Here are some ways to find out what is slowing them down.

Getting ready

Any questions of type "why is this different today than it was last week?", are much easier to answer if you have some kind of historic data collecting set up.

Things such as Cacti or Munin for monitoring general server characteristics (CPU and RAM usage, disk I/O, network traffic, load average) are very useful to see what has changed recently, and to try to correlate this with observed performance of some database operations.

Also, collecting historic statistics data from `pg_stat_*` tables, be that daily, hourly, or even every five minutes if you have enough disk space, is also very useful for detecting possible causes for sudden changes or gradual degradation in performance.

If you have both these statistics gatherings going on, then even better. If you have none, then the question is actually "Why is this query slow?".

But don't despair, because there are some things you can do to try to restore performance.

How to do it...

First, analyze your database as follows:

```
db_01=# analyse;
ANALYZE
Time: 6231.313 ms
db_01=#
```

This is the first thing to try, as it is usually cheap and is meant to be run quite often anyway.

If this restores the query performance, or at least improves current performance considerably, then it means that `autovacuum` is not doing its job well, and the next thing to do is to check why it is so.

How it works...

Analyze updates statistics about data size and data distribution in all tables. If a table size has changed significantly without its statistics being updated, then PostgreSQL's statistics-based optimizer can choose a bad plan. Running the ANALYZE command manually, updates the statistics for all tables.

There's more...

There are a few other common problems.

Do the queries return significantly more data than earlier?

If you initially tested your queries on almost empty tables, it is entirely possible that you are querying much more data than you need.

As an example, if you select all users items, and then show the first 10, then this runs very fast when user has 10 or even 50 items, but not so well when he/she has 50,000.

Check that you don't ask for more data than you need; use the LIMIT clause to return less data to your application (and to at least give the optimizer a chance to select a plan which processes less data when selecting and may also have lower startup cost).

Do the queries also run slowly when run alone?

If you can, then try to run the same slow query when the database has no or very little other queries running concurrently.

If it runs well in this situation, then it may be that the database host is just overloaded (CPU, memory, or disk I/O) and a plan that worked well under light load, is not so good any more. It may even be that it is not a very good query plan with which to begin, and you were fooled by modern computers being really fast.

```
db=# select count(*) from t;
  count
---------
 1000000
(1 row)
Time: 329.743 ms
```

As you can see, scanning one million rows takes just 0.3 seconds on a laptop, a few years old, if these rows are already cached.

But, if you have a few of such queries running in parallel, and also other queries competing for memory, this query can slow down an order of magnitude or two.

See chapter, *Performance & Concurrency* for general performance-tuning advice.

Is the second run of same query also slow?

This test is related to the previous one, and it checks if the slowdown may be caused by some of the needed data not fitting in memory, or being pushed out of memory by other queries.

If the second run of the query is fast, then you probably have developed a problem of not enough memory.

Again, see chapter *Performance & Concurrency*.

Table and index bloat

Something that can develop over time if some maintenance processes can't be run properly is table bloat. That is, due to the way **MVCC** works, your table will contain a lot of old versions of rows, in case these old versions can't be removed in a timely manner.

There are several ways this can develop, but all involve lots of updates or deletes, and inserts while the autovacuum is prevented from doing its job of getting rid of old tuples. And it is possible that even after the old versions are deleted, the table stays at its now acquired large size, thanks to visible rows being located at the end of table and preventing PostgreSQL from shrinking the file. There have been cases where a one-row table was grown to several gigabytes in size.

If you suspect some table may contain bloat, then run the following:

```
select pg_relation_size(relid) as tablesize,schemaname,relname,n_live_
tup
from pg_stat_user_tables
where relname = <tablename>;
```

And see if the relation of tablesize to n_live_tup makes sense.

For example, if the table size is tens of megabytes, and there are only a small number of rows, then you have bloat.

See also

- *Is anybody using a specific table/Collecting daily usage* statistics shows one way to collect info on table changes
- The whole Chapter, *Performance & Concurrency*

Investigating and reporting a bug

When you find out that PostgreSQL is not doing what it should, then it's time to investigate.

Getting ready

It is a good idea to make a full copy of your PostgreSQL installation before you start investigating. This will help you restart several times and be sure that you are in fact investigating the results of the bug and not chasing your own tail by looking at changes introduced by your last investigation and debugging attempt.

How to do it...

Try to make a minimal repeatable test scenario which exhibits this bug. Sometimes the bug disappears while doing it, but mostly it is needed for making it easier for the one who tries to fix it. It is almost impossible to fix a bug that you can't observe and repeat at will.

If it is about query processing, then usually you can provide minimal dump file (result of running `pg_dump`) of your database together with an SQL script that exhibits the error.

If you have corrupt data, then you may want to make (a subset of) the corrupted data files available to people who have knowledge and time to look at it. Sometimes, you can find such people on the PostgreSQL hackers list, and sometimes you have to hire someone or even fix it yourself. The more preparatory work you do yourself and the better you formulate your questions, the higher is the chance you have of finding help quickly.

If you suspect a data corruption bug and feel adventurous, then you can read about the data formats at `http://www.postgresql.org/docs/9.0/static/storage.html`, and investigate your data tables using the `pageinspect` package from contrib.

And always include at least the PostgreSQL version you are using and the operating system on which you are using it.

For a full guide, see the end of this chapter.

How it works...

If everything works really well, then it goes like the following:

- A user submits a well-researched bug report to the PostgreSQL hackers list
- Some discussions follow on the list and the user may be asked to provide some additional information
- Somebody finds out what is wrong, and proposes a fix
- The fix is discussed on the hackers list
- The bug is fixed, there is a patch for current version and, the fix will be included in the next version
- Sometimes the fix is backported to older versions

Unfortunately, this can go wrong at each step, due to various reasons, such as nobody feeling that this is his/her area of expertise, the right people not having time and hoping for someone else to deal with it, and these other people may just not be reading the list at the right moment.

If this happens, follow up your question in a day or two to try to understand why there was no reaction.

See also

The official PostgreSQL bug/problem reporting guides

If you follow the following URLs, you have a high chance of getting your questions answered:

```
http://wiki.postgresql.org/wiki/Guide_to_reporting_problems
```

```
http://wiki.postgresql.org/wiki/SlowQueryQuestions
```

Producing a daily summary of logfile errors

PostgreSQL can generate gigabytes of logs per day. Lots of data is good in case you want to investigate some specific event, but it is not what you will use for daily monitoring of database health.

Getting ready

Make sure that your PostgreSQL is set up to rotate the log files daily.

A default setup will do exactly the following:

```
log_rotation_age = 1d
```

Then get a PostgreSQL log processing program. Here, we describe how to do it using **pgFouine**.

For most Linux systems, you should be able to use your default package manager to install pgFouine.

Configure your PostgreSQL to produce `logfiles` in a format that pgFouine understands. Select logging to `syslog`. Use a modern version of `syslogd` for high-traffic databases.

How to do it...

Set up a cron job to run a few minutes after the default log rotation time. You can find the time by looking at timestamps of already rotated log files; they all have similar times.

Run the following:

```
pgfouine.php -file /var/log/postgressql/postgresql-9.0-main.log.1
-reports n-mostfrequenterrors > errors.html
```

You can also set it up to e-mail the generated error report to the DBA at that time.

How it works...

PgFouine condenses and ranks error messages for easy viewing, and produces a nicely formatted report in HTML. From that report, you can find out the most frequent errors.

As a rule, it is a good practice not to tolerate errors in database logs if you can avoid it. Once the errors start showing up in the log and report, you should find the cause of the errors and fix them.

While it is tempting to leave the errors there, as *they do no harm* and consider them just a small nuisance, it is often true, that simple errors are indication of other problems in the application, which if not found and understood may lead to all kinds of larger problems, such as security breaches or eventual data corruption at the logical level.

There's more...

Writing your own log processor

If you have only a small number of errors in your log files, then it may be sufficient to just run each logfile through `grep` to find errors:

```
user@dbhost: $ egrep "FATAL|ERROR" postgresql-9.0-main.log
```

See also

- ▶ Home page for pgFouine is at the following website:

  `http://pgfouine.projects.postgresql.org/`

- ▶ You can get much more information on setting up pgFouine at the following URL:

  `http://pgfouine.projects.postgresql.org/tutorial.html`

- ▶ Another similar tool is **PQA (Practical Query Analysis)**, available at the following URL:

  `http://pqa.projects.postgresql.org/`

PQA is written in **Ruby**, so if you are good at using Ruby, you may prefer this one.

In PostgreSQL 9.0, there is also a contrib module `pg_stat_statements` that captures query execution statistics in real time. See the documentation at the following URL:

`http://www.postgresql.org/docs/9.0/interactive/pgstatstatements.html`

9
Regular Maintenance

In this chapter, we will cover the following:

- ▶ Controlling automatic database maintenance
- ▶ Avoiding auto freezing and page corruptions
- ▶ Avoiding transaction wraparound
- ▶ Removing old prepared transactions
- ▶ Actions for heavy users of temporary tables
- ▶ Identifying and fixing bloated tables and indexes
- ▶ Maintaining indexes
- ▶ Finding unused indexes
- ▶ Carefully removing unwanted indexes
- ▶ Planning maintenance

Introduction

PostgreSQL prefers regular maintenance, and there is a recipe discussing planning maintenance.

We recognize that you're here for a reason and are looking for a quick solution to your needs. You're probably thinking fix me first and I'll plan later. So off we go.

PostgreSQL provides a utility command named VACUUM, which is a jokey name for a garbage collector that sweeps up all the bad things and fixes them, or at least most of them. That's the single most important thing you need to remember to do—I say single thing because closely connected to that is the ANALYZE command, that collects optimizer statistics. It's possible to run VACUUM and ANALYZE as a single joint command VACUUM ANALYZE, plus those actions are automatically executed for you when appropriate by autovacuum, a special background process that forms part of the PostgreSQL server.

VACUUM performs a range of clean up activities, some of them too complex to describe without a whole sideline into internals. VACUUM has been heavily optimized over a 10-year period to take the minimum required lock levels on tables, and execute in the most efficient manner possible, skipping all unnecessary work, and using L2 cache CPU optimizations when work is required.

Many experienced PostgreSQL DBAs will prefer to execute their own VACUUMs, though autovacuum now provides a fine degree of control, and that can save you much time by enabling and controlling it. Using both manual and automatic vacuuming gives you both control and a safety net.

Controlling automatic database maintenance

Autovacuum is enabled by default in PostgreSQL 9.0, and mostly does a great job of maintaining your PostgreSQL database. I say mostly because it doesn't know everything you do about the database, such as when would be the best time to perform maintenance actions.

Getting ready

Exercising control requires some thinking about what you actually want:

- Which are the best times of day to do things? When are system resources more available?
- Which days are quiet, and are which not?
- Which tables are critical to the application, and which are not?

How to do it...

The first thing to do is to make sure autovacuum is switched on. You must have both the following parameters enabled in your `postgresql.conf`:

- `autovacuum` = on
- `track_counts` = on

PostgreSQL controls autovacuum with 35 individually tunable parameters. That provides a wide range of options, though can be a little daunting.

The following parameters can be set in `postgresql.conf`:

- `autovacuum`
- `autovacuum_analyze_scale_factor`
- `autovacuum_analyze_threshold`

- ▸ `autovacuum_freeze_max_age`
- ▸ `autovacuum_max_workers`
- ▸ `autovacuum_naptime`
- ▸ `autovacuum_vacuum_cost_delay`
- ▸ `autovacuum_vacuum_cost_limit`
- ▸ `autovacuum_vacuum_scale_factor`
- ▸ `autovacuum_vacuum_threshold`
- ▸ `log_autovacuum_min_duration`

Individual tables can be controlled by "storage parameters", which are set using the following:

```
ALTER TABLE mytable SET (storage_parameter = value);
```

The storage parameters that relate to maintenance are as follows:

- ▸ `autovacuum_enabled`
- ▸ `autovacuum_vacuum_cost_delay`
- ▸ `autovacuum_vacuum_cost_limit`
- ▸ `autovacuum_vacuum_scale_factor`
- ▸ `autovacuum_vacuum_threshold`
- ▸ `autovacuum_freeze_min_age`
- ▸ `autovacuum_freeze_max_age`
- ▸ `autovacuum_freeze_table_age`
- ▸ `autovacuum_analyze_scale_factor`
- ▸ `autovacuum_analyze_threshold`

and "toast" tables can be controlled with the following parameters:

- ▸ `toast.autovacuum_enabled`
- ▸ `toast.autovacuum_vacuum_cost_delay`
- ▸ `toast.autovacuum_vacuum_cost_limit`
- ▸ `toast.autovacuum_vacuum_scale_factor`
- ▸ `toast.autovacuum_vacuum_threshold`
- ▸ `toast.autovacuum_freeze_min_age`
- ▸ `toast.autovacuum_freeze_max_age`
- ▸ `toast.autovacuum_freeze_table_age`
- ▸ `toast.autovacuum_analyze_scale_factor`
- ▸ `toast.autovacuum_analyze_threshold`

How it works...

If autovacuum is set, then autovacuum will wake up every autovacuum_naptime seconds, and decide whether to run `VACUUM` and/or `ANALYZE` commands.

There will never be more than autovacuum_max_workers maintenance processes running at any one time. As these autovacuum slaves perform I/O, they accumulate cost points, until they hit the autovacuum_vacuum_cost_limit, after which they sleep for autovacuum_vacuum_cost_delay. This is designed to throttle the resource utilization of autovacuum to prevent it from using all available disk performance, which it should never do. So, increasing autovacuum_vacuum_cost_delay will slow down each VACUUM to reduce the impact on user activity. Autovacuum will run an `ANALYZE` command when there have been at least autovacuum_analyze_threshold changes, and a fraction of the table defined by autovacuum_analyze_scale_factor has been inserted, updated, or deleted.

Autovacuum will run a `VACUUM` command when there have been at least autovacuum_vacuum_threshold changes, and a fraction of the table defined by autovacuum_vacuum_scale_factor has been updated or deleted.

If you set log_autovacuum_min_duration, then any autovacuum that runs for longer than this value will be logged to the server log, like the following:

```
2010-04-29 01:33:55 BST (13130) LOG:  automatic vacuum of table
"postgres.public.pgbench_accounts": index scans: 1
    pages: 0 removed, 3279 remain
    tuples: 100000 removed, 100000 remain
    system usage: CPU 0.19s/0.36u sec elapsed 19.01 sec
2010-04-29 01:33:59 BST (13130) LOG:  automatic analyze of table
"postgres.public.pgbench_accounts"
    system usage: CPU 0.06s/0.18u sec elapsed 3.66 sec
```

Most of the preceding global parameters can also be set at the table level. For example, if you think that you don't want a table to be autovacuumed, then you can set:

```
ALTER TABLE big_table SET (autovacuum_enabled = off);
```

It's also possible to set parameters for **toast** tables. The toast table is the location where oversize column values get placed, which the documents refer to as "supplementary storage tables". If there are no oversize values, then the toast table will occupy little space. Tables with very wide values often have large toast tables. Toast (stands for **the oversize attribute storage technique**) is optimized for UPDATE. If you have a heavily updated table, the toast table is untouched, so it may makes sense to turn off autovacuuming of the toast table as follows:

```
ALTER TABLE pgbench_accounts
SET ( autovacuum_vacuum_cost_delay = 20
        ,toast.autovacuum_enabled = off);
```

which will turn off autovacuuming of the "toast" table.

Note that autovacuuming of the toast table is performed completely separately from the main table, even though you can't ask for an explicit include/exclude of the toast table yourself when running VACUUM.

Use the following query to display the reloptions for tables and their toast tables:

```
postgres=# SELECT n.nspname, c.relname,
                pg_catalog.array_to_string(c.reloptions || array(
                  select 'toast.' ||
                  x from pg_catalog.unnest(tc.reloptions) x),', ')
                as relopts
FROM pg_catalog.pg_class c
  LEFT JOIN
          pg_catalog.pg_class tc ON (c.reltoastrelid = tc.oid) JOIN
          pg_namespace n ON c.relnamespace = n.oid
WHERE c.relkind = 'r'
AND nspname NOT IN ('pg_catalog', 'information_schema');
 nspname |      relname       |          relopts
---------+--------------------+-----------------------------
 public  | pgbench_accounts   | fillfactor=100,

                                autovacuum_enabled=on,

                                autovacuum_vacuum_cost_delay=20
 public  | pgbench_tellers    | fillfactor=100
 public  | pgbench_branches   | fillfactor=100
 public  | pgbench_history    |
 public  | text_archive       | toast.autovacuum_enabled=off
```

VACUUM allows inserts, updates, and deletes while it runs, though it prevents actions such as ALTER TABLE and CREATE INDEX. Autovacuum can detect if a user requests a conflicting lock on the table while it runs, and will cancel itself if it is getting in the user's way.

Note that VACUUM does not shrink a table when it runs, unless there is a large run of space at the end of a table, and nobody is accessing the table when we try to shrink it. To properly shrink a table, you need VACUUM FULL. That locks up the whole table for a long time, and should be avoided, if possible. VACUUM FULL will literally rewrite every row of the table, and completely rebuild all indexes. That process is faster in 9.0 than it used to be, though it's still a long time for larger tables.

There's more...

`postgresql.conf` also allows "include directives", which look like the following:

```
include 'autovacuum.conf'
```

These specify another file that will be read at that point, just as if those parameters had been included in the main file.

This can be used to maintain multiple sets of files for autovacuum configuration. Let's say we have a website that is busy, mainly during the daytime, with some occasional night time use. We decide to have two profiles, one for daytime, when we want only less aggressive autovacuuming, and another at night, where we allow more aggressive vacuuming.

We add the following lines to `postgresql.conf`:

- `autovacuum = on`
- `autovacuum_max_workers = 3`
- `include 'autovacuum.conf'`

and remove all other autovacuum parameters.

We then create one file named `autovacuum.conf.day`, containing the following parameters:

- `autovacuum_analyze_scale_factor = 0.1`
- `autovacuum_analyze_threshold = 50`
- `autovacuum_vacuum_cost_delay = 30`
- `autovacuum_vacuum_cost_limit = -1`
- `autovacuum_vacuum_scale_factor = 0.2`
- `autovacuum_vacuum_threshold = 50`

and another file named `autovacuum.conf.night`, that contains the following parameters:

- `autovacuum_analyze_scale_factor = 0.05`
- `autovacuum_analyze_threshold = 50`
- `autovacuum_vacuum_cost_delay = 10`
- `autovacuum_vacuum_cost_limit = -1`
- `autovacuum_vacuum_scale_factor = 0.1`
- `autovacuum_vacuum_threshold = 50`

To swap profiles, we would simply do the following actions:

```
$ ln -sf autovacuum.conf.night autovacuum.conf
$ pg_ctl -D datadir reload          # server reload command
```

(customized depending upon your platform).

This then allows us to switch profiles twice per day without needing to edit the configuration files. You can also tell easily which is the active profile simply by looking at the full details of the linked file (using ls –l). The exact details of the schedule are up to you; night/day was just an example, which is unlikely to suit everybody.

See also

`autovacuum_freeze_max_age` is explained in the recipe *Avoiding auto freezing*, as are the more complex table-level parameters.

Avoiding auto freezing and page corruptions

There are some aspects of VACUUM that are complex to explain why they exist, though have some occasional negative behaviors. Let's look more deeply at those and find some solutions.

Getting ready

PostgreSQL performs regular sweeps to clean out old transaction identifiers, which is known as "freezing". It does this to defer transaction wraparound, which is discussed in more detail in the next recipe.

There are two routes that a row can take in PostgreSQL: the row version dies and needs to be removed by VACUUM, or a row version gets old enough to need to be frozen, also performed by the VACUUM process.

Why do we care? Say we load a table with 100 million rows. Everything is fine. When those rows have been there long enough to begin being frozen, the next VACUUM on that table will re-write all of these rows to freeze their transaction identifiers. Put that another way, autovacuum will wake up and start using lots of I/O to perform the freezing.

How to do it...

The most obvious way to forestall that exact problem is to explicitly VACUUM a table after a major load. Of course that doesn't remove the problem entirely, and you might not have time for that.

Many people's knee-jerk reaction is to turn off autovacuum, because it keeps waking up at the most inconvenient times. My way is described in the recipe, *Controlling automatic database maintenance*.

Freezing takes place when a transaction identifier on a row becomes more than vacuum_ freeze_min_age transactions older than the current next value. Normal VACUUMs will perform a small amount of freezing as you go, and in most cases, you won't notice at all. As explained in the earlier example, large transactions leave many rows with the same transaction identifiers, so those might cause problems at freezing time.

VACUUM is normally optimized to look only at chunks of a table that require cleaning. When a table reaches vacuum_freeze_table_age, we ignore that optimization, and scan the whole table. While it does so, it's fairly likely to see rows that need freezing, which need to be re-written. So that is what causes the great increase in I/O.

If you fiddle with those parameters to try to forestall heavy VACUUMs, then you'll find that the `autovacuum_freeze_max_age` parameter controls when the table will be scanned by a forced VACUUM. To put that another way, you can't turn off the need to freeze rows, but you can get to choose when this happens. My advice is to control autovacuum as described in previous recipe, or perform explicit VACUUMs at a time of your choosing.

VACUUM is also an efficient way to confirm the absence of page corruptions, so it is worth scanning the whole database from time-to-time, every block. To do this, you can run the following script on each of your databases:

```
SET vacuum_freeze_table_age = 0;
VACUUM;
```

You can do this table-by-table as well; there's nothing special about whole database VACUUMs anymore—in earlier versions of PostgreSQL this was important, so you may read in random places on the web that this is a good idea.

If you've never had a corrupt block, then you may only need to scan maybe every two-to-three months. If you start to get corrupt blocks, then you may want to increase the scan rate to confirm everything is OK. Corrupt blocks are usually hardware-induced, though they show up as database errors. It's possible but rare that the corruption was instead from a PostgreSQL bug.

There's no easy way to fix page corruptions at present. There are ways to investigate and extract data from corrupt blocks, for example, using the contrib/pageinspect utility I wrote.

Avoiding transaction wraparound

To many users, "transaction wraparound" sounds like a disease from space. Mentioning "transaction wraparound" usually earns the speaker points for technical merit. Let's take a look at it, and how to avoid it.

Getting ready

First: have you seen the following message?

WARNING: database "postgres" must be vacuumed within XXX transactions.

HINT: To avoid a database shutdown, execute a database-wide VACUUM in that database.

You might also need to commit or roll back old prepared transactions.

Or even worse, the following message:

ERROR: database is not accepting commands to avoid wraparound data loss in database "template0"

HINT: Stop the postmaster and use a standalone backend to vacuum that database.

You might also need to commit or roll back old prepared transactions.

If not, then you don't need to do anything apart from normal planned maintenance. Those messages are reported to users, and they are also written to the server log.

How to do it...

If you have a support provider, now is a good time to call. Don't panic, but technical bravado can land you in worse situations than in which you already are. Let's continue to describe how to get out of this.

If you've received the WARNING, then follow both hints. First, let's do the suggested VACUUM on the appropriate database; it might not be "postgres", so replace the appropriate database name.

Either run the following:

```
$ vacuumdb postgres
```

or use the following:

```
psql -c "VACUUM" postgres
```

or use your admin tool to initiate a VACUUM on the appropriate database.

Next, find and follow the recipe, *Removing old prepared transactions*.

How it works...

PostgreSQL uses internal transaction identifiers that are four bytes long, so we only have 2^{31} transaction ids (about two billion). PostgreSQL wraps around and starts again from the beginning when that wraps around, allocating new identifiers in a circular manner. The reason we do this is that moving to an eight-byte identifier has various other negative effects and costs that we would rather not pay, so we keep the four-byte transaction identifier, which also has costs.

PostgreSQL is designed to continue using ids even after the system wraps. Properly maintained, everything will keep working forever and you'll never notice what happens on the inside. To allow that to happen we need to run regular VACUUMs.

There's more...

If you received the aforementioned ERROR, and the database is no longer accepting commands you're probably wondering what the phrase use a standalone backend to vacuum that database means.

A "standalone backend" means running the database server from just a single executable process. This is the equivalent of *nix run-level 1, also known as single user mode. We restrict access to the database to just a single user.

The command to do this is the following, noting that the --single must be the very first command on the command line:

```
$ postgres --single -D  /full/path/to/datadir postgres
```

which then returns the following command line prompt:

```
PostgreSQL stand-alone backend 9.0
backend>
```

and you can then run the VACUUM from there, as follows:

```
PostgreSQL stand-alone backend 9.0
backend> VACUUM;
backend>
```

when you're finished, type <CTRL>-D (or whatever you have set EOF to be for your terminal window) once or twice if you also used the -j option.

You should also check for old prepared transactions as described in *Removing old prepared transactions*.

See also

The recipe, *Avoiding auto freezing*, may also be relevant, or at least be an interesting read in a related area.

Removing old prepared transactions

You may have been routed here from other recipes, so you might not even know what prepared transactions are, let alone what an old one looks like.

The good news is that prepared transactions don't just happen, they happen in certain specific situations. If you don't know what I'm talking about, it's OK, you won't need to, and better still, you probably don't have any either.

Prepared transactions are part of the "two-phase commit" feature, also known as **2PC**. A transaction commits in two stages rather than one, allowing multiple databases to have synchronized commits. It's typical use is to combine multiple "resource managers" using the XA protocol, usually provided by a **Transaction Manager** (**TM**), as used by the **Java Transaction API** (**JTA**) and others. If none of that meant anything to you, then you probably don't have any prepared transactions.

Getting ready

First, check the setting of `max_prepared_transactions`. If this is zero, then you don't have any. If you still have no idea what I'm talking about, then set the parameter to zero.

```
SHOW max_prepared_transactions;
```

If your setting is more than zero, then look to see if you have any. As an example, you may find something like the following:

```
postgres=# SELECT * FROM pg_prepared_xacts;
-[ RECORD 1 ]-----------------------------
transaction | 121083
gid         | prep1
prepared    | 2010-03-28 15:47:57.637868+01
owner       | postgres
database    | postgres
```

where the `gid` ("global identifier") will usually have been automatically generated.

How to do it...

Removing a prepared transaction is also referred to as "resolving in-doubt transactions". The transaction is literally stuck between committing and aborting. The database or transaction manager crashed, leaving the transaction mid-way through the two-phase commit process.

If you have a connection pool of 100 active connections and something crashes, you'll probably find 1 to 20 transactions stuck in the prepared state, depending upon how long your average transaction is.

To resolve the transaction, we need to decide whether we want that change, or not. The best way is to check what happened externally to PostgreSQL. That should help you decide.

If you do need further help, look at the *There's more* section.

If you wish to commit the changes, then:

```
COMMIT PREPARED 'prep1';
```

or if you want to rollback the changes then:

```
ROLLBACK PREPARED 'prep1';
```

How it works...

Prepared transactions are persistent across crashes, so you can't just do a fast restart to get rid of them. They have both an internal transaction identifier and an external "global identifier". Either of those can be used to locate locked resources, and decide how to resolve the transactions.

There's more...

If you're not sure what the prepared transaction actually did, you can go and look, though it is time consuming. The pg_locks view shows locks are held by prepared transactions. You can get a full report of what is being locked using the following query:

```
postgres=# SELECT l.locktype, x.database, l.relation, l.page,
                  l.tuple,l.classid, l.objid, l.objsubid,
                  l.mode, x.transaction, x.gid, x.prepared,
                  x.owner
           FROM pg_locks l JOIN pg_prepared_xacts x
           ON l.virtualtransaction = '-1/' ||
                     x.transaction::text;
```

The documents mention that you can join `pg_locks` to `pg_prepared_xacts`, though they don't mention that if you join directly on the transaction id, all it tells you is that there is a transaction lock, unless there are some row-level locks. The table locks are listed as being held by a virtual transaction. A simpler query is the following:

```
postgres=# SELECT DISTINCT x.database, l.relation
              FROM pg_locks l JOIN pg_prepared_xacts x
              ON l.virtualtransaction = '-1/' ||
                  x.transaction::text
              WHERE l.locktype != 'transactionid';
 database | relation
----------+----------
 postgres |    16390
 postgres |    16401
(2 rows)
```

This tells you which relations in which databases have been touched by the remaining prepared transactions. We can't tell the names because we'd need to connect to those databases to check.

You can then fully scan each of those tables, looking for changes like the following:

```
SELECT * FROM table WHERE xmin = 121083;
```

which will show you all the rows in that table inserted by transaction `121083`, taken from the transaction column of `pg_prepared_xacts`.

Actions for heavy users of temporary tables

If you are a heavy user of temporary tables in your applications, then there are some additional actions you may need to perform.

How to do it...

There are four main things to check, which are as follows:

1. Make sure you run VACUUM on system tables, or enable autovacuum to do this for you.
2. Monitor running queries to see how many and how large temporary files are active.
3. Tune memory parameters. Think about increasing the temp_buffers parameter, though be careful not to overallocate memory by doing so.
4. Separate temp table I/O. In a query intensive system, you may find that read/write to temporary files exceeds reads/writes on permanent data tables and indexes. In this case, you should create new tablespace(s) on separate disks, and ensure that the `temp_tablespaces` parameter is configured to use the additional tablespace(s).

How it works...

In PostgreSQL 9.0, when we create a temporary table, we insert entries into the catalog tables pg_class and pg_attribute. These catalog tables and their indexes begin to grow and to bloat, an issue covered in later recipes. To control that growth, you can either VACUUM those tables manually, or set `autovacuum = on` in `postgreql.conf`. You cannot run `ALTER TABLE` against system tables, so it is not possible to set specific autovacuum settings for any of these tables.

If you VACUUM the system catalog tables manually, make sure you get all of the system tables. You can get the full list of tables to VACUUM using the following query:

```
postgres=# SELECT relname, pg_relation_size(oid)
              FROM pg_class
              WHERE relkind in ('i','r') and relnamespace = 11
              ORDER BY 2 DESC;
            relname                    | pg_relation_size
-----------------------------------+-------------------
 pg_proc                           |          450560
 pg_depend                         |          344064
 pg_attribute                      |          286720
 pg_depend_depender_index          |          204800
 pg_depend_reference_index         |          204800
 pg_proc_proname_args_nsp_index    |          180224
 pg_description                    |          172032
 pg_attribute_relid_attnam_index   |          114688
 pg_operator                       |          106496
 pg_statistic                      |          106496
 pg_description_o_c_o_index        |           98304
 pg_attribute_relid_attnum_index   |           81920
 pg_proc_oid_index                 |           73728
 pg_rewrite                        |           73728
 pg_class                          |           57344
 pg_type                           |           57344
 pg_class_relname_nsp_index        |           40960
 ...(partial listing)
```

The preceding values are for a newly created database. These tables can get very large if not properly maintained, with values of 11 GB of for one index being witnessed at one unlucky installation.

Identifying and fixing bloated tables and indexes

PostgreSQL implements **MVCC (Multi-Version Concurrency Control)**, that allows users to read data at the same time as writers make changes. This is an important feature for concurrency in database applications, as it can allow the following:

- Better performance because of fewer locks
- Greatly reduced deadlocking
- Simplified application design and management

MVCC is a core part of PostgreSQL and cannot be turned off, nor would you really want it to be. The internals of MVCC have some implications for the DBA that need to be understood. The price for these benefits is that SQL UPDATE command can cause tables and indexes to grow in size because they leave behind dead row versions. DELETEs and aborted INSERTs take up space that must be reclaimed by garbage collection. **VACUUM** is the mechanism by which we reclaim space, though there is also another internals feature named **HOT**, which does much of this work automatically for us.

Knowing this, many people become worried by and spend much time trying to rid themselves of dead row versions. Many users will be familiar with tools to perform tasks, such as defragmentation, shrinking, reorganization, and table optimization. These things are necessary, though you should not be unduly worried by the need for vacuuming in PostgreSQL. Many users execute VACUUM far too frequently, while at the same time complaining about the cost of doing so.

This recipe is all about understanding when you need to run VACUUM by estimating the amount of bloat in tables and indexes.

How to do it...

The best way to understand things is to look at things the same way that autovacuum does. Use the following query, derived by Greg Smith for his _PostgreSQL 9.0 High Performance_ book, also by _Packt_. The calculations are derived directly from the autovacuum documentation.

```
CREATE OR REPLACE VIEW av_needed AS
SELECT *,
  n_dead_tup > av_threshold AS "av_needed",
  CASE WHEN reltuples > 0
    THEN round(100.0 * n_dead_tup / (reltuples))
    ELSE 0
    END AS pct_dead
FROM
(SELECT
```

```
    N.nspname, C.relname,
    pg_stat_get_tuples_inserted(C.oid) AS n_tup_ins,
    pg_stat_get_tuples_updated(C.oid) AS n_tup_upd,
    pg_stat_get_tuples_deleted(C.oid) AS n_tup_del,
    pg_stat_get_tuples_hot_updated(C.oid)::real /
    pg_stat_get_tuples_updated(C.oid) AS HOT_update_ratio,
    pg_stat_get_live_tuples(C.oid) AS n_live_tup,
    pg_stat_get_dead_tuples(C.oid) AS n_dead_tup,
    C.reltuples AS reltuples,round(
      current_setting('autovacuum_vacuum_threshold')::integer
     +current_setting('autovacuum_vacuum_scale_factor')::numeric
  * C.reltuples)
      AS av_threshold, date_trunc('minute',greatest(pg_stat_get_last_
  vacuum_time(C.oid),pg_stat_get_last_autovacuum_time(C.oid))) AS last_
  vacuum, date_trunc('minute',greatest(pg_stat_get_last_analyze_time(C.
  oid),pg_stat_get_last_analyze_time(C.oid))) AS last_analyze
   FROM pg_class C LEFT JOIN
    pg_index I ON C.oid = I.indrelid
    LEFT JOIN pg_namespace N ON (N.oid = C.relnamespace)
    WHERE C.relkind IN ('r', 't')
      AND N.nspname NOT IN ('pg_catalog', 'information_schema') AND
      N.nspname !~ '^pg_toast'
) AS av
ORDER BY av_needed DESC,n_dead_tup DESC;
```

which we can then use to look at individual tables as follows:

```
postgres=# \x
postgres=# SELECT * FROM av_needed
                WHERE relation = 'public.pgbench_accounts';
-[ RECORD 1 ]----+------------------------
nspname          | public
relname          | pgbench_accounts
n_tup_ins        | 100001
n_tup_upd        | 117201
n_tup_del        | 1
hot_update_ratio | 0.123454578032611
n_live_tup       | 100000
n_dead_tup       | 0
reltuples        | 100000
av_threshold     | 20050
last_vacuum      | 2010-04-29 01:33:00+01
last_analyze     | 2010-04-28 15:21:00+01
av_needed        | f
pct_dead         | 0
```

How it works...

We can compare the number of dead row versions, shown as `n_dead_tup` against the required threshold, `av_threshold`.

The above query doesn't take into account table-specific autovacuum thresholds. It could do if you really need that, though the main purpose of the query is to give us information to understand what is happening, and then set the parameters accordingly, not the other way around.

Notice that the table query shows insert, updates and deletes, so you can understand your workload better. There is also something named the `HOT_update_ratio`. This shows the fraction of updates that take advantage of the HOT feature, which allows a table to self-vacuum as the table changes. If that ratio is high, then you may avoid VACUUMs altogether, or at least for long periods. If the ratio is low, then you will need to execute VACUUMs or autovacuums more frequently. Note that the ratio never reaches 1.0, so if you have better than 0.95, then that is very good, and you need not think about it further.

HOT updates take place when the UPDATE statement does not change any of the column values that are indexed by any index. If you change even one column that is indexed by just one index then it will be a non-HOT update, and there will be a performance hit. So careful selection of indexes can improve update performance and reduce the need for maintenance. Also, if HOT updates do occur, though not often enough for your liking, you might try to decrease the fillfactor storage parameter for the table. Remember that this will only be important on your most active tables. Seldom-touched tables don't need much tuning.

So, to recap: non-HOT updates cause indexes to bloat. The following query is useful in investigating index size, and how that changes over time. It runs fairly quickly, and can be used to monitor whether your indexes are changing in size over time.

```
SELECT
    nspname,relname,
    round(100 * pg_relation_size(indexrelid) /
            pg_relation_size(indrelid)) / 100
        AS index_ratio,
    pg_size_pretty(pg_relation_size(indexrelid))
        AS index_size,
    pg_size_pretty(pg_relation_size(indrelid))
        AS table_size
FROM pg_index I
LEFT JOIN pg_class C ON (C.oid = I.indexrelid)
LEFT JOIN pg_namespace N ON (N.oid = C.relnamespace)
WHERE
    nspname NOT IN ('pg_catalog', 'information_schema', 'pg_toast') AND
    C.relkind='i' AND
    pg_relation_size(indrelid) > 0;
```

Another route is to use the contrib/pgstattuple module, supplied with PostgreSQL. This provides overkill statistics about what's happening in your tables and indexes, which it derives by scanning the whole table or index, and literally counting everything. It's very good, and I am not dismissing it. Just use carefully: if you have time to scan the table, you may as well have VACUUMed the whole table anyway.

Scan tables using `pgstattuple()` as follows:

```
test=> SELECT * FROM pgstattuple('pg_catalog.pg_proc');
-[ RECORD 1 ]------+-------
table_len          | 458752
tuple_count        | 1470
tuple_len          | 438896
tuple_percent      | 95.67
dead_tuple_count   | 11
dead_tuple_len     | 3157
dead_tuple_percent | 0.69
free_space         | 8932
free_percent       | 1.95
```

and scan indexes using `pgstatindex()` as follows:

```
postgres=> SELECT * FROM pgstatindex('pg_cast_oid_index');
-[ RECORD 1 ]------+------
version            | 2
tree_level         | 0
index_size         | 8192
root_block_no      | 1
internal_pages     | 0
leaf_pages         | 1
empty_pages        | 0
deleted_pages      | 0
avg_leaf_density   | 50.27
leaf_fragmentation | 0
```

There's more...

You may want this as a Nagios plugin.

Look at **check_postgres_bloat** as part of the **check_postgres** plugins. That provides some flexible options to assess bloat. Unfortunately, its not that well documented, though if you've read this, it should make sense. You'll need to play with it to get the thresholding correct anyway, so that shouldn't be a problem.

Note also that the only way to know for certain the exact bloat of a table or index is to scan the whole relation. Anything else is just an estimate, and might lead to you running maintenance either too early or too late.

Maintaining indexes

Indexes can become a problem in many database applications that involve a high proportion of inserts/deletes. Just as tables can become bloated, so do indexes.

In the last recipe we saw that non-HOT updates can cause bloated indexes. Non-primary key indexes are also prone to some bloat from normal inserts, as is common in most relational databases.

Autovacuum does not detect bloated indexes, nor does it do anything to rebuild indexes. So we need to look at ways to maintain indexes.

Getting ready

PostgreSQL supports commands that will rebuild indexes for you. The client utility **reindexdb** allows you to execute the REINDEX command in a convenient way from the operating system:

```
$ reindexdb
```

This executes the SQL REINDEX command on every table in the default database. If you want to reindex all databases, then use the following:

```
$ reindexdb -a
```

That's what the manual says anyway. My experience is that most indexes don't need rebuilding, and even if they do, REINDEX puts a full table lock (AccessExclusiveLock) on the table while it runs. That locks up your database for possibly hours, and I advise that you think about *not* doing that.

Try this recipe *instead*.

First, let's create a test table with two indexes: a primary key and an additional index as follows:

- DROP TABLE IF EXISTS test;
- CREATE TABLE test
- (id INTEGER PRIMARY KEY
- ,category TEXT
- , value TEXT);
- CREATE INDEX ON test (category);

Now, let's look at the internal identifier of the tables, the `oid`, and the current file number, or `relfilenodes` as shown next:

```
SELECT oid, relname, relfilenode
FROM pg_class
WHERE oid in (SELECT indexrelid
              FROM pg_index
              WHERE indrelid = 'test'::regclass);
  oid  |      relname      | relfilenode
-------+-------------------+-------------
 16639 | test_pkey         |       16639
 16641 | test_category_idx |       16641
(2 rows)
```

How to do it...

PostgreSQL supports a command known as CREATE INDEX CONCURRENTLY, that builds an index without taking a full table lock. PostgreSQL also supports the ability to have two indexes, with different names, that have exactly the same definition. So, the trick is to build another index identical to the one you wish to rebuild, drop the old index, and then rename the new index to the same name as the old index had. Et voila, fresh index, no locking. Let's see that in slow motion:

```
CREATE INDEX CONCURRENTLY new_index
ON test (category);
BEGIN;
DROP INDEX test_category_idx;
ALTER INDEX new_index RENAME TO test_category_idx;
COMMIT;
```

and if we check our internal identifiers again, we get the following:

```
SELECT oid, relname, relfilenode
FROM pg_class
WHERE oid in (SELECT indexrelid
              FROM pg_index
              WHERE indrelid = 'test'::regclass);
  oid  |      relname      | relfilenode
-------+-------------------+-------------
 16639 | test_pkey         |       16639
 16642 | test_category_idx |       16642
(2 rows)
```

So, we can see that `test_category_idx` is now a completely new index.

That seems pretty good, yet it doesn't work on primary keys. Why not? Because you can't add a primary index to a table concurrently, in PostgreSQL 9.0 at least.

So we have another trick, slightly more complex than the last. First, we create another index with the same definition as the primary key as follows:

► `CREATE UNIQUE INDEX new_pkey ON test (id);`

and check internal identifiers again as follows:

```
SELECT oid, relname, relfilenode
FROM pg_class
WHERE oid in (SELECT indexrelid
                FROM pg_index
                WHERE indrelid = 'test'::regclass);
  oid  |        relname     |  relfilenode
-------+--------------------+-------------
 16639 | test_pkey          |      16639
 16642 | test_category_idx  |      16642
 16643 | new_pkey           |      16643
(3 rows)
```

Now we're going to swap the two indexes over, so that all the primary key constraints stay active and so do all of the foreign keys that depend upon them. So, we need to swap the `relfilenode` values as follws:

```
BEGIN;
LOCK TABLE test;
UPDATE pg_class SET relfilenode = 16643 WHERE oid = 16639;
UPDATE pg_class SET relfilenode = 16639 WHERE oid = 16643;
DROP INDEX new_pkey;
COMMIT;
```

which we confirm has succeeded using the following:

```
SELECT oid, relname, relfilenode
FROM pg_class
WHERE oid in (SELECT indexrelid
                FROM pg_index
                WHERE indrelid = 'test'::regclass);
  oid  |        relname     |  relfilenode
-------+--------------------+-------------
 16639 | test_pkey          |      16643
 16642 | test_category_idx  |      16642
 16643 | new_pkey           |      16639
(3 rows)
```

Yes, that's right. We just updated the core internal catalog tables of PostgreSQL. So make a mistake here, and you're in a big world of hurt. Make sure your backups are nicely polished before doing this.

How it works...

`CREATE INDEX CONCURRENTLY` allows inserts, updates, and deletes while the index is being created. It cannot be executed inside another transaction, and only one per table can be created at any time.

Swapping the indexes is easy and doesn't use any trickery.

Swapping the primary keys used some internals knowledge. The indexes themselves don't know which numbers they are, so you can swap them over without problems—as long as you swap the correct two indexes, and they really do have identical definitions. Be especially careful about creating the indexes in the same tablespace, as the above will fail if they're different.

There's more...

If you are fairly new to database systems, you might think rebuilding indexes for performance is something that only PostgreSQL needs to do. Other DBMS require this also, just maybe don't say so.

Indexes are designed for performance, and in all databases, deleting index entries causes contention and loss of performance. PostgreSQL does not remove index entries for a row when that row is deleted, so an index can fill with dead entries. PostgreSQL does attempt to remove dead entries when a block becomes full, though that doesn't stop small numbers of dead entries accumulating in many data blocks.

See also

I'm writing this just as PostgreSQL 9.0 is coming out. Its likely that in later versions, we will get a simple `REINDEX CONCURRENTLY` command that can be used more easily.

Finding the unused indexes

Selecting the correct set of indexes for a workload is known to be a hard problem. It usually involves trial and error by developers and DBAs to get a good mix of indexes.

Tools exist to identify slow queries and many `SELECT` statements can be improved by the addition of an index.

What many people forget is to check whether the mix of indexes remains valuable over time, which is something for the DBA to investigate and optimize.

How to do it...

PostgreSQL keeps track of each access against an index. We can view that information and use it to see if an index is unused as follows:

```
postgres=# SELECT schemaname, relname, indexrelname, idx_scan FROM pg_
stat_user_indexes ORDER BY idx_scan;
 schemaname  |          indexrelname           | idx_scan
-------------+---------------------------------+----------
 public      | pgbench_accounts_bid_idx |         0
 public      | pgbench_branches_pkey    |     14575
 public      | pgbench_tellers_pkey     |     15350
 public      | pgbench_accounts_pkey    |    114400
(4 rows)
```

As we can see in the preceding code, there is one index that is totally unused, alongside others that have some usage. You now need to decide whether "unused" means you should remove the index. That is a more complex question, and we first need to explain how it works.

How it works...

The PostgreSQL statistics accumulate various useful information. These statistics can be reset to zero using an administrator function. Also, as the data accumulates over time, we usually find that objects that have been there longer have higher apparent usage. So if we see a low number for `idx_scan`, then it might be that the index was newly created (as was the case in my preceding demonstration), or it might be that the index is only used by a part of the application that runs only at certain times of day, week, month, and so on.

Another important consideration is that the index may be a unique constraint index that exists specifically to safeguard against duplicate inserts. An INSERT does *not* show up as an `idx_scan`, whereas an UPDATE or DELETE might, because they have to locate the row first. So, a table that only has INSERTs against it will appear to have unused indexes.

Also, some indexes that show usage might be showing usage that was historical, and there is no further usage. Or, it might be the case that some queries use an index where they could just as easily and almost as cheaply use an alternative index. Those things are for you to explore and understand before you take action.

See also

You may decide from this that you want to remove an index. If only there was a way to try removing an index and then put it back again quickly if you cause problems! Rebuilding an index might take hours on a big table, so these decisions can be a little scary. No worries, just follow the next recipe, *Carefully removing unwanted indexes*.

Carefully removing unwanted indexes

Carefully removing? You mean press "enter" gently after typing DROP INDEX? err, no.

The thinking is that it takes a long time to build an index, and a short time to drop one. What we want is a way of removing the index that if we discover that removing it was a mistake, we can put the index back again quickly.

How to do it...

First, create the following function:

```
CREATE OR REPLACE FUNCTION trial_drop_index(iname TEXT)
RETURNS VOID
LANGUAGE SQL AS $$
UPDATE pg_index
SET indisvalid = false
WHERE indexrelid = $1::regclass;
$$;
```

then, run it to do a trial of dropping the index.

If you experience performance issues after dropping the index, then use the following function to "undrop" the index:

```
CREATE OR REPLACE FUNCTION trial_undrop_index(iname TEXT)
RETURNS VOID
LANGUAGE SQL AS $$
UPDATE pg_index
SET indisvalid = true
WHERE indexrelid = $1::regclass;
$$;
```

How it works...

This recipe also uses some inside knowledge. When we create an index using `CREATE INDEX CONCURRENTLY`, it is a two-stage process. The first phase builds the index, and then marks it invalid. Inserts, updates, and deletes now begin maintaining the index, but we do a further pass over the table to see if we missed anything before we declare the index valid. User queries don't use the index until it says valid.

Once the index is built and the flag is valid, then if we set the flag to invalid, the index will still be maintained, just not used by queries. This allows us to turn the index off quickly, though with the option to turn it back on again if we realize we actually do need the index after all. This makes it practical to test whether dropping the index will alter the performance of any of your most important queries.

Planning maintenance

In these busy times many people believe "if it ain't broke, don't fix it". I believe that also, though it isn't an excuse for not taking action to maintain your database servers and be sure that nothing will break.

Database maintenance is about making your database run smoothly.

Monitoring systems are not a substitute for good planning. They alert you to unplanned situations that need attention. The more unplanned things you respond to, the greater the chance that you will need to respond to multiple emergencies at once. And when that happens, something will break. Ultimately that is your fault. If you wish to take your responsibilities seriously you should plan ahead.

How to do it...

▶ **Let's break a rule**: If you don't have a backup, take one *now*. I mean now, go on, off you go. Then let's talk some more about planning maintenance. If you already do, well done. It's hard to keep your job as a DBA if you lose data because of missing backups, especially today when everybody's grandmother knows to keep her photos backed up.

▶ **First, plan your time**: Make a regular date on which to perform certain actions. Don't allow yourself to be a puppet of your monitoring system, running up and down every time the lights change. If you keep being dragged off on other assignments then you'll need to make it clear that you need to get a good handle on the database maintenance to make sure it doesn't bite you.

▶ **Don't be scared**: It's easy to worry about what you don't know and either overreact or underreact to the situation. Your database probably doesn't need to be inspected daily, but never is definitely a bad place also.

How it works...

Build a regular cycle of activity around the following tasks:

▶ **Capacity planning**: Observing long term trends in system performance and keeping track of growth of database volumes. Plan in to the schedule any new data feeds, new projects that increase rates of change. Best done monthly, so you monitor what has happened and what will happen.

▶ **Backups, recovery testing, and emergency planning**: Organize regular reviews of written plans, test scripts, check tape rotation, confirm that you still have the password to the off-site backups, and so on. Some sysadmins run a test recovery every night so they always know that a successful recovery is possible.

- **Vacuum and index maintenance**: To reduce bloat, including collecting optimizer statistics through ANALYZE.

- Consider VACUUM again, with the need to manage the less frequent **freezing** process. This is listed as a separate task so that you don't ignore this and have it bite you later.

- **Server log file analysis**: How many times has the server restarted? Are you sure you know about each incident?

- **Security and intrusion detection**: Has your database already been hacked? What did they do?

- **Understanding usage patterns**: If you don't know much about what your database is used for then I'll wager it is not very well tuned or maintained.

- **Long term performance analysis**: It's a common occurrence for me to get asked to come and tune a system which is slow. Often what happens is that a database server can get slower over a very long period. Nobody ever noticed any particular day when it got slow, it just got slower over time. Keeping records of response times over time can help confirm whether or not everything is as good now as it was months or years previously. This activity is where you might reconsider current index choices.

Many of these activities are mentioned in this chapter or throughout the rest of the cookbook. Some are not because they aren't so much technical tasks but more just planning and understanding of your environment.

You might also find time to consider the following things:

- **Data quality**: Are the contents of the database accurate and meaningful? Could the data be enhanced?

- **Business intelligence**: Is the data being used for everything that can bring value to the organization?

10
Performance & Concurrency

In this chapter, we will cover the following:

- ▸ Finding slow SQL statements
- ▸ Collecting regular statistics from `pg_stat*` views
- ▸ Finding what makes SQL slow
- ▸ Reducing the number of rows returned
- ▸ Simplifying complex SQL
- ▸ Speeding up queries without rewriting them
- ▸ Why queries do not use an index
- ▸ How do force a query to use an index
- ▸ Using optimistic locking
- ▸ Reporting performance problems

Introduction

Performance and concurrency are two problems that are often tightly coupled—when concurrency grows, performance usually degrades, in some cases a lot. And, if you take care of performance problems, you can achieve better concurrency.

In this chapter, we show you how to find slow queries, and also how to find queries that make other queries slow.

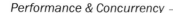

Performance tuning is unfortunately still not an exact science, so you may also encounter a performance problem not found by any of the given methods.

And, we show how to get help in the final chapter, Reporting Performance Problems, in case none of the other recipes here work.

Finding slow SQL statements

There are two main kinds of slowness which can manifest themselves in a database.

The first kind is a single query that can be too slow to be really useable, such as a customer information query in a CRM running for minutes, a password check query running in tens of seconds, or a daily data-aggregation query running for more than a day. These can be found by logging queries that take over a certain amount of time, either at the client end, or in the database.

The second kind is a query that is run frequently (say a few thousand times a second), and which used to run in single digit milliseconds, but now is running in several tens or even hundreds of milliseconds, and is slowing down the system. This kind of slowness is much harder to find.

Here, we will show several ways to find the statements that are either slow, or although not being slow by themselves, cause the database as a whole to slow down.

Getting ready

Connect to the database as the user whose statements you want to investigate, or as a superuser to investigate all users' queries.

Get access to PostgreSQL log files. They are usually located together with other log files, for example, on Debian/Ubuntu Linux, they are in directory /var/log/postgresql/.

You should also set up logging of queries taking over x seconds, or if you are not swamped with thousands of small and fast queries, you can also up logging all queries at least for some period of time, so you can get an overview of full database activity, and not just individual slow queries.

How to do it...

The easiest way for finding single, slow queries is to set up PostgreSQL to log them all. So, if you decide to monitor a query taking over 10 seconds, then set up logging queries over 10 seconds by defining the following:

```
log_min_duration_statement = 10000;
```

Remember that the duration is in milliseconds.

After doing this, and reloading PostgreSQL conf, all slow queries are logged.

You also want to make sure that `log_duration` is set to `on`, so that you can actually see the duration.

Another possibility to spot long queries is to look them up in system view `pg_stat_activity` by repeatedly running the following:

```
select now()-query_start as running_for, current_query from pg_stat_
activity order by 1 desc limit 5;
```

This query looks up top five currently running queries ordered by how long they have been running. You don't usually get the real run time this way, but spotting something here hints you that they may need optimizing.

Finding queries that make the server slow

Sometimes, a single query execution is not slow in itself, but the aggregate effect of running hundreds or even thousands of such queries per second has a net effect of making the server slow.

These queries do not show up in logs with slow query logging turned on, but there are other ways they can be found, which are as follows:

 ▶   Watch `pg_stat_activity`:

do this by repeatedly running `select now()-query_start as running_for, current_query from pg_stat_activity`. If the same query keeps coming up often, but the running for time remains slow, then there is a good chance that this is the query that consumes a lot of resources, and is at least partly responsible for general slow performance,

You can gather such statistics semi-automatically by running the following shell command (on one line)

```
while psql -qt -c "select current_query, now()-query_start as running_for
from pg_stat_activity" >>query_stats.txt ; do sleep 1; done
```

This issues the select query at one second intervals and collects the output in file `query_stats.txt`

after running it for a few seconds, you can stop it by pressing `Control-C` and then look at the sorted output

```
sort query_stats.txt | less
```

to find the repeating queries.

- ▸ Watch `pg_stat_user_tables` and `pg_statio_user_tables`:
- ▸ Another way to discover such queries is looking at suspicious behaviors in `pg_stat*` tables. Specific things to watch for as are follows:
  - ❑ In the `pg_stat_user_tables`, fast growth of `seq_tup_read` means that there are lots of sequential scans occurring. The ratio of `seq_tup_read/seq_scan` shows how many tuples each `seqscan` reads.
  - ❑ In the `pg_statio_user_tables`, watch the fields `heap_blks_hit` and `idx_blks_read`, which give you a fairly good idea on how much of your data is found in PostgreSQL shared buffers (`heap_blks_hit`), and how much had to be fetched from disk (`idx_blks_read`). If you continuously see large numbers of blocks being read from disk, you may want to tune those queries, or if you determine that the disk reads were justified, you can make the configured `shared_buffers` value bigger.

Once a suspect is found, make the query slow, so that it is logged

Once you have found out the query that you suspect is slowing you down, you can force the queries appear in slow query log by locking the any table involved in this query for a period slightly longer than configured by `log_min_duration_statement` in `postgresql.conf` file.

A sample psql session from logging all queries accessing `mysuspecttable` is as follows:

```
mydb=# begin;
BEGIN
mydb=# lock table mysuspecttable;
LOCK TABLE
select pg_sleep(12);
hannu=# rollback;
ROLLBACK
```

This also works when you have not found a single suspect query, but have found a table which is accessed in a suspicious manner, and you want to find out what queries use this table.

Finding slow queries run as prepared statements

If the slow query is not run as is, but is first prepared and then executed, then you need to be able to connect the `PREPARE` statement creating the prepared query plan with the actual invocation of the query using `EXECUTE`.

This can be done by configuring PostgreSQL to log all queries, and setting the configuration file parameter `log_line_prefix` so that it includes either process ID (`'%p'`) or session ID (`'%c'`). This will help you to trace back matching `PREPARE` statements if you see a slow `EXECUTE`.

See also

There is more information on tools for query analysis at the end of the Chapter, _Monitoring and Diagnosis_

Collecting regular statistics from pg_stat* views

This recipe describes how to collect the statistics needed to understand what is going on in the database system on a regular basis, so that they can be used for further optimizing the queries which are slow or which are becoming slow as the database changes.

The code to do is in file `pg_statlogs.tar.gz`

Getting ready

Find the package `pg_statlogs.tar.gz`.

Set up a directory as shown next for running the scripts:

```
mkdir /opt/pg_statlogs
cd /opt/pg_statlogs
tar xzvf pg_statlogs.tgz
```

Set up a schema for collecting the snapshots of statistics data and generating deltas from it as follows:

```
psql mydatabase <./pg_statlogs_prepare.sql
```

How to do it...

Run the following from command line:

```
psql mydatabase <./pg_statlogs_collect.sql
```

to collect the changes in `pg_stat*` tables since the last invocation.

You should probably set up a cron job to run on a regular basis, so that you have good coverage of what happens at what time of day and week. Running it at interval of 5 to 15 minutes should usually give you enough temporal resolution to understand what is going on with your tables.

How it works...

The scripts make static copies of tables `pg_stat_user_tables`, `pg_statio_user_tables`, `pg_stat_user_indexes`, and `pg_statio_user_indexes` at each run, then they compare the current copies with the ones saved at the last run, and save the timestamped deltas to log tables `stat_user_tables_delta_log` and `stat_user_indexes_delta_log`, which can then be analyzed later to learn about access and I/O patterns.

The latest set of deltas are also kept in tables `stat_user_tables_delta` and `stat_user_indexes_delta` which can be used for external monitoring systems, such as cacti, to get a graphical representation of it.

There's more...

These scripts just collect data indefinitely. This should not cause performance problems, as the large log tables are without indexes, and thus inserts into these are fast, but if you are low on disk space and have many tables, you may want to introduce a rotation scheme for these tables which throws away older data.

There is a script doing this in the downloaded package. Running the following:

```
psql mydatabase <./pg_statlogs_rotate.sql
```

each Sunday keeps four weeks of data.

Another statistics collection package

There is also a package available at at http://pgstatspack.projects.postgresql.org/ for similar data collecting.

Finding what makes SQL slow

A SQL statement can be slow for a lot of reasons. Following, we give a shortlist of these and at least one way for recognizing each of these.

Too much data is processed

Run the query with `explain analyse` to see how much data is processed for completing the query as follows:

```
mydb=# explain analyse select count(*) from t;
                      QUERY PLAN
-----------------------------------------------------------------
Aggregate  (cost=4427.27..4427.28 rows=1 width=0) \
                  (actual time=32.953..32.954 rows=1 loops=1)
   -> Seq Scan on t  (cost=0.00..4425.01 rows=901 width=0) \
                          (actual time=30.350..31.646 rows=901
loops=1)
  Total runtime: 33.028 ms
(3 rows)
```

and also see how many rows are processed, and how many blocks of data accessed by comparing the output of the following query before and after the query is run on idle system (the `pg_stat*` views are global, and collect info from all parallel queries):

```
select
    s.relid, s.schemaname, s.relname,
    seq_scan,seq_tup_read,
    idx_scan,idx_tup_fetch,
    heap_blks_read,heap_blks_hit,
    idx_blks_read,idx_blks_hit,
    toast_blks_read,toast_blks_hit
from pg_stat_user_tables s
join pg_statio_user_tables sio on s.relid = sio.relid
where s.schemaname = 'public' and s.relname = 't'
```

For example, if you want to get the three latest rows in a one million-row table, then run the following:

```
SELECT * FROM EVENTS ORDER BY ID DESC LIMIT 3;
```

You can either read through just three rows using an index on the serial id column, or you could be doing a sequential scan of all rows followed by a sort, as shown in the following code snippet, depending on whether you have a usable index on the field on which you want to get top three rows:

```
mydb=# create table events(id serial);
NOTICE:  CREATE TABLE will create implicit sequence "events_id_seq"
for serial column "events.id"
CREATE TABLE
mydb=# insert into events select generate_series(1,1000000);
INSERT 0 1000000
mydb=# explain analyse SELECT * FROM EVENTS ORDER BY ID DESC LIMIT 3;
                                    QUERY PLAN
------------------------------------------------------------------
Limit  (cost=25500.67..25500.68 rows=3 width=4) \
          (actual time=3143.493..3143.502 rows=3 loops=1)
   -> Sort  (cost=25500.67..27853.87 rows=941280 width=4)
                (actual time=3143.488..3143.490 rows=3 loops=1)
        Sort Key: id
        Sort Method:  top-N heapsort  Memory: 17kB
        -> Seq Scan on events
                    (cost=0.00..13334.80 rows=941280 width=4)
                    (actual time=0.105..1534.418 rows=1000000
loops=1)
 Total runtime: 3143.584 ms
(6 rows)
```

```
mydb=# create index events_id_ndx on events(id);
CREATE INDEX
mydb=# explain analyse SELECT * FROM EVENTS ORDER BY ID DESC LIMIT 3;
                                  QUERY PLAN
----------------------------------------------------------------------
 Limit  (cost=0.00..0.08 rows=3 width=4) (actual time=0.295..0.311
rows=3 loops=1)
    -> Index Scan Backward using events_id_ndx on events
(cost=0.00..27717.34 rows=1000000 width=4) (actual time=0.289..0.295
rows=3 loops=1)
 Total runtime: 0.364 ms
(3 rows)
```

This produces 10,000 times difference in query run time, even when all the data is in memory.

Too little of the data fits in the memory

If not enough of the data fits in shared buffers, lots of re-reading of the same data happens. This manifests as a big change in any of the fields `heap_blks_read`, `idx_blks_read`, `toast_blks_read` in the `pg_stat*` view before and after the query is run.

It is somewhat normal to have a big difference before and after the first run of the query, as some data may just not be accessed recently, but if you run the query immediately the second time and any of the `*_blks_read` fields still changes a lot, you have this problem for sure.

If your `shared_buffers` is tuned properly, and you can't rewrite the query to do less block I/O, you probably have to get a beefier computer.

The query returns too much data

Sometimes lazy programmers write a query that returns a lot more rows than needed. This usually goes unnoticed when the data volumes are small, but can quickly become problematic once more data appears in the database. For example, you have a picture database and an application showing a list of pictures. If you are showing only 10 pictures at a time, you should not request more than 10 from the database (or maybe 11 if you want to display the next link). For thousands of pictures it makes sense to have a separate `count(*)` query for determining the total number of pictures, and not select all pictures and count them in client. For high performance websites, you would want to replace even the count query with a separately maintained count in some table to further reduce work done at display time.

See also the recipe *Reducing the number of rows returned*.

Locking problems

Thanks to its MVCC design, PostgreSQL does not suffer from most locking problems, such as writers locking out readers or readers locking out writers, but it still has to take locks when more than one process wants to update the same row. And, it has to hold the write lock until the current writer's transaction finishes.

So, if you have a database design where many queries update the same record, you can have a locking problem.

The easiest way to find out if you do is to see if there are many backends waiting on locks by running the following:

```
SELECT * FROM pg_locks WHERE not granted;
```

If it comes up empty, or with only one or two rows, then you probably don't have this problem.

To see which queries are waiting on which other queries, run the following:

```
select
    a1.current_query as blocking_query,
    a2.current_query as waiting_query,
    t.schemaname ||'.'||t.relname as locked_table
  from pg_stat_activity a1
  join pg_locks p1 on a1.procpid = p1.pid and p1.granted
  join pg_locks p2 on p1.relation = p2.relation and not p2.granted
  join pg_stat_activity a2 on a2.procpid = p2.pid
  join pg_stat_all_tables t on p1.relation = t.relid;
    blocking_query      |       waiting_query       | locked_table
-----------------------+---------------------------+--------------
 <IDLE> in transaction | select * from t;          | public.t
 <IDLE> in transaction | select count(*) from t;   | public.t
(2 rows)
```

Here, the `<IDLE>` in transaction is an open-console connection, which has issued just the following commands:

```
BEGIN;
LOCK t;
```

and is waiting for further input.

Not enough CPU power or disk I/O capacity for the current load

These are usually caused by suboptimal query plans, but sometimes you just have not a powerful enough computer.

Here, `top` is your friend for quick checks, and from the command line, run the following:

```
user@host:~$ top
```

First, watch the CPU idle reading in the top. If this is in low single-digits for most of the time, you probably have problems with CPU power.

If you have a high load average with still lots of CPU idle left, you are probably out of disk bandwidth. In this case, you should also have lots of postgres processes in status D.

Reducing the number of rows returned

Although often the problem is producing many rows in the first place, it is made worse by returning all the unneeded rows to the client. This is especially true if client and server are not on the same host.

Here are some ways to reduce the traffic between the client and server.

A full text search returns 10,000 documents, but only first the 20 are displayed to user

In this case, order the documents by ranking on the server, and return only the top 20 actually displayed

```
SELECT title, ts_rank_cd(body_tsv, query, 20) AS text_rank
  FROM articles, plainto_tsquery('spicy potatoes') AS query
  WHERE body_tsv @@ query
  ORDER BY rank DESC
  LIMIT 20
;
```

If you need the next 20, don't just query with limit 40 and throw away the first 20, but use "OFFSET 20 LIMIT 20" to return just the next 20.

To have some stability, so that the documents with same rank still come out in the same order when using OFFSET 20, add a unique field (like id column of table articles) to ORDER BY in both queries.

```
SELECT title, ts_rank_cd(body_tsv, query, 20) AS text_rank
  FROM articles, plainto_tsquery('spicy potatoes') AS query
  WHERE body_tsv @@ query
  ORDER BY rank DESC, articles.id
  OFFSET 20 LIMIT 20
;
```

An application requests all products for a branch office to run a complex calculation over them

Try to do as much data analysis as possible inside the database.

So, instead of doing

```
SELECT * FROM ACCOUNTS WHERE BRANCH_ID = 7;
```

And counting and summing the rows in the client, do instead

```
SELECT count(*), sum(balance) FROM ACCOUNTS WHERE BRANCH_ID = 7;
```

With little research into the SQL language supported by PostgreSQL, you can do an amazingly large portion of your computation using plain SQL.

And if SQL is not enough, you can use PL/pgSQL or any other of PostgreSQL's supported embedded procedural languages for even more flexibility.

Application runs a huge number of small lookup queries

This can easily happen with modern ORM's (Object relational Mappers) and other toolkits, which do a lot of work for the programmer, but at the same time hide a lot of what is happening.

For example, if you define an HTML report over a query in a templating language, and then define a lookup function for resolving an ID inside the template, you may end up with a form that does a separate small lookup for each row displayed, even when most of the values looked up are the same. This does usually not pose a big problem for the database, as queries of the form "SELECT name FROM departments WHERE id = 7" are really fast when the row for id=7 is in shared buffers, but doing this query thousands of times still takes seconds, due to network latencies, process scheduling for each request, and other factors.

The two solutions are as follows:

- Make sure that the value is cached by your ORM
- Do the lookup inside the query that gets the main data, so it can be displayed directly

How exactly to do these depends on the toolkit, but they are both worth investigating, as they really can make a difference in speed and resource usage.

Simplifying complex SQL

There are two types of complexity which you can encounter in SQL queries.

First, the complexity can be directly visible in the query, having hundreds or even thousands of rows of SQL code in a single query code. This can cause both maintenance headaches and slow execution times as well.

The complexity can also be hidden in subviews, so that the SQL code of the query seems simple, but it uses other views and/or functions to do part of the work, which can in turn still use others. This is much better for maintenance, but still can cause performance problems.

Both types of queries can be either written manually by programmers or data analysts, or they can emerge as a result of a query generator.

Getting ready

First, verify that you really do have a complex query.

A query which simply returns lots of database field is not complex by itself. In order to be complex, the query has to join lots of tables in complex ways.

The easiest way to find out if the query itself is complex is to look at the output of EXPLAIN. If it has lots of rows, the query is complex, not just having lot of text.

How to do it...

Simplifying a query usually means restructuring it, so that parts of it can be defined separately and then used by other parts.

We illustrate the possibilities with rewriting the following query in several ways (full code is in file shop_database.tar.gz). It is a so-called "pivot" or "cross-tab" query, getting quarterly profit for non-local sales from all shops, as shown next:

```
SELECT shop.sp_name AS shop_name,
       q1_nloc_profit.profit as q1_profit,
       q2_nloc_profit.profit as q2_profit,
       q3_nloc_profit.profit as q3_profit,
       q4_nloc_profit.profit as q4_profit,
       year_nloc_profit.profit as year_profit
  FROM (SELECT * FROM salespoint ORDER BY sp_name) AS shop
  LEFT JOIN (
    SELECT
        spoint_id,
        sum(sale_price) - sum(cost) AS profit,
        count(*) AS nr_of_sales
    FROM sale s
    JOIN item_in_wh iw ON s.item_in_wh_id=iw.id
    JOIN item i ON iw.item_id = i.id
    JOIN salespoint sp ON s.spoint_id = sp.id
    JOIN location sploc ON sp.loc_id = sploc.id
    JOIN warehouse wh ON iw.whouse_id = wh.id
    JOIN location whloc ON wh.loc_id = whloc.id
    WHERE sale_time >= '2009-01-01'
      AND sale_time <  '2009-04-01'
      AND sploc.id != whloc.id
    GROUP BY 1
```

```
        ) AS q1_nloc_profit
      ON shop.id = Q1_NLOC_PROFIT.spoint_id
    LEFT JOIN (
< similar subquery for 2nd quarter >
      ) AS q2_nloc_profit
      ON shop.id = q2_nloc_profit.spoint_id
    LEFT JOIN (
< similar subquery for 3rd quarter >
      ) AS q3_nloc_profit
      ON shop.id = q3_nloc_profit.spoint_id
    LEFT JOIN (
< similar subquery for 4th  quarter >
      ) AS q4_nloc_profit
      ON shop.id = q4_nloc_profit.spoint_id
    LEFT JOIN (
< similar subquery for full year >
      ) AS year_nloc_profit
      ON shop.id = year_nloc_profit.spoint_id
ORDER BY 1
  ;
```

Moving part of the query into a view

As the preceding query has an almost identical repeating part for finding the sales for a period, it makes sense to move it into a separate view, and then use that view in the main reporting query as follows:

```
CREATE VIEW non_local_quarterly_profit AS
    SELECT
        spoint_id,
        extract('quarter' from sale_time) as sale_quarter,
        sum(sale_price) - sum(cost) AS profit,
        count(*) AS nr_of_sales
    FROM sale s
    JOIN item_in_wh iw ON s.item_in_wh_id=iw.id
    JOIN item i ON iw.item_id = i.id
    JOIN salespoint sp ON s.spoint_id = sp.id
    JOIN location sploc ON sp.loc_id = sploc.id
    JOIN warehouse wh ON iw.whouse_id = wh.id
    JOIN location whloc ON wh.loc_id = whloc.id
    WHERE sale_time >= '2009-01-01'
      AND sale_time <  '2010-01-01'
      AND sploc.id != whloc.id
    GROUP BY 1,2;
SELECT shop.sp_name AS shop_name,
```

```
            q1_nloc_profit.profit as q1_profit,
            q2_nloc_profit.profit as q2_profit,
            q3_nloc_profit.profit as q3_profit,
            q4_nloc_profit.profit as q4_profit,
            year_nloc_profit.profit as year_profit
    FROM (SELECT * FROM salespoint ORDER BY sp_name) AS shop
    LEFT JOIN non_local_quarterly_profit AS q1_nloc_profit
      ON shop.id = Q1_NLOC_PROFIT.spoint_id
      AND q1_nloc_profit.sale_quarter = 1
    LEFT JOIN non_local_quarterly_profit AS q2_nloc_profit
       ON shop.id = Q2_NLOC_PROFIT.spoint_id
    AND q2_nloc_profit.sale_quarter = 2
    LEFT JOIN non_local_quarterly_profit AS q3_nloc_profit
      ON shop.id = Q3_NLOC_PROFIT.spoint_id
    AND q3_nloc_profit.sale_quarter = 3
    LEFT JOIN non_local_quarterly_profit AS q4_nloc_profit
       ON shop.id = Q4_NLOC_PROFIT.spoint_id
    AND q4_nloc_profit.sale_quarter = 4
    LEFT JOIN (
          SELECT spoint_id, sum(profit) AS profit
            FROM non_local_quarterly_profit GROUP BY 1
      ) AS year_nloc_profit
      ON shop.id = year_nloc_profit.spoint_id
    ORDER BY 1;
```

Moving the subquery into a view made the query not only shorter, but also easier to understand and maintain.

Using the WITH statement instead of a separate view

Starting with PostgreSQL version 8.4, one can also use the new `WITH` statement for defining the view in-line, like the following:

```
WITH nlqp AS (
    SELECT
        spoint_id,
        extract('quarter' from sale_time) as sale_quarter,
        sum(sale_price) - sum(cost) AS profit,
        count(*) AS nr_of_sales
    FROM sale s
    JOIN item_in_wh iw ON s.item_in_wh_id=iw.id
    JOIN item i ON iw.item_id = i.id
    JOIN salespoint sp ON s.spoint_id = sp.id
    JOIN location sploc ON sp.loc_id = sploc.id
    JOIN warehouse wh ON iw.whouse_id = wh.id
    JOIN location whloc ON wh.loc_id = whloc.id
```

```
        WHERE sale_time >= '2009-01-01'
          AND sale_time <  '2010-01-01'
          AND sploc.id != whloc.id
        GROUP BY 1,2
)
SELECT shop.sp_name AS shop_name,
        q1_nloc_profit.profit as q1_profit,
        q2_nloc_profit.profit as q2_profit,
        q3_nloc_profit.profit as q3_profit,
        q4_nloc_profit.profit as q4_profit,
        year_nloc_profit.profit as year_profit
    FROM (SELECT * FROM salespoint ORDER BY sp_name) AS shop
    LEFT JOIN nlqp AS q1_nloc_profit
     ON shop.id = Q1_NLOC_PROFIT.spoint_id
     AND q1_nloc_profit.sale_quarter = 1
    LEFT JOIN nlqp AS q2_nloc_profit
     ON shop.id = Q2_NLOC_PROFIT.spoint_id
     AND q2_nloc_profit.sale_quarter = 2
    LEFT JOIN nlqp AS q3_nloc_profit
     ON shop.id = Q3_NLOC_PROFIT.spoint_id
     AND q3_nloc_profit.sale_quarter = 3
    LEFT JOIN nlqp AS q4_nloc_profit
     ON shop.id = Q4_NLOC_PROFIT.spoint_id
     AND q4_nloc_profit.sale_quarter = 4
    LEFT JOIN (
          SELECT spoint_id, sum(profit) AS profit
            FROM nlqp GROUP BY 1
    ) AS year_nloc_profit
     ON shop.id = year_nloc_profit.spoint_id
ORDER BY 1
;
```

Using temporary tables for parts of the query

PostgreSQL itself can choose to materialize parts of the query during the query optimization phase, but sometimes it fails to make the best choice for the query plan either due to insufficient statistics, or as it can happen for large query plans, where **genetic query optimization** (**GEQO**) is used, it may have just overlooked some possible query plans.

If you think that materializing (preparing separately) some parts of the query is a good idea, you can do it using a temporary table, simply by running `CREATE TEMPORARY TABLE mytemptable01 AS` <the part of the query you want to materialize>, and then using mytemptable01 in the main query instead of the part materialized. You can even create indexes on the temp table for PostgreSQL to use in the main query.

```
BEGIN;
CREATE TEMPORARY TABLE nlqp_temp ON COMMIT DROP
 AS
    SELECT
        spoint_id,
        extract('quarter' from sale_time) as sale_quarter,
        sum(sale_price) - sum(cost) AS profit,
        count(*) AS nr_of_sales
    FROM sale s
    JOIN item_in_wh iw ON s.item_in_wh_id=iw.id
    JOIN item i ON iw.item_id = i.id
    JOIN salespoint sp ON s.spoint_id = sp.id
    JOIN location sploc ON sp.loc_id = sploc.id
    JOIN warehouse wh ON iw.whouse_id = wh.id
    JOIN location whloc ON wh.loc_id = whloc.id
    WHERE sale_time >= '2009-01-01'
      AND sale_time <  '2010-01-01'
      AND sploc.id != whloc.id
    GROUP BY 1,2
 ;
```

You can create indexes on the table and analyze the temp table here:

```
SELECT shop.sp_name AS shop_name,
       q1_NLP.profit as q1_profit,
       q2_NLP.profit as q2_profit,
       q3_NLP.profit as q3_profit,
       q4_NLP.profit as q4_profit,
       year_NLP.profit as year_profit
  FROM (SELECT * FROM salespoint ORDER BY sp_name) AS shop
  LEFT JOIN nlqp_temp AS q1_NLP
   ON shop.id = Q1_NLP.spoint_id AND q1_NLP.sale_quarter = 1
  LEFT JOIN nlqp_temp AS q2_NLP
   ON shop.id = Q2_NLP.spoint_id AND q2_NLP.sale_quarter = 2
  LEFT JOIN nlqp_temp AS q3_NLP
   ON shop.id = Q3_NLP.spoint_id AND q3_NLP.sale_quarter = 3
  LEFT JOIN nlqp_temp AS q4_NLP
   ON shop.id = Q4_NLP.spoint_id AND q4_NLP.sale_quarter = 4
  LEFT JOIN (
        select spoint_id, sum(profit) AS profit FROM nlqp_temp GROUP
BY 1
   ) AS year_NLP
   ON shop.id = year_NLP.spoint_id
ORDER BY 1
;
COMMIT; -- here the temp table goes away
```

Use materialized views (long-living temp tables)

If the part you put in the temporary table is large, does not change very often, and/or is hard to compute, then you may be able to do it less often for each query by using a technique named **materialized views**. Materialized views are views that are prepared before they are used and are either fully regenerated as underlying data changes or in some cases can update only those rows that depend on the changed data. As of version 9.0, there is no explicit support for materialized views in PostgreSQL; that is, you can't just "CREATE MATERIALIZED VIEW AS ...", but there are several sample implementations for achieving exactly the same functionality. Visit `http://wiki.postgresql.org/wiki/Materialized_Views` for more discussion and examples.

Using set-returning functions for some parts of queries

Another possibility to achieve functionality similar to temp tables and/or materialized views is using a `set-returning` function for some part of the query.

For example, it is easy to have a materialized view freshness check inside a function.

There are also samples of materialized views and `set-returning` function usage in `shop_database.tar.gz`.

Speeding up queries without rewriting them

Often, you either can't or don't want to rewrite the query. In that case, you often can still speed up the query by the following techniques:

Providing better information to the optimizer

If `EXPLAIN ANALYSE` reveals that postgreSQL's estimates differ a lot from actual query execution statistics, you need to tell PostgreSQL to collect more fine-grained statistics.

The current default statistics target can be shown by:

```
show default_statistics_target ;
```

you can set it to a higher value either in the `postgresql.conf` file, or if you want to do it only for a single database, you can use `ALTER DATABASE` as follows:

```
alter database mydb set default_statistics_target = 200;
```

Usually, you don't want to set it too high for all tables and fields, as it slows down the `ANALYSE` command, so PostgreSQL gives you a more fine-grained way of doing it on a field-by-field basis.

```
alter table mytable alter col_with_bad_stats set statistics 500;
```

The new statistics values take effect at the next time `ANALYSE` is run on the table, so it makes sense to run `ANALYSE` after changing these values.

If you set the `default_statistics_target` for a database, then it takes effect the next time anyone connects to the database. So, you should either reconnect, or set it for current session with direct set `default_statistics_target` = 300 before `ANALYSE` if you want the new value to be used.

Adding a multi-column index tuned specifically for that query

If you have a query that for example selects rows from table `t1` on column `a`, and sorts on column `b`, then creating the following index enables PostgreSQL to do it all in one index scan:

```
CREATE INDEX t1_a_b_ndx ON t1(a,b);
```

Adding a special conditional index

If you `SELECT` on some condition (and especially if this condition only selects a small number of rows), you can use a conditional index on that expression like the following:

```
CREATE INDEX t1_proc_ndx ON t1(i1)
WHERE needs_processing = TRUE;
```

It is used in a query like the following for finding rows that need some processing to be done:

```
SELECT id, ... WHERE  needs_processing;
```

Cluster tables on specific indexes

Index access may still not be very efficient if the values accessed by the index are distributed randomly all over the table. If you know that some fields are likely to be accessed together, then cluster the table on an index defined on those fields. For a multi-column index shown above you can use the following command:

```
CLUSTER  t1_a_b_ndx ON t1
```

Clustering a table on index rewrites the whole table in index order, which can lock the table for a long time, so don't do it on a busy system. Also, `CLUSTER` is an one-time command, and new rows do not get inserted in cluster order, so to keep the performance gains, you may need to cluster the table every now and then.

Once a table is clustered on an index, you don't need to specify the index name in subsequent cluster commands, and can simply say:

```
CLUSTER t1;
```

It still takes time to rewrite the whole table, though it is probably a little faster once most of the table is in index order.

Use table partitioning and constraint exclusion

If you have a huge table, and a query select only a subset of that table, then you can partition that table and use constraint exclusion so that PostgreSQL knows which partitions it needs to access for a specific query.

Table partitioning is still not directly supported in PostgreSQL 9.0, but PostgreSQL has the basic capabilities in place to define it yourself. Unfortunately, it needs much longer explanation then we have space here. You can check out the official documentation on partitioning at the following URL:

```
http://www.postgresql.org/docs/9.0/interactive/ddl-partitioning.html
```

 There is a full chapter on table partitioning in another Packt book "High Performance PostgreSQL 9.0" which goes well beyond what is covered by the standard PostgreSQL documentation.

In case of many updates set fillfactor on table

If you often update only some table and can arrange so that you don't change any indexed fields, then setting `fillfactor` to a lower value than the default of 100 for that a table enables PostgreSQL to use HOT updates, which can be an order of magnitude faster than ordinary updates. HOT updates not only avoid creating new index entries but also can perform a fast mini-vacuum inside the page to make room for new rows.

```
ALTER TABLE t1 SET (fillfactor = 70);
```

Tells PostgreSQL to fill only 70% of each page in table `t1` when doing inserts, so that 30% is left for use by in-page (HOT) updates.

Rewriting the schema—a more radical approach

In some occasions, it may make sense to rewrite the database schema, and provide an old view for unchanged queries using views, triggers, rules, and functions.

One such case occurs when refactoring the database, and you want old queries to keep running while changes are made.

Another is an external application that is unusable with the provided schema, but can be made to perform OK with a different distribution of data between tables.

Why is my query not using an index?

This recipe explains what to do if you think your query should use an index, but it does not.

There can be several reasons for this, but most often it is that the optimizer believes that it is cheaper and faster to use a query plan that does not use an index.

How to do it...

Force index usage, and compare plan costs of using it with an index and without, using the following:

```
mydb=# create table itable(id int primary key );
NOTICE:  CREATE TABLE / PRIMARY KEY will create implicit index
"itable_pkey" for table "itable"
CREATE TABLE
mydb=# insert into itable select generate_series(1,10000);
INSERT 0 10000
mydb=# analyse;
ANALYZE
mydb=# explain analyse select count(*) from itable where id > 500;
                        QUERY PLAN
-----------------------------------------------------------------
Aggregate  (cost=188.75..188.76 rows=1 width=0)
          (actual time=37.958..37.959 rows=1 loops=1)
   -> Seq Scan on itable  (cost=0.00..165.00 rows=9500 width=0)
                          (actual time=0.290..18.792 rows=9500
loops=1)
         Filter: (id > 500)
 Total runtime: 38.027 ms
(4 rows)
mydb=# set enable_seqscan to false;
SET
mydb=# explain analyse select count(*) from itable where id > 500;
                        QUERY PLAN
-----------------------------------------------------------------
Aggregate  (cost=323.25..323.26 rows=1 width=0)
          (actual time=44.467..44.469 rows=1 loops=1)
   -> Index Scan using itable_pkey on itable
          (cost=0.00..299.50 rows=9500 width=0)
        (actual time=0.100..23.240 rows=9500 loops=1)
          Index Cond: (id > 500)
 Total runtime: 44.556 ms
(4 rows)
```

As you see, PostgreSQL estimates (rightly) that this query is better-served by performing a sequential scan.

How do I force a query to use an index

Here, we show how to force the database to use an index. In fact, it is not possible to tell PostgreSQL to use an index, but you can trick it into using one by telling the optimizer that all other options are prohibitively expensive.

Getting ready

First, you have to make sure that it is worth it to use the index. This is best done on a development or testing system, but if done carefully, can also be done on the production server. Sometimes it is very hard to generate a load similar to a live system in a test environment, and then your best option may be carefully testing on live.

As the PostgreSQL optimizer does not take into account the parallel load caused by other backends, it may make sense to lie to PostgreSQL about some statistics in order to make it use indexes.

How to do it...

set enable_seqscan to false

If you do:

```
set enable_seqscan to false;
```

you tell PostgreSQL that it is really very expensive to do sequential scans. It still does a `seqscan` (instead of failing) if it is the only way to do the query:

```
mydb=# create table table_with_no_index(id int);
CREATE TABLE
mydb=# set enable_seqscan to false;
SET
mydb=# explain select * from table_with_no_index where id > 10;
                    QUERY PLAN
---------------------------------------------------------------------
Seq Scan on table_with_no_index  (cost=10000000000.00..10000000040.00
rows=800 width=4)
   Filter: (id > 10)
(2 rows)
```

but it is very likely that it selects some other way of doing the query as cheaper:

```
mydb=# create index table_with_no_index_now_has_one on table_with_no_
index(id);
CREATE INDEX
```

```
mydb=# explain select * from table_with_no_index where id > 10;
                          QUERY PLAN
----------------------------------------------------------------------
Bitmap Heap Scan on table_with_no_index  (cost=10.45..30.45 rows=800
width=4)
    Recheck Cond: (id > 10)
    -> Bitmap Index Scan on table_with_no_index_now_has_one
(cost=0.00..10.25 rows=800 width=0)
          Index Cond: (id > 10)
(4 rows)
```

Once you enable `seqscans` again, it will use a sequential scan instead of the more costly (in this case) bitmap index scan as follows:

```
mydb=# set enable_seqscan to true;
SET
mydb=# explain select * from table_with_no_index where id > 10;
                                 QUERY PLAN
----------------------------------------------------------------------
  Seq Scan on table_with_no_index
      (cost=0.00..40.00 rows=800 width=4)
    Filter: (id > 10)
(2 rows)
```

Lower random_page_cost

For a softer nudge towards using indexes, set `random_page_cost` to a lower value, maybe even make it equal to `seq_page_cost`. This makes PostgreSQL prefer index scans on more occasions, but does still not produce entirely unreasonable plans, at least for cases where data is mostly cached in shared buffers or systems disk cache.

Default values for these parameters are as follows:

```
random_page_cost = 4;
seq_page_cost = 1;
```

Try setting:

```
set random_page_cost = 2;
```

and see if it helps; if not, set it to `1`.

Using optimistic locking

If you are doing lots of transactions which look like the following:

```
BEGIN;
SELECT * FROM ACCOUNTS WHERE HOLDER_NAME ='BOB' FOR UPDATE;
<do some calculations here>
UPDATE ACCOUNTS SET BALANCE = 42.00 WHERE HOLDER_NAME ='BOB';
COMMIT;
```

Then you may gain some performance by moving from explicit locking (SELECT ... FOR UPDATE) to optimistic locking.

Optimistic locking assumes that others don't update the same record, and checks this at update time, instead of locking the record for the time it takes to process the information on the client side.

How to do it...

Rewrite your application so that the preceding transaction is transformed into something like the following:

```
BEGIN;
SELECT A.*, (A.*::text) AS OLDACCINFO
   FROM ACCOUNTS A WHERE HOLDER_NAME ='BOB';
<do some calculations here>
UPDATE ACCOUNTS SET BALANCE = 42.00
 WHERE HOLDER_NAME ='BOB'
 AND   (A.*::text) = <OLDACCINFO from select above>;
COMMIT;
```

Then, check that the UPDATE did update one row in your application code. If it did not, then the account for bob was modified between SELECT and UPDATE, and you probably need to re-run your whole transaction.

How it works...

Instead of locking Bob's row for the time the data from select is processed in the client, it queries the old state of Bob's account record in variable OLDACCINFO, and then uses this value to check that the record has not changed.

You can also save all fields individually, and then check them all in UPDATE query, or if you can have an automatic last_change field, then you can use this. Or, if you actually care only about a few fields changing, such as BALANCE and can ignore others, say E_MAIL, then you can only check the relevant fields in UPDATE.

There's more...

Move the whole computation into the database function

If you can pass all the needed information into the database for processing as a database function, it will run even faster, as you save several roundtrips to database. If you use a PL/pgSQL function, you also benefit from automatically saving query plans on first call in a session, and using saved plans in subsequent calls.

So the preceding transaction is replaced by a function in the database as follows:

```
CREATE OR REPLACE FUNCTION consume_balance (
    i_username text, i_amount numeric(10,2), max_credit numeric(10,2),
    OUT success boolean, OUT remaining_balance numeric(10,2)) AS
$$
BEGIN
    UPDATE accounts SET balance = balance - i_amount
    WHERE username = i_username
        AND balance - i_amount > - max_credit
  RETURNING balance
        INTO remaining_balance;
    IF NOT FOUND THEN
        success := FALSE;
        SELECT balance
          FROM accounts
         WHERE username = i_username
           INTO remaining_balance;
    ELSE
        success := TRUE;
    END IF;
END;
$$ LANGUAGE plpgsql;
```

and you call it simply by running:

```
SELECT * FROM consume_balance ('bob', 7, 0);
```

from your client, returning the success variable telling you if there was high enough balance in Bob's account, and the number telling the balance Bob has left after this operation.

Reporting performance problems

If you need to get some advice on your performance problems, then the right place to do so is the performance mailing list at the following URL:

```
http://archives.postgresql.org/pgsql-performance/
```

You may want to first check that it is not a well known problem by searching the mailing list archives.

A very good description of what to include in your performance problem report is available at the following URL:

```
http://wiki.postgresql.org/wiki/Guide_to_reporting_problems
```

More performance related information can be found at the following URL:

```
http://wiki.postgresql.org/wiki/Performance_Optimization
```

Another good reference for all performance related information is the "High Performance PostgreSQL 9.0" book, also by Packt.

11
Backup & Recovery

In this chapter, we will cover the following:

- ▶ Understanding and controlling crash recovery
- ▶ Planning backups
- ▶ Hot logical backup of one database
- ▶ Hot logical backup of all databases
- ▶ Hot logical backup of all tables in a tablespace
- ▶ Backup of database object definitions
- ▶ Standalone hot physical database backup
- ▶ Hot physical backup & Continuous Archiving
- ▶ Recovery of all databases
- ▶ Recovery to a point in time
- ▶ Recovery of a dropped/damaged table
- ▶ Recovery of a dropped/damaged database
- ▶ Recovery of a dropped/damaged tablespace
- ▶ Improving performance of backup/recovery
- ▶ Incremental/Differential backup and restore

Introduction

Most people admit that backups are essential, though they also devote only a very small amount of time to thinking about the topic.

The first recipe is about understanding and controlling crash recovery. We need to understand what happens if the database server crashes, so we can understand when we might need to recover.

The next recipe is all about planning. That's really the best place to start before you go charging ahead to do backups.

The physical backup mechanisms here were initially written by me (*Simon Riggs*) for PostgreSQL in release 8.0 in 2004, and have been supported by him ever since then, now with increasing help from the community as its popularity grows. 2ndQuadrant has also been providing database recovery services since 2004 and regrettably many people have needed them as a result of missing or damaged backups.

Understanding and controlling crash recovery

Crash recovery is the PostgreSQL subsystem that saves us if the server should crash, or fail as a part of a system crash.

It's good to understand a little about it, and to do what we can to control it in our favor.

How to do it...

If PostgreSQL crashes there will be a message in the server log with severity-level `PANIC`. PostgreSQL will immediately restart and attempt to recover using the transaction log or **Write Ahead Log** (**WAL**).

The WAL consists of a series of files written to the `pg_xlog` subdirectory of the PostgreSQL data directory. Each change made to the database is recorded first in WAL, hence the name "write-ahead" log. When a transaction commits, the default and safe behavior is to force the WAL records to disk. If PostgreSQL should crash, the WAL will be replayed, which returns the database to the point of the last committed transaction, and thus ensures the durability of any database changes.

Note that the database changes themselves aren't written to disk at transaction commit. Those changes are written to disk sometime later by the "background writer" on a well-tuned server.

Crash recovery replays the WAL, though from what point does it start to recover? Recovery starts from points in the WAL known as "checkpoints". The duration of crash recovery depends upon the number of changes in the transaction log since the last checkpoint. A checkpoint is a known safe starting point for recovery, since at that time we write all currently outstanding database changes to disk. A checkpoint can become a performance bottleneck on busy database servers because of the number of writes required. There are a number of ways of tuning that, though please also understand the effect on crash recovery that those tuning options may cause. Two parameters control the amount of WAL that can be written before the next checkpoint. The first is checkpoint_segments, which controls the number of 16 MB files that will be written before a checkpoint is triggered. The second is time-based, known as checkpoint_timeout, and is the number of seconds until the next checkpoint. A checkpoint is called whenever either of those two limits is reached.

It's tempting to banish checkpoints as much as possible by setting the following parameters:

```
checkpoint_segments = 1000
checkpoint_timeout = 3600
```

though if you do you might give some thought to how long the recovery will be if you do and whether you want that.

Also, you should make sure that the `pg_xlog` directory is mounted on disks with enough disk space for at least 3 x 16 MB x checkpoint_segments. Put another way, you need *at least* 32 GB of disk space for `checkpoint_segments = 1000`. If wal_keep_segments > 0 then the server can also use up to 16MB x (wal_keep_segments + checkpoint_segments).

How it works...

Recovery continues until the end of the transaction log. We are writing this continually, so there is no defined end point; it is literally the last correct record. Each WAL record is individually CRC checked, so we know whether a record is complete and valid before trying to process it. Each record contains a pointer to the previous record, so we can tell that the record forms a valid link in the chain of actions recorded in WAL. As a result of that, recovery *always* ends with some kind of error reading the next WAL record. That is normal.

Recovery performance can be very fast, though it does depend upon the actions being recovered. The best way to test recovery performance is to setup a standby replication server, described in the chapter on *Replication*.

There's more...

It's possible for a problem to be caused replaying the transaction log, and for the database server to fail to start.

Some people's response to this is to use a utility named `pg_resetxlog`, which removes the current transaction log files and tidies up after that surgery has taken place.

pg_resetxlog destroys data changes and that means *data loss*. If you do decide to run that utility, make sure you take a backup of the `pg_xlog` directory first. My advice is to seek immediate assistance rather than do this. You don't know for certain that doing this will fix a problem, though once you've done it, you will have difficulty going backwards.

Planning backups

This section is all about thinking ahead and planning. If you're reading this section before you take a backup, well done.

The key thing to understand is that you should plan your recovery, not your backup. The type of backup you take influences the type of recovery that is possible, so you must give some thought to what you are trying to achieve beforehand.

If you want to plan your recovery, then you need to consider the different types of failures that can occur. What type of recovery do you wish to perform?

You need to consider the following main aspects:

- ▸ Full/Partial database?
- ▸ Everything or just object definitions only?
- ▸ Point In Time Recovery
- ▸ Restore performance

We need to look at the characteristics of the utilities to understand what our backup and recovery options are. It's often beneficial to have multiple types of backup to cover the different types of failure possible.

Your main backup options are

- ▸ logical backup—using `pg_dump`
- ▸ physical backup—file system backup

`pg_dump` comes in two main flavors: `pg_dump` and `pg_dumpall`. `pg_dump` has a `-F` option to produce backups in various file formats. The file format is very important when it comes to restoring from backup, so you need to pay close attention to that.

The following table shows the features available, depending upon the backup technique selected. The details of these techniques are covered in the remaining recipes in this chapter.

Table of Backup/Recovery options:

	SQL dump to an archive file pg_dump -F c	SQL dump to a script file pg_dump -F p or pg_dumpall	Filesystem backup using pg_start_backup
Backup type	Logical	Logical	Physical
Recover to point in time?	No	No	Yes
Backup all databases?	One at a time	Yes (pg_dumpall)	Yes
All databases backed up at same time?	No	No	Yes
Selective backup?	Yes	Yes	No (Note 3)
Incremental backup?	No	No	Possible (Note 4)
Selective restore?	Yes	Possible (Note 1)	No (Note 5)
DROP TABLE recovery	Yes	Yes	Possible (Note 6)
DROP TABLESPACE recovery	Possible (Note 2)	Possible (Note 6)	Possible (Note 6)
Compressed backup files?	Yes	Yes	Yes
Backup is multiple files?	No	No	Yes
Parallel backup possible?	No	No	Yes
Parallel restore possible?	Yes	No	Yes
Restore to later release?	Yes	Yes	No
Standalone backup?	Yes	Yes	Yes (Note 7)
Allows DDL during backup	No	No	Yes

How to do it...

1. If you've generated a script with pg_dump or pg_dumpall and need to restore just a single object, then you're going to need to go deep. You will need to write a Perl script (or similar) to read the file and extract out the parts you want. It's messy and time-consuming, but probably faster than restoring the whole thing to a second server, and then extracting just the parts you need with another pg_dump.

2. See recipe *Recovery of a dropped/damaged tablespace*.

3. Selective backup with physical backup is possible, though will cause later problems when you try to restore. See note 6.

4. See *Incremental/Differential backup*.

5. Selective restore with physical backup isn't possible with currently supplied utilities.

6. See recipe for *Recovery of a dropped/damaged tablespace*.

7. See recipe for *Standalone hot physical backup*.

How it works...

To backup all databases, you may be told you need to use the `pg_dumpall` utility. I have four reasons why you shouldn't do that, which are as follows:

- ▸ If you use `pg_dumpall`, then the only output produced is into a script file. Script files can't use the parallel restore feature of `pg_restore`, so by taking your backup in this way you will be forcing the restore to be slower than it needs to be.

- ▸ `pg_dumpall` produces dumps of each database, one after another. This means that:

  - ❑ `pg_dumpall` is slower than running multiple `pg_dump` tasks in parallel, one against each database.

  - ❑ The dumps of individual databases are not consistent to a particular point in time. If you start the dump at 04:00 and it ends at 07:00 then we're not sure exactly when the dump relates to—sometime between 0400 and 07:00.

- ▸ Options for `pg_dumpall` are similar in many ways to `pg_dump`, though not all of them exist, so some things aren't possible. In summary, `pg_dumpall` is slower to backup, slow to restore, and gives you less control over the dump. I suggest you don't use it for those reasons. If you have multiple databases, then I suggest you take your backup by doing either

- ▸ Dump global information for the database server using `pg_dumpall -g`. Then dump all databases in parallel using a separate `pg_dump` for each database, taking care to check for errors if they occur. Use the physical database backup technique instead.

Hot logical backup of one database

Logical backup makes a copy of the data in the database by dumping out the contents of each table.

How to do it...

The command to do this is simple and as follows:

```
pg_dump -F c > dumpfile
```

or

```
pg_dump -F c -f dumpfile
```

You can also do this through pgAdmin3 as shown in the following screenshot:

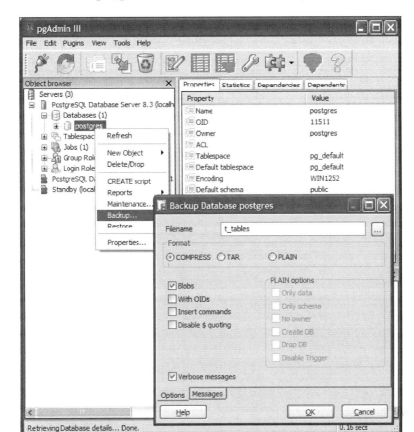

How it works...

`pg_dump` produces a single output file. The output file can use the split(1) command to separate the file into multiple pieces, if required.

`pg_dump` into custom format is lightly compressed by default. Compression can be removed or made more aggressive.

`pg_dump` runs by executing SQL statements against the database to unload data. When PostgreSQL runs an SQL statement we take a "snapshot" of currently running transactions, which freezes our viewpoint of the database. We can't (yet) share that snapshot across multiple sessions, so we cannot run an exactly consistent `pg_dump` in parallel in one database, nor across many databases.

The time of the snapshot is the only time we can recover to—we can't recover to a time either before or after that time. Note that the snapshot time is the start of the backup, not the end.

When `pg_dump` runs, it holds the very lowest kind of lock on the tables being dumped. Those are designed to prevent DDL from running against the tables while the dump takes place. If a dump is run at the point that other DDL are already running, then the dump will sit and wait. If you want to limit the waiting time you can do that by setting the `--lock-wait-timeout` option.

`pg_dump` allows you to make a selective backup of tables. The `-t` option also allows you to specify views and sequences. There's no way to dump other object types individually using `pg_dump`. You can use some supplied functions to extract individual snippets of information available at the following website:

```
http://www.postgresql.org/docs/9.0/static/functions-info.
html#FUNCTIONS-INFO-CATALOG-TABLE
```

`pg_dump` works against earlier releases of PostgreSQL, so it can be used to migrate data between releases.

`pg_dump` doesn't generally handle included modules very well. `pg_dump` isn't aware of additional tables that have been installed as part of an additional package, such as **PostGIS** or **Slony**, so it will dump those objects as well. That can cause difficulties if you then try to restore from the backup, as the additional tables may have been created as part of the software installation process in an empty server.

There's more...

What time was the `pg_dump` taken? The snapshot for a `pg_dump` is taken at the beginning of a run. The file modification time will tell you when the dump finished. The dump is consistent at the time of the snapshot, so you may want to know that time. If you are making a script dump, you can do a dump verbose as follows:

```
pg_dump -v
```

which then adds the time to the top of the script. Custom dumps store the start time as well and that can be accessed using the following:

```
pg_restore --schema-only -v dumpfile | head | grep Started
-- Started on 2010-06-03 09:05:46 BST
```

See also

Note that `pg_dump` does not dump the roles (such as users/groups) and tablespaces. Those two things are only dumped by `pg_dumpall`; see the next recipes for more detailed descriptions.

Hot logical backup of all databases

If you have more than one database in your PostgreSQL server, you may want to backup all databases together.

How to do it...

My recommendation is that you do exactly what you did for one database on each database in your cluster.

You can run those individual dumps in parallel if you want to speed things up.

Once complete, dump the global information also, using the following:

```
pg_dumpall -g
```

How it works...

To backup all databases, you may be told you need to use the `pg_dumpall` utility. I have four reasons why you shouldn't do that which are as follows:

▸   If you use `pg_dumpall`, then the only output produced is into a script file. Script files can't use the parallel restore feature of `pg_restore`, so by taking your backup in this way, you will be forcing the restore to be slower than it needs to be.

▸   `pg_dumpall` produces dumps of each database one after another. This means that

   ❑   `pg_dumpall` is slower than running multiple `pg_dump` tasks in parallel, one against each database.

▸   The dumps of individual databases are not consistent to a particular point in time. If you start the dump at 04:00 and it ends at 07:00 then we're not sure exactly when the dump relates to—sometime between 0400 and 07:00.

▸   Options for `pg_dumpall` are similar in many ways to pg_dump, though not all of them exist, so some things aren't possible.

See also

Also, look at *Hot physical backup* options.

Hot logical backup of all tables in a tablespace

Sometimes we may wish to make a dump of tables and data in a tablespace. Unfortunately, there isn't a simple command to do this, so we need to write some reusable scripts.

How to do it...

It is possible for a tablespace to contain objects from more than one database, so run the following query to see which databases from which you need to dump:

```
SELECT datname
FROM pg_database
WHERE   oid IN (
    SELECT pg_tablespace_databases(ts.oid)
    FROM pg_tablespace ts
    WHERE spcname = 'mytablespacename');
```

The following procedure allows you to dump all tables that reside on one tablespace and within *one* database only.

Create a file named `onets.sql` that contains the following SQL, which extracts the list of tables in a tablespace:

```
SELECT 'pg_dump'
UNION ALL
SELECT '-t ' || spcname || '.' || relname
FROM pg_class t JOIN pg_tablespace ts
ON reltablespace = ts.oid AND spcname = :TSNAME
JOIN pg_namespace n ON n.oid = t.relnamespace
WHERE relkind = 'r'
UNION ALL
SELECT '-F c > dumpfile';  -- dumpfile is the name of the output file
```

Execute the query to build the `pg_dump` script:

```
psql -t -v TSNAME="'mytablespace'" -f onets.sql > get_my_ts
```

From the recovered database server, dump the tables in the tablespace, including data and definitions. The output file is named "dumpfile", from last line in the first step.

```
chmod 755 get_my_ts
./get_my_ts
```

How it works...

`pg_dump` allows you to specify more than one table on the command line, so it's possible to generate a list of tables directly from the database.

We use the named parameter in psql to create a parameterized script, which we then execute to create a dump.

Backup of database object definitions

Sometimes it's useful to get a dump of the object definitions that make up a database. This is useful for comparing what's in the database against the definitions in a data or object-modeling tool. It's also useful to make sure you can recreate objects in exactly the correct schema, tablespace, and database with the correct ownership and permissions.

How to do it...

The basic command to dump the definitions only is to use the following:

```
pg_dumpall --schema-only > myscriptdump.sql
```

Which includes all objects, including roles, tablespaces, databases, schemas, tables, indexes, triggers, constraints, views, functions, ownership, and privileges.

If you want to dump PostgreSQL role definitions, you can use the following:

```
pg_dumpall --roles-only > myroles.sql
```

If you want to dump PostgreSQL tablespace definitions, you can use the following:

```
pg_dumpall --tablespaces-only > mytablespaces.sql
```

Or if you want to dump both roles and tablespaces, then you can use the following:

```
pg_dumpall --globals-only > myglobals.sql
```

The output is a human-readable script file that can be re-executed to re-create each of the databases.

There's more...

In PostgreSQL, the word "schema" is also used to describe a set of related database objects similar to a directory, also known as a "namespace". Be careful that you don't confuse what is happening here. The `--schema-only` option makes a backup of the "database schema" - the definitions of all objects in the database (and in all namespaces). To make a backup of the data and definitions in just one namespace, use the –s option. Or, to make a backup of only the definitions, in just one namespace, use both –s and --schema-only together.

Standalone hot physical database backup

Hot physical backup is an important capability for databases.

Physical backup allows us to get a completely consistent view of all database changes at once. Physical backup also allows us to backup even while DDL changes are being executed on the database. Apart from resource constraints, there is no additional overhead or locking with this approach.

Physical backup procedures are slightly more complex than logical backup procedures. So, let's start with a simple procedure to produce a standalone backup.

How to do it...

The following steps assume that a number of environment variables have been set:

1. $PGDATA is the path to the PostgreSQL data directory, ending with /

2. $BACKUPNAME is the filename of a backup file

3. All required PostgreSQL connection parameters have been set

> The initial procedure is steps 1 onwards. If running subsequent backups, start at step 6.

4. Create a new archive directory, if not already present, as follows:
   ```
   cd $PGDATA
   mkdir -p ../ standalone
   ```

5. Set an `archive_command`. In `postgresql.conf` you will need to add the following lines and restart the server, or just confirm they are present:
   ```
   archive_mode = on
   archive_command = 'test ! ../standalone/archiving_active ||
                       cp -i %p ../standalone/archive/%f'
   ```

6. Start archiving as follows:
   ```
   mkdir ../standalone/archive
   touch ../standalone/archiving_active
   ```

7. Start the backup as follows:
   ```
   psql -c "select pg_start_backup('standalone')"
   ```

8. Base backup—copy the data files (excluding the pg_xlog directory) as follows:
   ```
   tar -cv --exclude=$PGDATA/pg_xlog \
   -f ../standalone/$BACKUPNAME   $PGDATA
   ```

9. Stop the backup as follows:

```
psql -c "select pg_stop_backup(), current_timestamp"
```

10. Stop archiving as follows:

```
rm ../standalone/archiving_active
```

11. Move the files to the archive subdirectory, ready for recovery as follows:

```
mv ../standalone/archive/ archive/
```

12. Add the archived files to the standalone backup as follows:

```
tar -rzf  ../standalone/$BACKUPNAME  archive/
```

13. Write a `recovery.conf` with which to recover. Note that the archive directory mentioned here must match the location files to which are copied in step 8.

```
echo "restore_command = 'cp archive/%f %p'" > recovery.conf
```

14. Add the `recovery.conf` to the archive as follows:

```
tar -rf  ../standalone/$BACKUPNAME  recovery.conf
echo "recovery_end_command = 'rm -R archive' " >> recovery.conf
```

15. Store $BACKUPNAME somewhere *safe*. A safe place is definitely *not* on the same server.

The procedure ends with a file named $BACKUPNAME in the standalone directory. So, you need to remember to copy it somewhere safe. The file contains everything that you need to recover, including a recovery parameter file.

How it works...

The backup produced by the preceding procedure allows you to restore only to a single point in time. That point is the time of the `pg_stop_backup()` function.

Physical backup takes a copy of all files in the database (step 8, the "base backup"). That alone is not sufficient as a backup, and you need the other steps as well. A simple copy of the database produces a time-inconsistent copy of the database files. To make the backup time-consistent, we need to add to it all the changes that took place from the start to the end of the backup. That's why we have steps 7 and 9 to bracket our backup step.

The changes made are put into the standalone/archive directory as a set of archived transaction log/write-ahead log (WAL) files. Step 6 creates the archive directory. Steps 1, 2, 3, and 5 set the parameters that copy the files to the archive. Changing `archive_mode` requires us to restart the database server, so there is a trick to avoid that. These parameters are conditional upon the existence of a file named `archiving_active`, whose presence enables or disables the archiving process. Note this choice of parameters is configurable, so PostgreSQL doesn't always need to work this way.

Steps 6 and 10 enable and disable archiving, so that we only store copies of the WAL files created during the period of the backup. So, steps 1 to 5 are setup, and steps 6 to 10 are where the backup happens. Steps 11 onwards are gift wrapping, so that the backup script ends with everything in one neat file.

Step 11 moves the archived files under the data directory, a more convenient location from which to restore. Step 12 appends the WAL files to the backup file, so it is just one file.

Steps 3-14 add a `recovery.conf` file with its parameters setup so that there are no manual steps when we recover from this backup. This isn't explained here; look at the recipe on *Recovery of all databases*.

The key to understanding this is that we need both the base backup and the appropriate archived WAL files to allow us to recover. Without both of those things, we have nothing. Most of the steps are designed to ensure that we really will have the appropriate WAL files in all cases.

See also

It's common to use continuous archiving when using the physical backup technique, because that allows you to recover to any point in time, should you need that.

Hot physical backup & Continuous Archiving

This recipe describes how to set up a hot physical backup with a continuous archiving mechanism. The purpose of the continuous archiving is to allow us to recover to any point in time from the time of the backup to the time onwards.

Getting ready

This recipe builds upon the previous recipe to take a *Standalone hot physical backup*. You should read that first before following this recipe.

You need to decide a few things, which are as follows:

- ▶ Where will you store the WAL files (known as the "archive")?
- ▶ How will you send WAL files to the archive?
- ▶ Where will you store your base backups?
- ▶ How will you take my base backups?
- ▶ How many backups will you keep? What is your policy for maintaining the archive?

These are hard questions to answer immediately. So, we give a practical example as a way of explaining how this works, and then let the user decide how they would like it to operate.

How to do it...

The rest of this recipe assumes the following answers to the key questions:

▸ Archive is a directory on a remote server named $OTHERNODE

▸ We send WAL files to the archive using scp

▸ Base backups are also stored on $OTHERNODE

▸ Base backups are made using rsync

▸ We'll keep two backups, overwriting alternate backups as we take new ones and backups are taken weekly on Sundays

The following steps assume that a number of environment variables have been set:

▸ $PGDATA is the path to the PostgreSQL data directory, ending with /

▸ $OTHERNODE is the name of the remote server

▸ $BACKUPNAME is either b1/ or b2/, and we alternate this each time we take a backup. Two backups is the minimum; you may wish to use more copies.

▸ All required PostgreSQL connection parameters have been set

The procedure is as follows:

1. Create the archive and backup directories on a backup server.

2. Set an archive_command. In postgresql.conf, you will need to add the following lines and restart the server, or just confirm they are present.

```
archive_mode = on
archive_command = 'scp %p $OTHERNODE:/archive/%f'
```

3. Start the backup as follows:

```
psql -c "select pg_start_backup('my backup')"
```

4. Copy the data files (excluding the pg_xlog directory) as follows:

```
rsync -cva --inplace --exclude=*pg_xlog* \
${PGDATA}/  $OTHERNODE:$BACKUPNAME/$PGDATA
```

5. Stop the backup as follows:

```
psql -c "select pg_stop_backup(), current_timestamp"
```

6. It's also good practice to put a README.backup file into the data directory prior to the backup, so that it forms part of the set of files that make up the base backup. This should say something intelligent about the location of the archive, including any identification numbers, names, and so on.

Notice that we don't put a `recovery.conf` into the backup this time. That's because we're assuming we want flexibility at the time of recovery, rather than a gift-wrapped solution. The reason for that is we don't know when or where or how we will be recovering, nor do we need to make a decision on that yet.

How it works...

The key point here is that we must have both the base backup and the archive in order to recover. Where you put them is completely up to you. You can use any file system backup technology and/or file system backup management system to do this.

Many backup management systems have claimed that they have a PostgreSQL interface/plugin, though this most often means they support logical backup. However, there's no need for them to officially support PostgreSQL; there isn't any "Runs on PostgreSQL" badge or certification required. If you can copy files, then you can run the preceding processes to keep your database safe.

The preceding procedure uses a simple secure file copy, though it could also use `rsync`. If the network or backup server goes down, then the command will begin to fail. When the `archive_command` fails, it will repeatedly retry until it succeeds. PostgreSQL does not remove WAL files from `pg_xlog` until the WAL files have been successfully archived, so the end result is that your `pg_xlog` directory fills up. It's a good idea to have an `archive_command` that reacts better to that condition, though that is left as an improvement for the sysadmin. Typical action is to make that an emergency call out so we can resolve the problem manually. Automatic resolution is difficult to get right as this condition is one for which it is hard to test.

When continuously archiving, we will generate a considerable number of WAL files. If `archive_timeout` is set to 30 seconds, we will generate a minimum of 2*60*24 = 2880 files per day, each 16 MB in size, so a total volume of 46 GB per day (minimum). With a reasonable transaction rate, a database server might generate 100 GB of archive data per day, so you should use that as a rough figure for calculations before you have better measurements. Of course the rate could be much higher, with rates of 1 TB per day or higher being possible. Clearly we would only want to store WAL files that are useful for backup, so when we decide we no longer wish to keep a backup we will also want to remove files from the archive. In each base backup you will find a file called backup_label. The earliest WAL file required by a physical backup is the filename mentioned on the first line of the backup_label file. We can use a contrib module called pg_archivecleanup to remove any WAL files earlier than the earliest file.

The size of the WAL archive is clearly something we would want to compress. Ordinary compression is only reasonably effective. As is typically the case, a domain-specific compression tool is usually better at compressing archives. `pg_lesslog` is available at the following website to do this.

```
http://pgfoundry.org/frs/?group_id=1000310
```

Recovery of all databases

Recovery of a complete database server, including all of its databases, is an important feature. This recipe covers how to do that in the simplest way possible.

Some complexities are discussed here, though most are covered in later recipes.

Getting ready

Find a suitable server on which to perform the restore.

Before you recover onto a live server, always take another backup. Whatever problem you thought you had could be just about to get worse.

How to do it...

LOGICAL (from custom dump `-F c`):

- ▸ Restore of all databases means simply restoring each individual database from each dump you took. Confirm you have the correct backup before you restore:

  ```
  pg_restore --schema-only -v dumpfile | head | grep Started
  ```

- ▸ Reload globals from script file as follows:

  ```
  psql -f myglobals.sql
  ```

- ▸ Reload all databases. Create the databases using parallel tasks to speed things along. This can be executed remotely without needing to transfer dumpfile between systems. Note that there is a separate dumpfile for each database.

  ```
  pg_restore -d postgres -j 4 dumpfile
  ```

LOGICAL (from script dump created by `pg_dump -F p`):

As above, though with this command to execute the script. This can be executed remotely without needing to transfer dumpfile between systems.

- ▸ Confirm you have the correct backup before you restore. If the following command returns nothing, then the file is not timestamped, and you'll have to identify it in a different way:

  ```
  head myscriptdump.sql | grep Started
  ```

- ▸ Reload globals from script file as follows:

  ```
  psql -f myglobals.sql
  ```

▶ Reload all scripts like the following:

```
psql -f myscriptdump.sql
```

LOGICAL (from script dump created by `pg_dumpall`):

We need to follow the procedure, which is shown next.

▶ Confirm you have the correct backup before you restore. If the following command returns nothing, then the file is not timestamped, and you'll have to identify it in a different way:

```
head myscriptdump.sql | grep Started
```

▶ Find a suitable server, or create a new virtual server.

▶ Reload script in full

```
psql -f myscriptdump.sql
```

PHYSICAL:

▶ If you used the *Standalone hot physical database backup* recipe then recovery is very easy. Restore the backup file onto the target server.

▶ Extract the backup file into the new data directory.

▶ Confirm that you have the correct backup before you restore.

```
$ cat backup_label
START WAL LOCATION: 0/12000020 (file 000000010000000000000012)
CHECKPOINT LOCATION: 0/12000058
START TIME: 2010-06-03 19:53:23 BST
LABEL: standalone
```

▶ Check all file permissions and ownerships are correct and links are valid. That should already be the case if you are using the postgres userid everywhere, which is recommended.

▶ Start the server

That procedure is so simple because in the *Standalone* recipe we gift wrapped everything for you. That also helps us understand that we need both a base backup and the appropriate WAL files.

If you used other techniques, then we need to step through the tasks to make sure we cover everything required as follows:

▶ Shutdown any server running in the data directory.

▶ Restore the backup so that any files in the data directory that have matching names are replaced with the version from the backup. (The manual says delete all files and then restore backup—that might be a lot slower than running an rsync between your backup and the destination without the `--update` option). Remember that this step can be performed in parallel to speed things up, though it is up to you to script that.

- ▶ Check that all file permissions and ownerships are correct and links are valid. That should already be the case if you are using the postgres userid everywhere, which is recommended.

- ▶ Remove any files in `pg_xlog/`. If you've been following my recipes, you'll be able to skip this step, because we never backed them up in the first place.

- ▶ Copy in any latest WAL files from a running server, if any.

- ▶ Add in a `recovery.conf` and set its file permissions correctly also.

- ▶ Start the server.

The only part that requires some thought and checking is which parameters you select for the `recovery.conf`. There's only one that matters here, and that is the `restore_command`.

`restore_command` tells us how to restore archived WAL files. It needs to be the command that will be executed to bring back WAL files from the archive.

If you are forward-thinking, there'll be a `README.backup` file for you to read to find out how to set the `restore_command`. If not, then presumably you've got the location of the WAL files you've been saving written down somewhere.

Say, for example, that your files are being saved to a directory named `/backups/pg/servername/archive`, owned by the postgres user.

On a remote server named `backup1`, we would then write this all on one line of the `recovery.conf` as follows:

```
restore_command = 'scp backup1:/backups/pg/servername/archive/%f %p'
```

How it works...

PostgreSQL is designed to require very minimal information to perform a recovery. We try hard to wrap all the details up for you.

- ▶ **Logical recovery**: Logical recovery executes SQL to re-create the database objects. If performance is an issue, look at the recipe on recovery performance.

- ▶ **Physical recovery**: Physical recovery re-applies data changes at the block level so tends to be much faster than logical recovery. Physical recovery requires both a base backup and a set of archived WAL files.

There is a file named `backup_label` in the data directory of the base backup. This tells us to retrieve a `.backup` file from the archive that contains the start and stop WAL locations of the base backup. Recovery then starts to apply changes from the starting WAL location, and must proceed as far as the stop address for the backup to be valid.

After recovery completes, the `recovery.conf` file is renamed to `recovery.done` to prevent the server from re-entering recovery.

The server log records each WAL file restored from the archive, so you can check progress and rate of recovery. You can query the archive to find out the name of the latest archived WAL file to allow you to calculate how many files to go.

The `restore_command` should return 0 if a file has been restored and non-zero for failure cases. Recovery will proceed until there is no next WAL file, so there will eventually be an error recorded in the logs.

If you have lost some of the WAL files, or they are damaged, then recovery will stop at that point. No further changes after that will be applied, and you will likely lose those changes; that would be the time to call your support vendor.

There's more...

You can start and stop the server once recovery has started without any problem. It will not interfere with the recovery.

You can connect to the database server while it is recovering and run queries, if that is useful. That is known as **Hot Standby mode**, and is discussed in a later chapter.

See also

Once recovery reaches the stop address you can stop the recovery at any point, as discussed in *Recovery to a point in time*.

Recovery to a point in time

If your database suffers a problem at 15:22 p.m. and yet your backup was taken at 04:00 a.m. you're probably hoping there is a way to recover the changes made between those two times. What you need is known as "point-in-time recovery".

Regrettably, if you've made a backup with `pg_dump` at 04:00 a.m. then you won't be able to recover to any other time than 04:00. As a result, the term **point-in-time recovery** (**PITR**) has become synonymous with the physical backup and restore technique in PostgreSQL.

Getting ready

If you have a backup made with `pg_dump`, then give up all hope of using that as a starting point for a point in time recovery. It's a frequently asked question, but the answer is still "no"; the reason it gets asked is *exactly* why I'm pleading with you to plan your backups ahead of time.

First, you need to decide what the point of time is that to which you would like to recover. If the answer is "as late as possible", then you don't need to do a PITR at all, just recover until end of logs.

How to do it...

How do you decide to what point to recover? The point where we stop recovery is known as the "recovery target". The most straightforward way is to do this based upon a timestamp.

In the `recovery.conf`, you can add (or uncomment) a line that says the following:

```
recovery_target_time = '2010-06-01 16:59:14.27452+01'
```

or similar. Note that you need to be careful to specify the time zone of the target, so that it matches the time zone of *the server that wrote the log*. That might differ from the time zone of the current server, so check.

After that, you can check progress during a recovery by running queries in Hot Standby mode.

How it works...

Recovery works by applying individual WAL records. These correspond to individual block changes, so there are many WAL records to each transaction. The final part of any successful transaction is a commit WAL record, though there are abort records as well. Each transaction completion record has a timestamp on it that allows us to decide whether to stop at that point or not.

You can also define a recovery target using a **transaction id** (**xid**), though finding out which xid to use is somewhat difficult, and you may need to refer to external records if they exist.

The recovery target is specified in the `recovery.conf` and cannot change while the server is running. If you want to change the recovery target, you can shutdown the server, edit the `recovery.conf`, and then restart the server. Be careful though, if you change the recovery target and recovery is already passed the point, it can lead to errors. If you define a recovery_target_timestamp that has already passed, then recovery will stop almost immediately, though this will be later than the correct stopping point. If you define a recovery_target_xid that has already passed, then recovery will just continue to the end of logs. Restarting recovery from the beginning using a fresh restore of the base backup is always safe.

Once a server completes recovery, it will assign a new "timeline". Once a server is fully available, we can write new changes to the database. Those changes might differ from changes we made in a previous "future history" of the database. So we differentiate between alternate futures using different timelines. If we need to go back and run recovery again, we can create a new server history using the original or subsequent timelines. The best way to think about this is that it is exactly like a *Sci-Fi* novel—you can't change the past but you can return to an earlier time and take a different action instead. But you'll need to be careful not to confuse yourself.

There's more...

`pg_dump` cannot be used as a base backup for a PITR. The reason is that a log replay contains the physical changes to data blocks, not logical changes based upon Primary Keys. If you reload a `pg_dump` the data will likely go back into different data blocks, so the changes wouldn't correctly reference the data.

WAL doesn't contain enough information to reconstruct all SQL fully that produced those changes. Later feature additions to PostgreSQL may add the required information to WAL.

See also

Planned in 9.1 is the ability to pause/resume/stop recovery, and to set recovery targets while the server is up dynamically. This will allow you to use the Hot Standby facility to locate the correct stopping point more easily.

You can trick Hot Standby into stopping recovery, which may help. See the recipe on managing Hot Standby.

Recovery of a dropped/damaged table

You may drop or even damage a table in some way. Tables could be damaged for physical reasons, such as disk corruption, or they could also be damaged by running poorly specified UPDATEs/DELETEs, which update too many rows or overwrite critical data.

It's a common request to recover from this situation from a backup.

How to do it...

The methods differ, depending upon the type of backup you have available. If you have multiple types of backup, you have a choice.

LOGICAL (from custom dump `-F c`):

If you've taken a logical backup using `pg_dump` into a custom file, then you can simply extract the table you want from the dumpfile like the following:

```
pg_restore -t mydroppedtable dumpfile | psql
```

or connect direct to the database using `-d`.

The preceding command tries to re-create the table and then load data into it. Note that `pg_restore -t` option does *not* dump out any of the indexes on the table selected. That means we need a slightly more complex procedure than it would first appear, and the procedure needs to vary depending upon whether we are repairing a damaged table or putting back a dropped table.

To repair a damaged table we want to replace the data in the table in a single transaction. There isn't a specific option to do this, so we need to do the following:

- ▶ Dump the table to a script file as follows:

```
pg_restore -t mydroppedtable dumpfile > mydroppedtable.sql
```

- ▶ Edit a script named `restore_mydroppedtable.sql` with the following code:

```
BEGIN;
TRUNCATE mydroppedtable;
\i mydroppedtable.sql
COMMIT;
```

- ▶ Then, run it using the following:

```
psql -f restore_mydroppedtable.sql
```

- ▶ If you've dropped a table then you need to:

  - ❑ Create a new database in which to work, name it `restorework`, as follows:

    ```
    CREATE DATABASE restorework;
    ```

  - ❑ Restore the complete schema to the new database as follows:

    ```
    pg_restore --schema-only -d restorework dumpfile
    ```

- ▶ Now, dump just the definitions of the dropped table into a new file, which will contain CREATE TABLE, indexes, other constraints and grants. Note that this database has no data in it, so specifying `--schema-only` is optional, as follows:

```
pg_dump -t mydroppedtable --schema-only restorework >
mydroppedtable.sql
```

- ▶ Now, recreate the table on the main database as follows:

```
psql -f mydroppedtable.sql
```

- ▶ Now, reload just the data into database `maindb` as follows

```
pg_restore -t mydroppedtable --data-only -d maindb dumpfile
```

If you've got a very large table, then the fourth step can be a problem, because it builds the indexes as well. If you want you can manually edit the script into two pieces, one before the load ("pre-load") and one after the load ("post-load"). There are some ideas for that at the end of the recipe.

LOGICAL (from script dump):

The easy way to restore a single table from a script is as follows:

- ▶ Find a suitable server, or create a new virtual server.

- ▶ Reload the script in full, as follows:

```
psql -f myscriptdump.sql
```

- From the recovered database server, dump the table, its data, and all the definitions of the dropped table into a new file as follows:

```
pg_dump -t mydroppedtable -F c mydatabase > dumpfile
```

- Now, recreate the table into the original server and database, using parallel tasks to speed things along. This can be executed remotely without needing to transfer dumpfile between systems.

```
pg_restore -d mydatabase -j 2 dumpfile
```

The only way to extract a single table from a script dump without doing all of the preceding is to write a custom Perl script to read and extract just the parts of the file you want. That can be complicated, because you may need certain SET commands at the top of the file, the table, and data in the middle of the file, and the indexes and constraints on the table are near the end of the file. It's complex; the safe route is the one already mentioned.

PHYSICAL:

To recover a single table from a physical backup, we need to:

- Find a suitable server, or create a new virtual server.

- Recover the database server in full, as described in previous recipes on physical recovery, including all databases and all tables. You may wish to stop at a useful point in time, in which case you can look at the recipe on that topic later in the chapter.

- From the recovered database server, dump the table, its data, and all the definitions of the dropped table into a new file as follows:

```
pg_dump -t mydroppedtable -F c mydatabase > dumpfile
```

- Now, recreate the table into the original server and database using parallel tasks to speed things along. This can be executed remotely without needing to transfer dumpfile between systems as follows:

```
pg_restore -d mydatabase -j 2 dumpfile
```

How it works...

At present, there's no way to restore a single table from a physical restore in just a single step.

See also

Splitting a pg_dump into multiple sections, "pre" and "post" was proposed by me for an earlier release of PostgreSQL, though I haven't had time to complete that yet. It's possible to do that using an external utility also; the best script I've seen to split a dump file into two pieces is available at the following website:

```
http://bucardo.org/wiki/split_postgres_dump
```

It's extremely likely that we get changes to `pg_dump` in this area for PostgreSQL 9.1, with a few developers interested in following up on my earlier ideas.

Recovery of a dropped/damaged tablespace

Recovering a complete tablespace is also sometimes required. It's actually a lot easier than recovering a single table.

How to do it...

The methods differ depending upon the type of backup you have available. If you have multiple types of backup, you have a choice.

LOGICAL (from custom dump `-F  c`):

If you've taken a logical backup using `pg_dump` into a custom file, then you can simply extract the tables you want from the dumpfile, like the following:

```
pg_restore -t mytab1 -t mytab2 …  dumpfile | psql
```

or connect direct to the database using `–d`.

Of course, you may have difficulty remembering which exact tables were there. So, you may need to proceed, like the following:

- Find a suitable server, or create a new virtual server.
- Reload the script in full, using four parallel tasks as follows:

  ```
  pg_restore -d mydatabase -j 4 dumpfile
  ```

- Once the restore is complete, you can then dump the tables in the tablespace by following the recipe *Hot logical backup of all tables in a tablespace*.
- Now, recreate the tables into the original server and database, using parallel tasks to speed things along. This can be executed remotely without needing to transfer dumpfile between systems as follows:

  ```
  pg_restore -d mydatabase -j 2 dumpfile
  ```

LOGICAL (from script dump):

There's no easy way to extract the required tables from a script dump.

We need to follow the procedure which is as follows:

- Find a suitable server, or create a new virtual server.
- Reload the script in full

  ```
  psql -f myscriptdump.sql
  ```

- ▶ Once the restore is complete, you can then dump the tables in the tablespace by following the recipe *Hot logical backup of all tables in a tablespace*.

- ▶ Now, recreate the tables into the original server and database, using parallel tasks to speed things along. This can be executed remotely without needing to transfer dumpfile between systems like the following:

```
pg_restore -d mydatabase -j 2 dumpfile
```

PHYSICAL:

To recover a single tablespace from a physical backup, we need to:

- ▶ Find a suitable server, or create a new virtual server.

- ▶ Recover database server in full, as described in previous recipes on physical recovery, including all databases and all tables. You may wish to stop at a useful point in time, in which case you can look at the recipe on that topic later in the chapter.

- ▶ Once the restore is complete, you can then dump the tables in the tablespace by following the recipe *Hot logical backup of all tables in a tablespace*.

- ▶ Now, recreate the tables into the original server and database, using parallel tasks to speed things along. This can be executed remotely without needing to transfer dumpfile between systems like the following:

```
pg_restore -d mydatabase -j 2 dumpfile
```

There's more...

When recovering from a custom backup file (`-F c`), you can also use the `-l` option to list out the contents of the archive. You can then edit that file to remove, comment out, or reorder the actions. `pg_restore` can then reuse the list file as input, using the `-L` option.

Recovery of a dropped/damaged database

Recovering a complete database is also sometimes required. It's actually a lot easier than recovering a single table. Many users choose to place all their tables in a single database; in that case this recipe isn't relevant.

How to do it...

The methods differ depending upon the type of backup you have available. If you have multiple types of backup, you have a choice.

LOGICAL (from custom dump `-F c`):

Recreate the database into the original server using parallel tasks to speed things along. This can be executed remotely without needing to transfer dumpfile between systems like the following:

```
pg_restore -d myfreshdb -j 4 dumpfile
```

LOGICAL (from script dump created by `pg_dump`):

Recreate the database into the original server. This can be executed remotely without needing to transfer dumpfile between systems like the following:

```
psql -f myscriptdump.sql myfreshdb
```

LOGICAL (from script dump created by `pg_dumpall`):

There's no easy way to extract the required tables from a script dump.

We need to follow the procedure, which is as follows:

- Find a suitable server, or create a new virtual server.
- Reload script in full, as follows:

```
psql -f myscriptdump.sql
```

- Once the restore is complete, you can then dump the tables in the tablespace by following the recipe *Hot logical backup of one database*.
- Now recreate the database as described for logical dumps earlier in this recipe.

PHYSICAL:

To recover a single database from a physical backup we need to:

- Find a suitable server, or create a new virtual server.
- Recover database server in full, as described in previous recipes on physical recovery including all databases and all tables. You may wish to stop at a useful point in time, in which case you can look at the recipe on that topic later in the chapter.
- Once the restore is complete, you can then dump the tables in the database by following the recipe *Hot logical backup of one database*.
- Now, recreate the database as described for logical dumps, earlier in this recipe.

Improving performance of backup/restore

Performance is often a concern in any medium or large database.

Backup performance is often a delicate issue, because the resource usage may need to be limited to within certain boundaries. There may also be a restriction on the maximum run-time for the backup, for example, if the backup runs each Sunday.

Again, restore performance may be more important than backup performance, even if backup is the more obvious concern.

Getting ready

If performance is a concern or is likely to be one, then you should read the recipe about planning first.

How to do it...

- **Physical backup**: Improving performance of a physical backup can be done by taking the backup in parallel. That is, copying away the files using more than one task. The more tasks you use, the more it will impact the current system. When backing up, you can skip certain files. You won't need (in order) the following:

    - any files placed there by DBA that shouldn't actually be there

    - any files in `pg_xlog`

    - any old server log files in `pg_log` (even the current one)

    Remember, it's safer not to try to exclude files at all, as if you miss something critical you may get data loss. Also remember that your backup speed may be bottlenecked by your disks or your network. Some larger systems have dedicated networks in place purely for backups.

- **Logical backup**: As explained in a previous recipe, if you want to backup all databases in a database server, then you should use multiple pg_dump tasks running in parallel. If you want to speed up the dump speed of a pg_dump task, there really isn't an easy way of doing that right now. If you're using compression, look at the notes at the bottom of this recipe.

- **Physical restore**: Just as with physical backup, it's possible for us to put everything back quicker if we use parallel restore.

- **Logical restore**: Whether you use psql or `pg_restore`, you can speed up the program by assigning `maintenance_work_mem = 128MB` or more either in `postgresql.conf` or on the user that will run the restore. If neither of those ways is easily possible, you can specify the option using the `PGOPTIONS` environment variable, as follows:

❑   export PGOPTIONS ="-c work_mem = 128000"

This will then be used to set that option value for subsequent connections.

If you are running, archiving, or streaming replication, then transaction log writes may become a problem. Set `wal_buffers` between `2,000` and `10,000`, and set `checkpoint_segments` to `1024`, so it has room to breathe.

If you aren't running archiving or streaming replication, or you can turn it off during the restore, then you'll be able to minimize the amount of transaction log writes. In that case, you may wish to use the `--single-transaction` option, as that will also act to improve performance.

If a pg_dump was made using `-F` (custom format), then we can restore in parallel as follows:

```
pg_restore -j NumJobs
```

You'll have to be careful about how you select what degree of parallelism to use. A good starting point is the number of CPUs. Be very careful that you don't overflow available memory when using parallel restore: each job will use up to `maintenance_work_mem`, so the whole restore could begin swapping when it hits larger indexes later in the restore. Plan out the size of `shared_buffers` and `maintenance_work_mem` according to the number of jobs specified.

Whatever you do, make sure you run `ANALYZE` afterwards on every object created. This will happen automatically if autovacuum is enabled. It often helps to disable autovacuum completely while running a large restore, so double-check that you have it switched on again following the restore. The consequences of skipping this step will be extremely poor performance when you start your application again, which can easily set everybody off in a panic.

How it works...

Physical backup and restore is completely up to you. Copy those files away as fast as you like, anyway you like. Put them back the same or a different way.

Logical backup and restore involves moving data into and out of the database. That's typically going to be slower than physical backup and restore. Particularly with a restore, rebuilding indexes and constraints takes time, even when run in parallel. Plan ahead, measure the performance of your backup and restore techniques, so you have a chance when you need your database back in a hurry.

There's more...

Compressing backups is often considered as a way to reduce the size of the backup for storage. Even mild compression can use large amounts of CPU. In some cases, this might offset network transfer costs, so there isn't any hard rule as to whether compression is always good.

Compression for WAL files from physical backups was discussed earlier: pg_lesslog, available at the following website. `http://pgfoundry.org/frs/?group_id=1000310`. Physical backups can be compressed in various ways, depending upon the exact backup mechanism used. By default, the custom dump format for logical backups will be compressed. Even when compressed, the objects can be accessed individually if required.

Using `--compress` with script dumps will result in a compressed text file, just as if you had dumped the file, and then compressed it. Access to individual tables is not possible.

PostgreSQL utilities do have a compress/decompress option, though this isn't always that efficient. Put another way:

```
pg_dump --compress=0
```

will typically be slower than:

```
pg_dump | gzip
```

Of course, feel free to use your favorite fast compression tool instead, which is likely to vary, depending upon the type of data in use.

Using multiple processes is known as pipeline parallelism. If you're using physical backup, then you can copy the data away in multiple streams, which also allows you to take advantage of parallel compression/decompression.

See also

If taking a backup is an expensive operation, then one way around that is to take the backup from a replica instead that offloads the cost of the backup operation away from the master. Look at the recipes in the chapter on *Replication* to see how to set up a replica.

Incremental/Differential backup and restore

If you have performance problems with backup of a large PostgreSQL database, then you may ask about incremental or differential backup.

An incremental backup is a backup of all files that have changed since the last full backup. In order to restore, you must restore the full backup and then each set of incremental changes.

A differential backup is a backup of all individual changes since the last full backup. Again, restoration requires you to restore the full backup and then apply any changes since then.

How to do it...

To perform a differential physical backup, you can use `rsync` to compare the existing files against the previous full backup, and then overwrite just changed data blocks. It's a bad plan to overwrite your last backup, so keep two or more copies. An example backup schedule would be as follows:

Day of Week	Backup Set 1	Backup Set 2
Sunday	New full backup to Set 1	New full backup to Set 2
Monday	Differential to Set 1	Differential to Set 2
Tuesday	Differential to Set 1	Differential to Set 2
Wednesday	Differential to Set 1	Differential to Set 2
Thursday	Differential to Set 1	Differential to Set 2
Friday	Differential to Set 1	Differential to Set 2
Saturday	Differential to Set 1	Differential to Set 2

You should keep at least two full backup sets.

Many large databases have tables that are insert-only. In that case, it's easy to store away parts of those tables. If the tables are partitioned by insertion/creation date or a similar field, it makes doing that much simpler. Either way, you're still going to need a good way of recording what data is where in your backup.

In the general case, there's no easy way to run a differential backup using `pg_dump`.

How it works...

PostgreSQL doesn't explicitly keep track of last changed date or similar information for a file or table. PostgreSQL tables are held as files, so you should be able to rely on the *modification time (mtime)* of the files on the filesystem. If, for some reason, you don't trust that or that has been disabled, then incremental backup is not for you.

`pg_dump` doesn't allow `WHERE` clauses to be specified, so even if you add your own columns to track `last_changed_date` you'll still need to perform that manually somehow.

There's more...

`http://en.wikipedia.org/wiki/Backup_rotation_scheme` gives further useful information.

While thinking about incremental backup, you should note that replication techniques work by continually applying changes onto a full backup. This could be considered a technique for an incremental updated backup, also known as an "incremental forever" backup strategy. The changes are applied ahead of time, so that you can restore easily and quickly. You should still take a backup, but you can take the backup from the replication standby instead.

It's possible to write a utility that makes a differential backup of data blocks. You can read each data block and check the block's **Log Sequence Number** (**LSN**) to see if it has changed since a previous copy.

pg_rman is an interesting project, and you can get more information at the following website:

`http://code.google.com/p/pg-rman/`

pg_rman reads changed data blocks and compresses them, using detailed knowledge of the internals of PostgreSQL data blocks. Any bugs that exist there could cause data loss in your backups. Issues aren't resolved by the main PostgreSQL project, so I personally wouldn't advise using this utility without a formal support contract. Various companies support this; ask them.

pg_rman 1.1.2 will certainly produce smaller backups, though creating those backups is not yet a parallel process. As a result, it can be much faster to use a full or incremental backup with parallel streams.

pg_rman is certainly a project to watch in the future.

12
Replication & Upgrades

In this chapter, we will cover the following:

- ► Replication concepts
- ► Replication best practices
- ► Setting up file-based log shipping replication
- ► Setting up streaming log replication
- ► Managing log shipping replication
- ► Managing Hot Standby
- ► Selective replication using Londiste 3.0
- ► Selective replication using Slony 2.0
- ► Load balancing with pgpool II 3.0
- ► Upgrading to a new minor release (for example, 9.0.0 to 9.0.1)
- ► In-place major upgrades (for example, 8.4 to 9.0, or 9.0 to 9.1)
- ► Major upgrades online using replication tools

Introduction

Replication isn't magic, though it can be pretty cool. It's even cooler when it works, and that's what this chapter is all about.

Replication requires understanding, effort, and patience. There are a significant number of points to get right. My emphasis here is on providing simple approaches to get you started, and some clear best practices on operational robustness.

PostgreSQL has included some form of native replication since Version 8.2, though that support has steadily improved over time. External projects and tools have always been a heavy part of the PostgreSQL landscape, with most of them being written and supported by very strong PostgreSQL technical developers. Some people with a negative viewpoint have observed that this weakens PostgreSQL or emphasizes shortcomings. My view would be that PostgreSQL has been lucky enough to be supported by a huge range of replication tools, together offering a wide set of supported use cases from which to build practical solutions. That view extends throughout this chapter on replication, with around half of the recipes mentioning tools that are not part of the core PostgreSQL project.

All of the tools mentioned in this chapter are maintained and actively enhanced by current core PostgreSQL developers. The pace of change in this area is high, and it is likely that some of the restrictions mentioned here could well be removed by the time you read this. Please double-check the documentation for each tool or project.

Which is best? is a question that gets asked many times. The answer varies on the exact circumstances. In many cases, people use one technique on one server and a different technique to protect other servers. Even the developers of particular tools use the other tools when it is appropriate. Use the right tools for the job. All of the tools and techniques listed in this chapter have been recommended by me at some time, in relevant circumstances. If something isn't mentioned here by me that does probably imply it is less favorable for various reasons, and there are some tools and techniques that I would personally avoid altogether in their present form or level of maturity.

Understanding replication concepts

Replication technology can be confusing. You might be forgiven for thinking that people have a reason to keep it that way. My observation is that there are many techniques, each with their own advocates, and the strengths and weaknesses are often hotly debated.

There are some simple underlying concepts that can help us to understand the various options available. The terms used here are designed to avoid favoring any particular technique, as well as using standard industry terms when available.

How it works...

Database replication is the term we use to describe the technology for maintaining a copy of a set of data on a remote system.

There are usually two main reasons for wanting to do this, and often those reasons are combined:

- ▶ **High availability**: Reducing the chances of data unavailability by having multiple systems each holding a full copy of the data.

> ▸ **Data movement**: Allowing data to be used by additional applications or workloads on additional hardware. Examples are **Reference Data Management**, where a single central server might provide information to many other applications, and also **Business Intelligence/Reporting Systems**.

Of course, both of those topics are complex areas, and there are many architectures and possibilities for doing each of those.

What we will talk about here is data movement, where there is *no transformation* of the data—we simply copy the data from one PostgreSQL database server to another. So, we are specifically avoiding all discussion on ETL tools, EAI tools, inter-database migration, data warehousing strategies, and so on. Those are valid topics in IT architecture, we just don't cover them here.

Let's look at the basic architecture. Typically, the individual database servers are referred to as nodes. The whole group of database servers involved in replication is known as a Cluster. That is the common usage of the term, though be careful that the term Cluster is also used for two other quite separate meanings elsewhere in PostgreSQL. First, cluster is sometimes used to refer to the whole database instance, though I prefer the term "database server". Second, there is a command named CLUSTER, which is designed to sort data into a specific order within a table.

The first database server is also known as the *Master*, *Primary*, *Provider*, *Sender*, or the *Source server*.

The second database server is also known as the *Standby*, *Slave* or *Subscriber*, or *Receiver*. There can be multiple Standbys, if desired.

The replication systems described here are all Single Master, Multiple Standby systems. Multi-Master architectures are discussed briefly later.

The designations Master and Standby are just roles that any node can take at some point. To move the Master role to another node, we perform a procedure named **Switchover**. If the Master dies, and does not recover, then the more severe role change is known as a **Failover**. In many ways, they may be similar, but it helps to use different words for the two situations.

Software that manages the cluster, and in some cases automatically initiates the failover process, is sometimes referred to as clusterware. Clusterware may also perform other functions, such as load balancing.

The key aspect of replication is that data changes are captured on the Master, and then transferred to the Standby nodes. In some cases, a Standby node may send data changes onto later Standbys, a process known as relay.

After a transaction commits on the Master, the time taken to transfer data changes are sent from Master to Standby is important, and is usually referred to as the **latency**, or replication delay. Replication delay is best measured as a time (in seconds). Changes must then be applied to the Standby, which takes an amount of time known as the apply delay. Data changes are often sent in batches. Increasing batch size may increase transfer efficiency, though will also increase replication delay, and also the apply delay of the data changes towards the end of the batch. The total time a record takes from Master to Standby is the replication delay plus the apply delay. Be careful to note that some authors describe those times differently, and sometimes confuse the two, which is easy to do. In some cases, you may see the apply delay expressed in terms of the total volume of changes currently outstanding, expressed in bytes (usually MB). Please note that the throughput, or rate of data transfer, measured in MBs, is interesting, but not the same thing as the latency or replication delay, though may often be loosely related.

If data changes are acknowledged as sent from Master to Standby before transaction commit is acknowledged, we refer to that as synchronous replication. If data changes are sent after a transaction commits, we name that asynchronous replication. With synchronous replication, the replication delay directly affects performance on the Master. With asynchronous replication the Master may continue at full speed, though this opens up a possible risk that the Standby may not be able to keep pace with the Master. All asynchronous replication must be monitored to ensure that a significant lag does not develop, which is why we must be careful to monitor the replication delay.

All forms of Single-Master replication are initialized in roughly the same way. First, you enable change capture, and then make a full replica of the data set onto the Standby. After that, we begin applying the changes. As a result, the replication delay immediately following the initial copy task will be equal to the duration of the initial copy task. The Standby will then begin to catch-up with the Master, and the replication delay will begin to get smaller. This is known as the catch up period. If the Master is busy, it will continue to produce many new changes, and that can lengthen the time it takes the Standby to catch up. Note that in some cases, the catch-up period will be too long to be acceptable. Be sure to include this understanding in your planning and monitoring. Replication tuning may often be different during the catch-up period from the tuning you may need during normal running.

Replication will either copy all tables, or in some cases, we can copy a subset of tables, in which case we call this selective replication. When using selective replication we can group selected objects together into a replication set. If you choose selective replication, you should note that the management overhead increases as the number of objects managed increases. Additional administration time should be planned, especially if more than a few hundred objects are being managed.

There's more...

Multi-Master database architectures cause a number of problems that are difficult to resolve in the general case. Jim Gray's classic paper on multi-Master database architectures, *The Dangers of Replication and a Solution*, is considered the clearest explanation of the problems that can occur with the multi-Master approach. To quote from the Summary of the paper directly:

> *Replicating the data at many nodes and letting anyone update the data is problematic.*

The main problem is also stated clearly:

> *Update anywhere-anytime-anyway transactional replication has unstable behavior as the workload scales.*

 Visit the following URL:
http://books.google.co.uk/ The Dangers of Replication and a Solution

My own personal experience of clustering solutions that provide multi-Master architectures has not been rosy. Operational instability is not a good thing in a transactional database system, and can be difficult to predict and tune. Usually, I find the people that are the keenest to implement these architectures are the people that haven't ever tried them *yet*. The difficulties are practical problems, and may one day be easily solvable, though my observation is that this hasn't happened yet in production-quality software.

Single master replication architectures are both simple and robust. They also respond well under heavy load without sensitivity to application design, and are well-suited to general-purpose use cases.

Jim Gray's paper describes what is now known as sharding. Shared nothing scale-out can be a viable option in some cases, though again is not a general panacea. Those options aren't required by most people and so we skip covering the necessary details in this book. PL/Proxy has been specifically designed to allow sharding of PostgreSQL. There is much that can and will be written on these topics for which we do not have space here. Necessarily, this means that we also neglect to mention a number of projects associated with PostgreSQL replication and clustering. The main single Master replication solutions are covered here.

See also

Visit the following URL for more information:

http://en.wikipedia.org/wiki/Replication_(computer_science)

Replication best practices

Some general best practices for running replication systems are described in this chapter.

How to do it...

▶ **Use similar hardware and OS on all systems**: Replication allows nodes to switch roles. If we switchover or failover to different hardware, we may get performance issues and it will be hard to maintain a smoothly running application.

▶ **Configure all systems identically, as far as possible**: Use the same mount points, same directory names, same users; keep everything possible the same. Don't be tempted to make one system more important than the others in some way. It's just a single point of failure and gets confusing.

▶ **Give systems good names to reduce confusion**: Never, ever call one of your systems "Master" and the other one "Slave". When you do a switchover, you will get very confused. Try to pick system *names* that have nothing whatsoever to do with their role. Replication roles will inevitably change. System names should not. If one system fails, and you add a new system, never reuse the name of the old system: pick another one. It will be too confusing. Don't pick names that relate to something in the business. Colors are a bad choice, because if you have two servers named *yellow* and *red*, you then end up saying things like "there is a red alert on server yellow" which can easily be confusing. Don't pick place names, otherwise you'll be confused trying to remember that London is in Edinburgh and Paris is in Rome.

▶ **Keep the system clocks synchronized**: This helps you to keep sane when looking at log files produced by multiple servers. You can either use *ntp* or manually *resync* them on a regular basis.

▶ **Use a single, unambiguous timezone**: Use **UTC (Coordinated Universal Time)** or similar. Don't pick a timezone that has *Daylight Savings Time*, especially in regions that have complex DST rules. This just leads to (human) confusion with replication, as servers are often in different countries, and timezone differences vary throughout the year. Do this even if you start with all servers in one country, because over the lifetime of the application, you may add new servers in different locations. Think ahead.

▶ **Monitor each of the database servers**: If you want high availability, then you'll need to regularly check that your servers are operational. I speak to many people who would like to regard replication as a one-shot deal. Think of it more as a marriage, and plan for it to be a happy one.

▶ **Monitor the replication delay between servers**: All forms of replication are only useful if the data is flowing correctly between the servers. Monitoring the time it takes data to go from one server to another is essential to understanding whether replication is working for you, or not. Replication can be bursty, so you'll need to watch to make sure it keeps within sensible limits. You may be able to set tuning parameters to keep things low, or you may need to look at other factors.

The essential point is that your replication delay is directly related to the amount of data you're likely to lose when running asynchronous replication. Be careful here, because it is the replication delay, not the apply delay that affects data loss. A long apply delay may be more acceptable as a result.

As described previously, your initial replication delay will be high and should reduce down to a lower and more stable value over a period of time. For large databases this could take days, so be careful to monitor during the catch-up period.

File-based log-shipping replication

Log shipping is a replication technique used by many database management systems. The Master records database changes in its transaction log and then the log files are shipped from the Master to the Standby, where the log is replayed.

File-based log shipping has been available since PostgreSQL 8.2, which is more than four years before 9.0 was released. It's a simple, very low overhead, and trustworthy form of replication.

The technique is mostly superseded by streaming replication in 9.0, though is still useful as part of a comprehensive backup strategy. It is also worth understanding how this works, as this technique can also be used as the starting phase for a large streaming replication setup. Look at the next recipes for some further details on that.

Getting ready

If you haven't read the recipes on *Replication Concepts* and *Replication best practice* at the start of this chapter, please go and read them now. Replication is complex, and even if you think "no problem, I know that", its worth just checking the basic concepts and names that I'll be using here. Note that log shipping replication refers to the Master node as the primary node, and the two terms are used interchangeably.

How to do it...

Follow these steps for initial configuration of file-based log shipping:

► Identify your archive location and ensure that it has sufficient space. This recipe assumes that the archive is a directory on the Standby node, identified by the $PGARCHIVE environment variable. This is set on both the Master and Standby nodes, as the Master must write to the archive, and the Standby must read from it. The Standby node is identified on the Master using $STANDBYNODE.

► Configure replication security. Perform a key exchange to allow the Master and the server to run the rsync command in either direction. See a later step.

- ► Adjust Master parameters in `postgresql.conf` as follows:

```
wal_level = 'archive'
archive_mode = on
archive_command = <scp %p $STANDBYNODE:$PGARCHIVE/%f>
archive_timeout = 30
```

- ► Adjust hot Standby parameters if required (see later recipe).

- ► Take a base backup, very similar to the process for taking a physical backup as described in the *Backup* chapter.

  - ❑ Start the backup by running the following:

```
psql -c "select pg_start_backup('base backup for log shipping')"
```

  - ❑ Copy the data files (excluding the `pg_xlog` directory). Note that this requires some security configuration to ensure that `rsync` can be executed without needing to provide a password when it executes. If you skipped step 2, do this now as follows:

```
rsync -cva --inplace --exclude=*pg_xlog* \
${PGDATA}/ $STANDBYNODE:$PGDATA
```

  - ❑ Stop the backup by running the following:

```
psql -c "select pg_stop_backup(), current_timestamp"
```

- ► Set the `recovery.conf` parameters on the Standby server as follows:

```
standby_mode = 'on'
restore_command = <cp $PGARCHIVE/%f %p>
archive_cleanup_command = <pg_archivecleanup $PGARCHIVE %r>
trigger_file = </tmp/postgresql.trigger.5432>
```

- ► Start the Standby server.

- ► Carefully monitor replication delay until catch-up period is over. During the initial catch-up period, the replication delay will be much higher than we would normally expect it to be. You are advised to set `hot_standby` = `off` for the initial period only.

Use a script; don't do this by hand, even when testing or just exploring the capabilities. If you make a mistake, you'll want to re-run things from the start again quickly, and doing things manually is both laborious and an extra source of error.

How it works...

Transaction log (WAL) files will be written on the Master. Setting `wal_level` ensures that we collect all changed data, and that WAL is never optimized away. WAL is sent from the Master to the archive using `archive_command` and from there the Standby reads WAL files using `restore_command`, and then replays the changes.

Files are sent when a file becomes full, or `archive_timeout` seconds have passed since the transaction log was written by any user. If the server is writing no new transaction log data for an extended period, then files will switch every `checkpoint_timeout` seconds; this is normal, and not a problem.

The preceding configuration assumes that the archive is on the Standby, so the `restore_command` shown is a simple copy command (cp). If the archive was on a third system, then we would either need to mount the filesystem remotely, or use a network copy command.

The `archive_cleanup_command` ensures that the archive only holds the files the Standby needs to restart if it should stop for any reason. Files older than the last file required are deleted regularly to ensure that the archive does not overflow. Note that if the Standby is down for any extended period, then the number of files in the archive will continue to accumulate and eventually overflow. The number of files in the archive should also be monitored.

In the configuration shown, a contrib module named `pg_archivecleanup` is used to remove files from the archive. This is a supplied module with PostgreSQL 9.0. `pg_archivecleanup` is designed to work with one Standby node at a time. Note that `pg_archivecleanup` requires two parameters: the archive directory and "%r", with a space between them. PostgreSQL transforms `%r` into the cut-off filename.

If you wish to have multiple Standby nodes, then a shared archive would be a single point of failure and should be avoided, so each Standby should maintain its own archive. We must modify the `archive_command` to be a script, rather than executing the command directly. This allows us to handle archiving to multiple destinations:

```
archive_command = 'myarchivescript %p %f'
```

and then we would write myarchivescript that looked somewhat like the following, though with additional error checking to handle cases with down Standbys more cleanly:

```
scp $1 $STANDBYNODE1:$PGARCHIVE/$2
scp $1 $STANDBYNODE2:$PGARCHIVE/$2
scp $1 $STANDBYNODE3:$PGARCHIVE/$2
```

The initial copy, or base backup, is performed using the rsync utility, which may require you to have direct security authorization, for example, using SSH and key exchange. You may also choose to perform the base backup a different way; if so, feel free to substitute your preferred method.

There's more...

Monitoring file-based log shipping can be performed in a number of ways. You can look at the current files on both Master and Standby as follows:

```
ps -ef | grep archiver                        on master
postgres: archiver process  last was  000000010000000000000040
```

```
ps -ef | grep startup                     on standby
postgres: startup process  waiting for  000000010000000000000041
```

Prior to PostgreSQL 9.0, it was difficult to measure the replication delay precisely and some hackish methods needed to be used. Those aren't presented here.

Monitoring replication is covered in more detail in the recipe on *Managing log shipping replication* later in this chapter.

Some of the tuning advice on compressing WAL files from the *Backup* chapter may apply here, though in general WAL may not be around long enough to build up a large enough volume to worry you. In that case, the compression might just slow you down instead.

See also

If you have configuration instructions written for PostgreSQL 8.2 to 8.4, then they will work almost exactly the same in PostgreSQL 9.0 onwards. The only difference is that you will also need to specify `wal_level`. Note that the procedures covered here are not the default configuration, and do differ from earlier releases. In PostgreSQL 9.0, the utility `pg_Standby` is no longer required, as many of its features are now performed directly by the server. If you prefer to continue using `pg_Standby` with PostgreSQL 9.0, then you do not need to use the `archive_cleanup_command`, `Standby_mode`, or `trigger_file` parameters at all.

You may also be interested in an improved version of `pg_standby` that is available as part of the 2warm project.

 Visit the following URL to know more about the 2warm toolset:
`http://projects.2ndQuadrant.com/2warm`

Setting up streaming log replication

Log shipping is a replication technique used by many database management systems. The Master records changes in its transaction log (WAL), and then the log data is shipped from the Master to the Standby, where the log is replayed.

Streaming log replication is new in PostgreSQL 9.0 and by time of release will have been through nearly three years of design, development, and beta-testing. The key feature in PostgreSQL 9.0 is that the data is transferred directly from Master to Standby, giving us integrated security and reduced replication delay.

There are two main ways to set up streaming replication: with or without an additional archive. Set up without an external archive is presented here, as it is both the most simple and efficient way. There is one downside that suggests the simple approach may not be appropriate for larger databases, explained later in the recipe.

Getting ready

If you haven't read the recipes on *Replication concepts* and *Replication best practice* at the start of this chapter, please go and read them now. Note that streaming replication refers to the Master node as the primary node, and the two terms are used interchangeably.

How to do it...

Carry out the following steps:

1. Identify your Master and Standby nodes, and ensure that they have been configured according to the best practice recipe.

2. Configure replication security. Create or confirm the existence of the replication user on Master node

   ```
   CREATE USER repuser
          SUPERUSER
          LOGIN
          CONNECTION LIMIT 1
          ENCRYPTED PASSWORD 'changeme';
   ```

3. Allow the replication user to authenticate. The following example allows access from any ip address using encrypted password authentication; you may wish to consider more restrictive options. Add the following line to the

   ```
   host            replication  repuser      127.0.0.1/0         md5
   ```

4. Set logging options in postgresql.conf on both Master and Standby, so that you get increased information regarding replication connection attempts and associated failures.

   ```
   log_connections = on
   ```

5. Set max_wal_senders on Master in postgresql.conf, or increment if the value is already non-zero.

   ```
   max_wal_senders = 1
   wal_mode = 'archive'
   archive_mode = on
   archive_command = 'cd .'
   ```

6. Adjust wal_keep_segments on Master in postgresql.conf. Set this to a value no higher than the amount of freespace on the drive on which the pg_xlog directory is mounted, divided by 16MB. If pg_xlog isn't mounted on a separate drive, then don't assume all of the current freespace is available for transaction log files.

   ```
   wal_keep_segments = 10000        # e.g. 160 GB
   ```

7. Adjust hot Standby parameters if required (see later recipe)

8. Take a base backup, very similar to the process for taking a physical backup as described in the backup chapter.

   a. Start the backup

   ```
   psql -c "select pg_start_backup('base backup for streaming
   rep')"
   ```

   b. Copy the data files (excluding the pg_xlog directory)

   ```
   rsync -cva --inplace --exclude=*pg_xlog* \
   ${PGDATA}/ $STANDBYNODE:$PGDATA
   ```

   c. Stop the backup

   ```
   psql -c "select pg_stop_backup(), current_timestamp"
   ```

9. Set the `recovery.conf` parameters on the Standby. Note that the `primary_conninfo` must not specify a database name, though can contain any other PostgreSQL connection option. Note also that all options in `recovery.conf` are enclosed in quotes, whereas postgresql.conf parameters need not be.

   ```
   Standby_mode = 'on'
   primary_conninfo = 'host=192.168.0.1 user=repuser'
   trigger_file = '/tmp/postgresql.trigger.5432'
   ```

10. Start Standby server

11. Carefully monitor replication delay until the catchup period is over. During the initial catchup period, the replication delay will be much higher than we would normally expect it to be. You are advised to set hot_Standby = off for the initial period only.

How it works...

Multiple Standby nodes can connect to a single Master. If you use multiple Standbys, be sure to set `max_wal_senders` correctly. You may wish to set up an individual user for each Standby node, though it may be sufficient just to set the `application_name` parameter in the `primary_conninfo`.

Standby nodes cannot connect to other Standby nodes, only to the current Master. A Standby that connects to a different Master will receive an error message.

The architecture for streaming replication is that on the Master, one WALSender process is created for each Standby that connects for streaming replication. On the Standby node, a WALReceiver process is created to work co-operatively with the Master. Data transfer has been designed and measured to be very efficient—data is typically sent in 8192-byte chunks without additional buffering at the network layer.

Both the WALSender and WALReceiver will work continuously on any outstanding data to be replicated until the queue is empty. If there is a quiet period, then the WALReceiver will sleep for 100ms at a time, and the WALSender will sleep for `wal_sender_delay`. Typically, the value of `wal_sender_delay` need not be altered, because it only affects behavior during momentary quiet periods. The default value is a good balance between efficiency and data protection. If the Master and Standby are connected by a low bandwidth network, and the write rate on the Master is high, you may wish to lower this value to perhaps 20ms or 50ms. Reducing this value will reduce the amount of data loss if the Master becomes permanently unavailable, though will also marginally increase the cost of streaming the transaction log data to the Standbys.

The Standby connects to the Master using native PostgreSQL libpq connections. That means that all forms of authentication and security work for replication, just as they do for normal connections. Note that for replication sessions the Standby is the "client" and the Master is the "server", if any parameters need to be configured. Using standard PostgreSQL libpq connections also means that normal network port numbers are used, so no additional firewall rules are required. You should also note that if the connections use SSL, then encryption costs will slightly increase the replication delay and CPU resources required.

There's more...

If the connection drops between Master and Standby, it will take some time for that to be noticed across an indirect network. To ensure that a dropped connection is noticed as soon as possible, you may wish to adjust the `keepalive` settings.

If you want a Standby to notice that the connection to the Master has dropped, you need to set the `keepalives` in the `primary_conninfo` in the `recovery.conf` on the Standby as follows:

```
primary_conninfo = '....keepalives_idle= 60 ...'
```

If you want the Master to notice that a streaming Standby connection has dropped, you can set the `keepalive` parameters in `postgresql.conf` on the Master, such as:

```
tcp_keepalives_idle = 60              # time before we send keepalives
```

That setting will then apply to all connections from users and replication. If you want to be very specific, and just set that for replication, you must supply this as an option to be passed to the Master, which is specified like the following:

```
primary_conninfo = '....options="-c tcp_keepalives_idle= 60" ...'
```

All of the preceding examples set the length of time the connection will be idle before we start sending keepalives to be 60 seconds. The default is two hours, and is not recommended. There are multiple keepalive parameters we can set; I have avoided showing those here for clarity. A related option is `connection_timeout`. Remember, you can hide all of this complexity in a connection service file, so that `primary_conninfo` only refers to a single service name, as described in the *First Steps* chapter.

You may also wish to increase `max_wal_senders`, so that it will be possible to reconnect even before a dropped connection is noted; this allows a manual restart to re-establish connections more easily. If you do this, then also increase the connection limit for the replication user.

Data transfer may stop because the connection drops or the Standby server or the Standby system is shutdown. If replication data transfer stops for any reason, it will attempt to restart from the point of last transfer.

For streaming replication, the Master keeps a number of files that is at least `wal_keep_segments`. If the Standby database server has been down for long enough, the Master will have moved on and will no longer have the data for the last point of transfer. If that should occur, then the Standby needs to be re-configured using the same procedure with which we started.

Note that the Standby database server will not be streaming during the initial base backup, so if the base backup is long enough, we might end up with a situation where replication will never start because the desired starting point is no longer available on the Master. This is the error that you'll get:

```
FATAL:  requested WAL segment 000000010000000000000002 has already
been removed
```

It's very annoying, and there's no way out of that. You need to start over. So, start with a very high `wal_keep_segments`. If you still get that error, then we need to increase `wal_keep_segments` and try again, possibly also using techniques to speed up the base backup, discussed in the *Backup* chapter. If you can't set `wal_keep_segments` high enough, then we must move to a configuration where the archive is on a third server with increased disk storage capacity. The Master will need to have an `archive_command` that places files on the archive server, rather than the dummy command shown in the preceding procedure, in addition to parameter settings to allow streaming to take place. The Standby will need to retrieve files from the archive using `restore_command`, as well as streaming using `primary_conninfo`. Thus, both Master and Standby have two modes for sending and receiving, and can switch between them should failures occur. This is the typical configuration for large databases. Note that this means that WAL data will be copied twice: once to the archive and once directly to the Standby. Two copies are more expensive, but also more robust.

The reason for setting `archive_mode = on` in the preceding procedure is that altering that parameter requires a restart, so you may as well set it on just in case you need it later. All we need to do is use a dummy `archive_command` to ensure everything still works OK; by dummy command, I mean a command that will do nothing and then return `rc=0`.

One thing that is a possibility is to set `archive_command` only until the end of the catch up period. After that you can reset it to the dummy value ("cd") and then continue just with streaming replication. Data is only transferred from the Master to the Standby once that data has been written (or more precisely, fsynced) to disk. So setting `synchronous_commit = off` will not improve the replication delay, even if that improves performance on the Master. Once WAL data is received by the Standby, the WAL data is fsynced to disk on the Standby to ensure that it is not lost if the Standby system restarts.

Monitoring streaming replication is very important and noted previously. `WALSender`
processes don't show up in `pg_stat_activity`, though the details are there if you want to
access them. Use the following view:

```
CREATE OR REPLACE VIEW pg_stat_replication AS
    SELECT
            S.procpid,
            S.usesysid,
            U.rolname AS usename,
            S.application_name,
            S.client_addr,
            S.client_port,
            S.backend_start
    FROM pg_stat_get_activity(NULL) AS S, pg_authid U
    WHERE S.usesysid = U.oid AND S.datid = 0;
```

Managing log shipping replication

Whether you use file-based or streaming replication as the transport mechanism, managing a
log shipping replication cluster is in many ways very similar.

Getting ready

Discussion here assumes you have already set up file-based log shipping, streaming
replication, or both.

How to do it...

Monitoring

Monitoring of log shipping is essential. You'll find it best to enable Hot Standby mode, as the
information is both easier to obtain and more accurate if you do.

Repmgr and pgpool both provide replication monitoring facilities. Munin plugins are available
for graphing replication and apply delay.

You may wish to calculate the delays yourself. To do that, we request current values from Master
and Standby, and then compare the values. On the Master, execute the following query:

```
SELECT pg_current_xlog_location();
```

On the Standby, execute the following query:

```
SELECT pg_last_xlog_receive_location();
```

You can then compare the results to understand the replication delay. You can calculate the apply delay by comparing the preceding value from Master with the following:

```
SELECT pg_last_xlog_apply_location();
```

The comparison can be a little fiddly, as you must use hex arithmetic to convert the two parts of the file name. You can do this in Perl, Python, Java, C, and so on, or if you are brave you can have a go at this in SQL, using a function to do the hex-to-decimal conversion as follows:

```
CREATE OR REPLACE FUNCTION hex2dec(text)
RETURNS bigint LANGUAGE SQL AS
$$
SELECT sum(digit * 16 ^ (length($1)-pos)) ::bigint
  FROM (SELECT case
             when digit between '0' and '9' then ascii(digit) - 48
             when digit between 'A' and 'F' then ascii(digit) - 55
             end,
             pos as i
             FROM (SELECT substring(c from x for 1), x
                     FROM (values(upper($1))) as a(c),
                          generate_series(1,length($1)) as t(x))
                  as u(digit, pos)
        ) as v(digit, pos);
$$;
```

Switchover and Failover

Switchover is a controlled switch from Master to Standby. If performed correctly, there will be no data loss. To be safe, simply shutdown the Master node cleanly, using either smart or fast shutdown modes. Do not use immediate mode shutdown, because you will almost certainly lose data that way.

Failover is a forced switch from the Master node to a Standby because of the loss of the Master. So in that case, there is no action to perform on the Master; we presume it is not there anymore.

Next, we need to promote one of the Standby nodes to be the new Master. A Standby node can be triggered into becoming a Master node by creating the trigger file specified in the parameter `trigger_file`. For example:

```
touch /tmp/postgresql.trigger.5432
```

The trigger file will be deleted again when the transition is complete. Note that the Standby will only become the Master once it has fully caught up. If you haven't been monitoring replication, this could take some time.

To move from a Standby to a Master, the database performs an immediate checkpoint, which may take some time on database servers with large caches and high rate of changes being replicated from the Master.

Once the ex-Standby becomes a Master, it will begin to operate all normal functions, including starting to archive files if configured. Be careful to check that you have all the correct settings for when this node begins to operate as Master. It is likely that the settings will be different from those on the original Master from which they were copied.

Note that I refer to this new server as "a Master" not "the Master". It is up to you to ensure that the previous Master doesn't continue to operate, a situation known as a *split-brain* situation. You must be careful to ensure that the previous Master stays down.

Management of complex failover situations is not provided with PostgreSQL, nor is automated failover. Situations can be quite complex with multiple nodes, and clusterware is used in many cases to manage this.

Switchback

Following switchover from one node to another, it is common to want to do a switchover back to the old Master again, which I call switchback.

Once a Standby has become a Master, it cannot go back to being a Standby again. So with log replication, there is no explicit switchback operation. This is a surprising situation for many people, though it is quick to work around. Once you have performed a switchover, all you need to do is the following:

▶ Reconfigure the old Master again, repeating same process as before
▶ Switchover from current to old Master

The important part here is that if we perform the first without deleting the files on the old Master, this allows the rsync to go much faster. When no files are present on the destination, rsync just performs a copy. When similar named files are present on the destination, then rsync will compare the files, and send only changes. So, the rsync we perform on a switchback operation performs much less data transfer than in the original copy. It is likely that this will be enhanced in later releases of PostgreSQL. There are also ways to avoid this, as shown in the repmgr utility, discussed next.

How it works...

Note that the *trigger file* has nothing whatsoever to do with trigger-based replication. The trigger file is a mechanism to allow us to specify that the Standby should change role to become the Master. The trigger file name can be anything you like, though the preceding recipe uses a suffix of 5432 to ensure that we only trigger one server if there are multiple PostgreSQL servers operating on the same system.

The role of the `recovery_end_command` is to clean up at the end of the switchover or failover process. You do not need to remove the trigger file explicitly, as was recommended in previous releases.

See also

Clusterware may provide additional features, such as automated failover, monitoring, or ease of management of replication.

Repmgr is an open source tool designed specifically for PostgreSQL replication. To get additional information about repmgr visit the following URL:

`http://projects.2ndQuadrant.com/repmgr/`

Continuent Tungsten is a commercial clusterware product that also supports PostgreSQL, and is available at the following URL:

`http://www.continuent.com/`

Managing Hot Standby

Hot Standby is the name for the PostgreSQL feature that allows us to connect to a Standby database and execute read-only queries. Most importantly, Hot Standby allows us to run queries while the Standby is being continuously updated through either file-based or streaming replication.

Hot Standby allows you to offload larger queries or parts of your read-only workload onto the Standby nodes. Should you need to failover to the Standby node, your queries will keep executing during the failover process to avoid any interruption of service.

There are some complexities that need to be understood to manage Hot Standby successfully, as in some cases user queries can conflict with the continuous application of changes from the Master. If no new changes arrive, no conflicts will arise.

There are two main roles we need to consider with hot Standby. First, that the Standby node provides a secondary node in case the primary node fails. Second, that we can run queries on that node. In some cases, those two roles can come into conflict with each other, and we need to decide ahead of time the importance we attach to each role.

In most cases, the role of Standby will take priority: queries are good, but its OK to cancel them to ensure we have a viable Standby. If we have more than one hot Standby node, it may be possible to have one node nominated as Standby and others dedicated to serving queries, without regard for their need to act as Standbys.

Getting ready

Hot Standby is usable with the following:

- ▸ File-based replication
- ▸ Streaming replication

> ▶ While performing a point in time recovery
> ▶ When using a permanently frozen Standby

For the first two replication mechanisms, you will need to configure replication as described in earlier recipes. In addition, you will need to configure the following parameters:

On the Master set:

```
wal_level = 'hot_Standby'    in postgresql.conf
```

On the Standby set:

```
hot_Standby = on             in postgresql.conf
```

Neither of those settings are the default, so you will need to make changes. You will need to do a clean restart of the database server on both the Master and the Standby for these changes to take effect.

You will need to allow a short delay between the restarts, as the new mode is not immediately picked up on the Standby. The delay is usually the same duration as `checkpoint_timeout`, though may in some cases be longer. If you restart the Standby too quickly, it will still be reading older transaction log data, and it will fail to start and give a log message saying "you need to enable Hot Standby", so please be patient. You only need to configure this once, not every time you restart.

Optional parameters on the Standby node are set in `postgresql.conf` as follows:

> ▶ `max_Standby_archive_delay`
> ▶ `max_Standby_streaming_delay`
> ▶ `vacuum_defer_cleanup_age`
> ▶ `trace_recovery_messages`

A permanently frozen Standby can be created by specific settings in the `recovery.conf` file. Neither `restore_command` nor `primary_conninfo` should be set, while `Standby_mode = on`. In this mode, the server will start, but always remain at the exact state of the database as it was when the `pg_stop_backup()` function completes.

Another point to note is that during the initial catch-up period, the replication delay will be much higher than we would normally expect it to be. You are advised to set `hot_Standby = off` for the initial period immediately following creation of the Standby only. User connections during that initial period may use system resources or cause conflicts that could extend the catch-up delay. When the Standby is fully caught up with the primary, then we can set `hot_Standby = on`, and restart.

How to do it...

Queries that run on the Standby node see a version of the database that is slightly behind the primary node. We describe this as eventually consistent. How long is "eventually"? That time is exactly the replication delay plus the apply delay, as discussed in the recipe on replication concepts. You can set an upper limit on the acceptable apply delay by controlling two similar parameters: `max_Standby_streaming_delay` and `max_Standby_archive_delay`.

To understand how to set these parameters, we must understand the forces that act to increase the apply delay: query conflicts. There are four main types of conflicts that can occur between the Master and queries on the Standby, which are as follows:

- ▶ Resources—CPU, I/O, and so on
- ▶ Locks—AccessExclusiveLocks
- ▶ Cleanup records
- ▶ Other special cases

Resource conflicts are the easiest to understand: if the server is busy applying changes from the Master, then you will have fewer resources to use for queries. That means if there are no changes arriving, then you'll get more query throughput. If there are predictable changes in the write workload on the Master, then you may need to throttle back your query workload on the Standby when that occurs.

Resource conflicts can slow down queries on the Standby, and can be thought of as soft conflicts. Other forms of conflict are hard conflicts, causing queries on the Standby to be canceled or disconnected.

Lock conflicts are also easy to understand: if you wish to run a command on the Master, such as `ALTER TABLE ... DROP COLUMN`, then you must first lock the table to prevent all access. The lock request is sent through to the Standby server as well, which will then cancel Standby queries that are currently accessing that table after a configurable delay.

On high-availability systems, making DDL changes to tables that cause long periods of locking on the Master can be difficult. You may want the tables on the Standby to stay available for read during the period while the changes on the Master are being made. To do that, temporarily set `max_Standby_streaming delay = -1` and `max_Standby_archive_delay = -1`, and then reload the server. As soon as the first lock record is seen on the Standby, all further changes will be held. Once the locks are released on the Master, you can then reset the original parameter values on the Standby, which then will allow the changes to be made there.

Using `max_Standby` parameter settings of `-1` may not be useful for normal running because this is a very timid setting. No user query will ever be canceled if it conflicts with applying changes, causing the apply process to wait indefinitely. As a result, the apply delay can increase significantly over time, depending upon the frequency and duration of queries, and the frequency of conflicts. To work out an appropriate setting for these parameters, we need to understand more about the other types of conflict, though there is also a simple way to avoid this problem entirely.

Cleanup records and other special cases also conflicts. The special cases are rare and/or obvious, for example, if you drop a database on the Master, then queries running on Standby will be canceled.

Cleanup records remove old tuple versions from the database, as part of the internal workings of MVCC. The easiest way to understand this is to review what happens on the Master node. When a VACUUM runs, it will only remove row versions that can no longer be seen by any current query. To do this, the VACUUM asks for and receives feedback about which queries are running, and then ensures that it doesn't remove expired row versions too early. When running in Hot Standby mode, the Master doesn't receive visibility feedback about what queries are running on the Standby nodes. As a result, it is possible that the tasks running on the Master node will remove row versions that may be required on the Standby nodes. When those row versions are removed they generate *cleanup records* in the transaction log that cause conflicts with queries running on the Standby.

You can provide some protection against canceled queries by setting `vacuum_defer_cleanup_age` to a value higher than 0. That parameter is fairly hard to set accurately, though I would suggest starting with a value of 1,000 and tune upwards. A vague and inaccurate assumption would be to say that each 1,000 will be approximately 1 second of additional delay. A vague and inaccurate assumption is probably helpful more often than it is wrong, though it will often be wrong.

The repmgr project provides a mechanism to provide more accurate visibility feedback, and is specifically designed to help Hot Standby in PostgreSQL 9.0. repmgr will reduce cancelations caused by cleanup record conflicts by providing dynamic and accurate visibility feedback from the Standby node to the Master.

If you want to completely *freeze* a Standby database, so that no further changes are applied, then you can do this by stopping the server, modifying `recovery.conf` so that neither `restore_command` and `primary_conninfo` are set, yet `Standby_mode` = on, then restarting the server. You can come back out of this mode, though, only if the archive contains the required WAL files to catch up, otherwise you will need to re-configure the Standby from a base backup again.

If cancelations do occur, they will throw either an *error* or *fatal* level errors. These will be marked with `SQLSTATE 40001 SERIALIZATION FAILURE`. That could be trapped by an application, and the SQL can be resubmitted.

If you attempt to run a non-read only query, then you will receive an error marked with SQLSTATE 25006 READ ONLY TRANSACTION. That might be used to re-direct SQL to the Master, where it can execute successfully.

How it works...

On the Standby, node changes from the Master are read from the transaction log and applied to the Standby database. Hot Standby works by emulating running transactions from the Master, so that queries on the Standby have the visibility information they need to fully respect MVCC. This makes Hot Standby mode particularly suitable for serving a large workload of short/fast SELECT queries. If the workload is consistently short, then few conflicts will delay the Standby, and the server will run smoothly.

When running longer selects in reporting mode, then you will probably need to play with the configuration settings to suit you, or use a utility, such as the repmgr, to minimize query conflicts from cleanup records.

There's more...

Changes made by a transaction on the Master will not be visible until the commit is applied onto the Standby. So, for example, we have a Master and a Standby with a replication delay of four seconds between them. A long-running transaction may take one hour to make changes on the Master. How long does it take before those changes are visible on the Standby? With Hot Standby, the answer is *four* seconds after the commit on the Master. This is because the changes made during the transaction on the Master have been streamed while the transaction is still in progress, and in most cases already applied on the Standby when the commit record arrives. Note that this is a very different situation for trigger-based replication, such as Slony and Londiste, where the data does not start transferring until after a transaction commits on the Master. So, with trigger-based replication, the data would likely only become visible many minutes after the commit on the Master. Which means that with trigger-based replication the effective apply delay also depends upon, transaction duration on the Master.

Hot Standby can also be used when running a *Point-in-Time Recovery*, so the WAL records applied to the database need not be arriving immediately from a live database server. We would just use file-based recovery in that case, not streaming replication.

Also note that a Standby node can be shutdown and restarted normally using the commands already described in earlier chapters.

See also

Repmgr project contains a component to minimize query conflicts available at the following URL:

http://projects.2ndQuadrant.com/repmgr/

Selective replication using Londiste

Londiste is part of the Skytools suite of software, produced by and used by **Skype** for their production transactional databases. Londiste is a replication system built on top of a generic event-queuing system named **PgQ** (pronounced as pg-queue), a PostgreSQL extension module.

It's simple, easy, and robust.

One of the most important features is that Londiste achieves eventual consistency between Master and Standby in a relaxed manner, ensuring that operations on the Master are lock-free.

Getting ready

If you haven't read the recipes on *Replication Concepts* and *Replication best practice* at the start of this chapter, please go and read them now. Replication is complex, and even if you think "no problem, I know that", it's worth just checking the basic concepts and names that I'll be using here.

How to do it...

Carry out the following steps to configure Londiste replication:

1. Install the software and create directories: On Debian/Ubuntu the software installed using the names without the `.py` suffix, so just pgqadm and Londiste.

2. Configure `clustname_ticker.ini` as follows:

```
[pgqadm]
job_name = clustname_ticker
db = dbname=ticker
# how often to run maintenance [seconds]
maint_delay = 600
# how often to check for activity [seconds]
loop_delay = 0.1
logfile = /var/log/londiste/%(job_name)s.log
pidfile = /var/log/londiste/%(job_name)s.pid
```

3. Configure `clustname_londiste.ini` as follows:

```
[londiste]
job_name = clustname_londiste
provider_db = dbname=source port=6000 host=groucho
subscriber_db = dbname=target port=6000 host=zeppo
pgq_queue_name = clustname_queue
pgq_lazy_fetch = 500
logfile = /var/log/londiste/%(job_name)s.log
pidfile = /var/run/londiste/%(job_name)s.pid
```

Test connection to provider and subscriber as mentioned in the `clustname_londiste.ini` file for `provider_db` and `subscriber_db`.

4. Create the database infrastructure. Run all the following on Provider node:

    ```
    pgqadm.py clustname_ticker.ini install
    londiste.py clustname_londiste.ini provider install
    londiste.py clustname_londiste.ini subscriber install
    ```

5. Start ticker daemon on Provider node by running the following:

    ```
    pgqadm.py clustname_ticker.ini ticker -d
    ```

6. Start Londiste daemon on Subscriber node as follows:

    ```
    londiste.py clustname_londiste.ini replay -d
    ```

7. Define a replication set on Provider node. For a replication set consisting of tables a, b, and c use the following:

    ```
    londiste.py clustname_londiste.ini provider add a b c
    ```

8. Copy the replicated objects to the subscriber node. The definitions need to be the same, though indexes and Foreign Keys may differ. If you want to make changes on the Subscriber side, produce a manual script of additional changes. On the Provider node, run the following:

    ```
    pg_dump --schema-only -t a -t b -t c > clustname_schema.sql
    ```

9. On the Subscriber node, run the following:

    ```
    psql -f clustname_schema.sql
    ```

10. If you have additional changes on the subscriber, add them now. An example might be that the subscriber can have a completely different set of indexes to the provider, allowing it to support different kinds of workloads:

    ```
    psql -f clustname_subscriber_changes.sql
    ```

11. Subscribe: on subscriber node, run the following:

    ```
    londiste.py clustname_londiste.ini subscriber add a b c
    ```

12. That's it, your done. Londiste will eventually catch up. If you really want to know exactly when, then you can watch

    ```
    londiste.py clustname_londiste.ini subscriber tables
    ```

13. until all tables show as «OK». Or run the following on the provider:

    ```
    SELECT * FROM pgq.get_consumer_info();
    ```

14. Then you should wait for all Foreign Keys to be re-added onto the subscriber tables by monitoring using the following query run on the subscriber:

```
SELECT count(*) FROM londiste.subscriber_pending_fkeys;
```

That covers how to set up *selective* replication with Londiste.

If you want *all tables* in one replication set, you should set up scripts to perform the preceding steps for all tables:

1. Follow steps 1 to 6, and 10 as described in the preceding sequence.
2. Define a replication set on Provider node as follows:

```
londiste.py clustname_londiste.ini provider add table1
londiste.py clustname_londiste.ini provider add table2
...
londiste.py clustname_londiste.ini provider add tableN
```

3. Copy the replicated objects to the subscriber node. On the Provider node, run the following:

```
pg_dump --schema-only > clustname_schema.sql
```

4. On the Subscriber node, run the following:

```
psql -f clustname_schema.sql
```

5. If you have additional changes on the subscriber, add them now by using the following:

```
psql -f clustname_subscriber_changes.sql
```

6. Subscribe: on the subscriber node, run the following:

```
londiste.py clustname_londiste.ini subscriber add table1
londiste.py clustname_londiste.ini subscriber add table2
...
londiste.py clustname_londiste.ini subscriber add tableN
```

How it works...

All related tables that form one replication set must use a single queue. There's no problem in having multiple queues and multiple Londiste daemons connecting the same provider/subscribers, though obviously that is a more complex configuration, and seldom necessary, unless performance is a significant issue. Each provider database needs only one pgqadm as all that provides is the *ticker*.

When adding tables without explicit schema, Londiste assumes the schema *public*. Londiste does not use a search path. If you want another schema, you'll need to fully qualify tablenames like the following:

```
schemaname.tablename
```

Londiste uses an efficient `COPY` command to move data across, and then carefully applies changes, so that the set of tables all eventually match. You don't need to have all tables in a single replication set listed on the same command line. The Foreign Keys are restored once consistency is achieved.

Eventual consistency is probably the most important aspect of this system of replication. Tables are copied separately, so that there is no need to lock all of the tables on the provider using one big transaction, such as occurs during a `pg_dump`.

For Londiste, each row change creates one event row in the queue table using special triggers. Triggers are placed automatically on each database table by the Londiste commands. Londiste uses almost identical triggers to Slony, and so shares many of the characteristics of that project; they are both offer *trigger-based replication*.

Changed rows are brought across to the subscriber in batches. The batches are defined on the provider by the ticker as demanded by the subscriber, so if the ticker fails, then you will get very large batches.

There are downsides to this form of replication. First, there is an overhead to triggers and writing to queue tables, though this will vary from workload-to-workload, it is best to plan for a 10 to 20% overhead. Second, queue tables take up space and RAM. Third, that you need to take special administrative actions to add, change, or remove tables from the replication set.

The benefit of using Londiste is that it allows you to make a selective replica of your database. Not all tables need to be copied.

There's more...

You can stop Londiste safely by using the following:

```
londiste.py clustname_londiste.ini --stop
```

or you can stop in an emergency using the following:

```
londiste.py clustname_londiste.ini --kill
```

If you want to change the configuration while server is online, you can reload the configuration using the following:

```
londiste.py clustname_londiste.ini --reload
```

Check status using the following command:

```
SELECT queue_name, consumer_name, lag, last_seen
FROM pgq.get_consumer_info();
```

The `lag` column helps monitor the replication delay.

If replication drops or needs to be restarted, you can use the following command on the subscriber:

```
londiste.py clustname_londiste.ini repair table1
```

See also

```
http://skytools.projects.postgresql.org/doc/
```

Thanks to *Marko Kreen* and *Dimitri Fontaine* for additional advice, especially `http://wiki.postgresql.org/wiki/Londiste_Tutorial`, which was the starting point for most people's first steps with Londiste.

Selective replication using Slony 2.0

Slony is one of the longest running and best known replication projects for PostgreSQL. It provides advanced features, though as a result is considered complex by many users.

Slony is also known as Slony-I because there were once plans for a Slony-II, though that doesn't exist (at least so far). Slony-I was first released as 1.0, though there is now a Version 2.0. So when we talk about Slony 2.0, we mean Slony-I Version 2.0.

Getting ready

If you haven't read the recipes on *Replication Concepts* and *Replication best practice* at the start of this chapter, please go and read them now. Replication is complex.

The first question to look at is whether to use Slony. Slony still has some advantages, even alongside streaming replication, for specific-use cases. Some of its advantages are as follows:

- ▶ Slony can replicate data between different PostgreSQL major versions.
- ▶ Slony can replicate data between different hardware or operating systems.
- ▶ Slony can record changes into a file, so that those changes can be replicated in bulk by some mechanism. This can be used to replicate by regular transfer of tapes, and is also useful when network connection is not always available. This offers the capability for periodic updates from remote or mobile users.
- ▶ Slony allows you to perform selective replication.
- ▶ Slony also allows a Master to replicate some tables to one Standby and other tables to a different Standby. We name that *fan-out*. The reverse is also true: a Standby can receive tables from multiple Masters. We can name that *fan-in*, or maybe "*roll-up*" capability.
- ▶ Slony allows relay replication, so that the Master (or Origin) sends changes to a Standby node (a Subscriber), which then sends it onwards (as a Provider) to other Standbys (also Subscribers).

These last abilities mean that we can have very complex cluster configurations if we need them. Such clusters are well beyond the scope of this book, regrettably.

Sounds very cool, and it definitely is. Please be very careful here: complexity is your enemy when building robust and highly available solutions. If you definitely need some of the preceding features, go with Slony. If you don't or you are unsure, use a simpler alternative: streaming replication.

Next, consider which version of Slony to use. Version 1.2 is a very mature version of Slony with many production installations. Many features have been enhanced in Version 2.0, and that is now the recommended version for PostgreSQL 8.3 and above. Slony 2.0 offers somewhat reduced locking and smoother, more efficient replication. Slony 2.0.5 has grown through many of the teething problems in early releases, and is in use by many production systems.

How to do it...

As you might guess, Slony configuration is complex. There have been a few attempts to simplify configuration, though there is no accepted standard there. Here, we choose to use a project named Slony1-ctl available at the following URL:

```
http://pgfoundry.org/projects/slony1-ctl/
```

The benefits of using Slony1-ctl are that it allows:

- ▶ Management of even complex replication with cascading, several sets of replication, several Masters, and so on
- ▶ Failover/switchover (even in cascading)
- ▶ Add/drop objects (table, sequence) to replication in 1 script, very easily
- ▶ Add/manage nodes and paths between nodes
- ▶ Add replication sets
- ▶ Upgrade Slony

Probably the key point is that all actions happen in two stages. Stage one is a create script, stage two is an execution script. This gives the replication administrator the opportunity to edit the scripts if necessary, or simply to stop and check things.

Scripts produced are autonomous: they don't need any Slony-ctl script or run-time component to be executed. Some people just use these scripts to create the scripts and then deploy them separately. The execution script also provides error handling as well.

Full replication process

This recipe will configure Slony replication from a single Master to a single Slave/Standby. Once this process is mastered, you can think about further complexity. Carry out the following steps:

1. Ensure that all tables that will be replicated have a Primary Key or Unique index defined.

2. Install Slony on each node in the configuration.

3. Create a PostgreSQL user to perform replication. You need to create a PostgreSQL user in each PostgreSQL cluster. This user is dedicated to the Slony replication system, and must have a robust md5 password for login. Log in each server involved in the replication, and execute the following command as postgresql Unix user:

    ```
    createuser -s -W -E my_slony_user
    ```

4. Update your PostgreSQL `pg_hba.conf`. On each server involved in the replication system, adjust authorization to login so that `my_slony_user` is able to connect from each servers to each others to the databases you want to replicate.

    ```
    host    my_db  my_slony_user 192.168.1.111/32    md5
    host    my_db  my_slony_user 192.168.1.112/32    md5
    ```

5. Provide password in `.pgpass`. Edit the the `~/.pgpass` file, and add lines for each host, like the following:

    ```
    192.168.0.1:5432:my_db:my_slony_user:my_slony_pass
    ```

6. Edit `etc/slony_include.h` in the marked places for the following entries:
    - Edit the file, and adjust the path.
    - Edit the Slony user

7. Edit `etc/bases.h`. This file holds the connection information for each database involved in the replication. There can be a different database name for the same replication or the same database name for different replication.

    ```
    # CLUSTER     NODE          BASE      HOST            PORT
    my_replica    1             my_db     192.168.1.12    5432
    my_replica    2             my_db     192.168.1.13    5432
    ```

8. Edit `etc/relations.h`. Edit the tables that you wish to replicate as follows:

    ```
    # CLUSTER     SET    MASTER        SLAVE
    my_replica    1      1             2
    ```

9. Optionally, edit `etc/slon.cfg`. Edit the file if you want to change the defaults. Slony will be launch with this configuration file.

10. Use slony-ctl:

    ```
    ./01_create_init.sh -c my_replica
    ./create_struct.sh -c my_replica
    ./02_exec_init.sh -c my_replica
    ```

These last three steps are where the actual execution takes place. After all of these have executed, the databases are fully replicated with slon daemons running.

- `01_create_init.sh` creates the bash scripts for later use. You can edit `$SLON_TMP/my_replica.sh` and add/remove tables, if needed. So selective replication is a simple matter of editing those files.

- `create_struct.sh` performs a dump from Master and a restore to the slave of the database schema. This dumps the whole database schema.

- `02_exec_init.sh` executes the scripts. This copies the data, so may take a while.

Maintaining replication

Slony doesn't replicate the following items:

- Table definition changes (DDL commands)
- Changes to users and roles
- Changes to large objects (BLOBS)
- Changes made by the TRUNCATE command (may change in future)

So, once you've set up Slony, you'll need to make any further changes to the replicated tables onto each of the nodes in the configuration. Slony provides a tool named **slonik** which allows you to perform EXECUTE SCRIPT, which executes a change script in a single transaction on each node.

You can create new non-unique indexes of any kind onto tables onto the subscriber without a problem. This can be used to tune the Standby for different workloads. Make sure you don't put unique indexes on the subscriber side that don't exist on the Master, because this can cause replication failures.

Non-replicated tables on the Standby can still be written to, allowing post-processing of incoming changes or creation of materialized view-style tables.

How it works...

When data changes are made, they are placed in log tables named `sl_log_1` and `sl_log_2` using database triggers on the origin. Slony will flip/flop between those two tables, so it can perform truncate data on the non-current log table. That avoids the need for deletion and vacuuming of the log tables. Triggers are also placed on replicated tables on the Standby to prevent writes to tables.

For each node in the cluster, there will be one slon process which sends data and configuration changes from the Master to the Standby. The slon daemon reads the log table on the Origin/Provider, and then executes the SQL onto the Subscriber (Standby). Changes are applied in batches, with batch size as a tunable parameter.

With Slony 1.2, all replicated tables got locked with every EXECUTE SCRIPT call, even if they were in different replication sets. With Slony 2.0, locking is more relaxed, though this means it is possible to use too little locking and cause yourself errors.

There's more...

Slony support in available through pgAdmin and phppgadmin GUIs, though Slony management is probably too complex to make sense to control it through that route. Opinions will no doubt differ on that point.

See also

For more information visit the following URL:

```
http://slony.info
```

Load balancing with pgpool-II 3.0

Pgpool-II is middleware that can perform the following major functions:

- Connection pooling
- Load balancing
- Replication management
- Parallel query

The only aspect of pgpool we cover here is load-balancing mode, which is designed to work with the other forms of replication discussed in this chapter. Pgpool is actively developed and contains many new features for PostgreSQL 9.0. Load balancing mode allows an application to connect to pgpool once, and then spread certain kinds of work across multiple nodes. As a result, it is possible to use pgpool with an existing application with minimal changes. There are other ways of load balancing across multiple servers, though those utilize features of non-PostgreSQL related software, so aren't covered here.

Getting ready

Before we use pgpool, we need to understand how the load balancing works, and whether it will act as we would like.

In load-balancing mode, pgpool makes intelligent routing decisions based upon the type of SQL statement.

SQL Statement type	Master	Standby
Straightforward SELECT	Load is split between Master and Standby, if possible	
Other/Non-SELECT	Sent to Master only	Never sent to Standby

`Straightforward SELECT` statements are easily load balanced. `Straightforward` is defined here as being a `SELECT` statement that:

▶ is issued as a top-level `SELECT`, so selects issued within functions do not get replicated

▶ is not issued as a part of an explicit/extended transaction

▶ doesn't use row-level locking: `SELECT ... FOR SHARE/UPDATE`

▶ doesn't use `nextval()` or `setval()` functions

▶ doesn't access volatile functions

▶ doesn't access system catalog tables

You can look for further details of pgpool at the following URL:

`http://pgfoundry.org/projects/pgpool/`

Other pgpool features are as follows:

▶ Standby servers can be added without restarting pgpool

▶ Pgpool can also be used to automate failover

▶ A query cache is available in all modes

How to do it...

If using Pgpool with streaming log replication, then Hot Standby must be enabled.

We setup pgpool, and then point the applications at the pgpool server, which responds to them like a PostgreSQL server. Pgpool then connects to the Master and Standbys. You can use a `pool_hba.conf` file to control access, just as with the normal server's `pg_hba.conf` file.

You'll need the following settings in the `pgpool.conf.sample-stream`:

```
replication_mode = false
Master_slave = true
replicate_select = false
load_balance_mode = true
```

These purely set up the load-balancing mode. In addition, pgpool supports the following directives:

- ▶ `delay_threshold` specifies the accepted replication delay of the Standby against the primary server in bytes. If the delay exceeds `delay_threshold` then load balancing is interrupted momentarily and all queries are sent to the Master. If you don't want this, just set it to zero.

- ▶ `log_Standby_delay` provides an option to log the Standby delay, so you can review it over time. If always, we log the delay every time health checking is performed. If `if_over_threshold` is specified, then we compare against `delay_threshold` before logging.

- ▶ `health_check_period` defines the time between measurements of the Standby delay. `health_check_user` specifies the username that will be used for health check access.

There are additional parameters for automated failover and other features. You may want to read the `pgpool.conf.sample-stream` file for more detail on those and the many other parameters you can control.

Pgpool can be controlled using the command line, like the following:

```
pgpool -f pgpool.conf -a pool_hba.conf
pgpool -m fast stop
pgpool -f pgpool.conf -a pool_hba.conf reload
```

The replication delay can be requested dynamically by issuing the following:

```
SHOW POOL_STATUS;
```

which is a dummy SQL command that is intercepted by pgpool and returns information about the dynamic status. Other `SHOW` commands provide various other feedback.

How it works...

Pgpool parses SQL statements to understand their type and contents. The parsing needs to go quite deep to understand whether `SELECT` statements contain volatile function calls. Pgpool doesn't know about user-defined functions, though you can explicitly include or exclude functions using the new parameters `white_function_list` (to include) and `black_function_list` (to exclude).

Pgpool implements the health checking feature in a separate worker process, so it can continue to work without blocking incoming SQL.

Special thanks to *Tatsuo Ishii* for providing detailed feedback on my questions about the new features of pgpool II 3.0, which was released shortly before publication.

There's more...

Pgpool-II is middleware that can perform the following major functions:

- ▸ Connection pooling
- ▸ Load balancing
- ▸ Replication management
- ▸ Parallel query

I've ignored some of the other features here, so I need to say a few words about my thoughts on that. Connection pooling is also provided by pgbouncer. Replication management features are probably superseded by other forms of replication covered here.

The parallel query features are regrettably out-classed by popular products, such as Greenplum, which offers a free-to-use edition that performs very well, and is in production use at a number of PostgreSQL user sites. Visit the following URL:

```
http://www.greenplum.com/products/single-node/
```

Upgrading (minor)

Minor release upgrades are released regularly by all software developers and PostgreSQL has its share of corrections. When a minor release occurs, we bump the last number, usually by one.

So ,the first release of major release 9.0 is 9.0.0. The first set of bug fixes is 9.0.1, then 9.0.2, and so on.

This recipe is about moving from minor release to minor release.

Getting ready

First, get hold of the new release, either by downloading the source or downloading fresh binaries.

How to do it...

In most cases, PostgreSQL aims for minor releases to be trivial upgrades. We make great efforts to keep the on-disk format the same for both data/index files and transaction log (WAL) files. Some temporary files can sometimes change.

The upgrade process is as follows:

1. Read the release notes to see if there are any special actions that need to be taken for this release.

2. If you have professional support, speak to your support vendor to see if additional safety checks over and above the upgrade instructions are required or recommended, if any. Check also that the target release is fully supported by your vendor on your hardware and OS and OS release level; it may not be, yet.

3. Apply any special actions or checks, for example if WAL format has changed, then you may need to reconfigure log based replication following the upgrade. You may need to scan tables, rebuild indexes or some other action. Not every release has such actions, but watch closely for them, because if they exist, then they are important.

4. If you are using replication, test the upgrade by shutting down one of your Standby or slave servers.

5. Follow the instructions for your OS distribution and binary packager to complete the upgrade. These can vary considerably.

6. Startup the database server being used for a test, apply any post-upgrade special actions, and check that things are working for you.

7. Follow steps 4 to 6 for other Standby servers.

8. Follow steps 4 to 6 for the Primary server.

How it works...

Minor upgrades mostly affect the binary files, so it should be a simple matter of replacing those files and restarting. But check.

Major upgrades in-place

New in PostgreSQL 9.0 is a utility named `pg_upgrade`, supplied as a contrib module. `pg_upgrade` allows you to migrate to new major versions of PostgreSQL, such as from 8.4 to 9.0, or from 9.0 to 9.1.

In-place upgrades means upgrading your database without moving to a new system. That does sounds good, though `pg_upgrade` has a few things that you may wish to consider as potential negatives, which are as follows:

▶ Database server must be shut down while upgrade takes place.

▶ Your system must be big enough to hold two copies of the database server: old and new copies. If it's not, then you have to use the link option of `pg_upgrade`, or use the recipe on upgrading using replication tools. If you use the link option on `pg_upgrade`, then there is no *pg_downgrade* utility. The only option is a restore from backup, and that means extended unavailability if that occurs.

▶ If you copy the database, then upgrade, time will be proportional to the size of the database.

▶ `pg_upgrade` only supports PostgreSQL 8.3+.

- ▶ pg_upgrade (for 9.0) does not validate all of your additional add-in modules, so you will need to set up a test server and confirm that these work ahead of performing the main upgrade. (Sorry, no tricks yet to make that easy!)

Getting ready

Find out the size of your database (using an earlier recipe). If the database is large or you have an important requirement for availability, you should consider doing the major upgrade using replication tools instead. Check out the next recipe.

How to do it...

- ▶ Read the release notes for the new server version to which you are migrating. Pay careful attention to the incompatibilities section; PostgreSQL does change from release-to-release.

- ▶ Set up a test server with the old software release on it. Upgrade that system to the new release to check there are no conflicts from software dependencies. Test your application. Make sure you identify and test each add-in PostgreSQL module you were using to confirm it still works at the new release level.

- ▶ Backup your server. Prepare for the worst; hope for the best.

- ▶ Write a test script that will confirm the database has been upgraded successfully. Include some commands that will only work at the new release, so you know it really is the new release, such as the following:

```
SELECT (string_to_array(version(), ' '))[2] = '9.0.1';
```

- ▶ Most importantly, work out who you will call if things go badly, and exactly how to restore from that backup you just took.

- ▶ Install new versions of all required software on the production server, and create a new database server.

- ▶ Don't disable security while doing the upgrade. Your security team will do backflips if they hear about this. Keep your job.

- ▶ Shutdown the database servers.

- ▶ Run pg_upgrade, and then run any required post-upgrade scripts. Make sure you check to see whether any were required.

- ▶ Startup the new database server, and immediately run a server-wide ANALYZE.

- ▶ Run through your tests to check whether it worked or you need to start performing the contingency plan.

- ▶ If all is OK, re-enable wide access to the database server. Restart applications.

- ▶ Don't delete your old server directory if you used the link method. The old data directory still contains the data for the new database server. Confusing, so don't get caught by this.

How it works...

`pg_upgrade` works easily because the data block format hasn't changed between some releases. That won't always be the case; however, replication might not work across major upgrades as well, though has done so for the last seven releases of PostgreSQL.

`pg_upgrade` works by creating a new set of database catalog tables, and then creating the old objects again in the new tables. This works well for common cases.

There's more...

If you're upgrading more than one major release, then we hope it should be possible. We do this by allowing a chain of upgrade steps that takes you through the versions one-by-one. It will be more complex to do things that way, though its the same general procedure.

Whatever you do, carefully plan the tests that will tell you whether the upgrade was successful and whether it will be safe to continue.

Major upgrades online using replication tools

Upgrading between major releases is hard, and should be deferred until you have some good reasons and sufficient time to get it right.

You can use replication tools to minimize the downtime required for an upgrade, so we refer to the following recipe as *online upgrade*.

How to do it...

The following general points should be followed, allowing at least a month for the complete process to ensure that everything is tested, and everybody understands the implications:

▸ Set up a new release of software on a new system

▸ Take a standalone backup from main system, and build a test server. Test applications extensively against the new release on the test system. When everything works and performs correctly, then:

    ❏ Set up a connection pooler to main database (may have already)

    ❏ Set up replication using Londiste or Slony to the new system, as described previously

    ❏ Re-test application extensively against the new release on live data, then when ready for final cut-over we can:

        ▸ Prepare a new connection pool config to point at the new system

        ▸ Pause the connection pool

        ▸ Switchover to the new system

        ▸ Point the connection pool to the new system, and reload

How it works...

Slony and Londiste both work against multiple releases of PostgreSQL, so you can be sure that cross-release replication works and works well. The preceding recipe allows for online upgrade with zero data loss, because of the use of the clean switchover process. There's no need for lengthy downtime during the upgrade, and there's much reduced risk in comparison with an in-place upgrade. It works best with new hardware, and is a good way to upgrade the hardware or change the disk layout at the same time. This is also very useful for changing server encoding.

Index

user connection
  NOLOGIN users, disconnecting 132
  preventing temporarily 131
  verifying 193
user passwords
  encrypting 135

V

VACUUM command 215
versions, PostgreSQL
  PostgreSQL 8.2 33
  PostgreSQL 8.3 33
  PostgreSQL 8.4 33
  PostgreSQL 9.0 33

views
  about 182
  making updateable 182, 184
  working 185
VPN (Virtual private Network) 145

W

WAL receiver process 72
WAL writer process 71
Windows
  database server files, locating 35
Write Ahead Log (WAL) 268

Thank you for buying
PostgreSQL 9 Administration Cookbook

About Packt Publishing

Packt, pronounced 'packed', published its first book "*Mastering phpMyAdmin for Effective MySQL Management*" in April 2004 and subsequently continued to specialize in publishing highly focused books on specific technologies and solutions.

Our books and publications share the experiences of your fellow IT professionals in adapting and customizing today's systems, applications, and frameworks. Our solution based books give you the knowledge and power to customize the software and technologies you're using to get the job done. Packt books are more specific and less general than the IT books you have seen in the past. Our unique business model allows us to bring you more focused information, giving you more of what you need to know, and less of what you don't.

Packt is a modern, yet unique publishing company, which focuses on producing quality, cutting-edge books for communities of developers, administrators, and newbies alike. For more information, please visit our website: www.packtpub.com.

About Packt Open Source

In 2010, Packt launched two new brands, Packt Open Source and Packt Enterprise, in order to continue its focus on specialization. This book is part of the Packt Open Source brand, home to books published on software built around Open Source licences, and offering information to anybody from advanced developers to budding web designers. The Open Source brand also runs Packt's Open Source Royalty Scheme, by which Packt gives a royalty to each Open Source project about whose software a book is sold.

Writing for Packt

We welcome all inquiries from people who are interested in authoring. Book proposals should be sent to author@packtpub.com. If your book idea is still at an early stage and you would like to discuss it first before writing a formal book proposal, contact us; one of our commissioning editors will get in touch with you.

We're not just looking for published authors; if you have strong technical skills but no writing experience, our experienced editors can help you develop a writing career, or simply get some additional reward for your expertise.

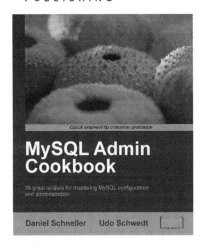

MySQL Admin Cookbook

ISBN: 978-1-847197-96-2   Paperback: 376 pages

99 great recipes for mastering MySQL configuration and administration

1. Set up MySQL to perform administrative tasks such as efficiently managing data and database schema, improving the performance of MySQL servers, and managing user credentials

2. Deal with typical performance bottlenecks and lock-contention problems

3. Restrict access sensibly and regain access to your database in case of loss of administrative user credentials

Mastering phpMyAdmin 3.3.x for Effective MySQL Management

ISBN: 978-1-84951-354-8   Paperback: 412 pages

A complete guide to get started with phpMyAdmin 3.3 and master its features

1. The best introduction to phpMyAdmin available

2. Written by the project leader of phpMyAdmin, and improved over several editions

3. A step-by-step tutorial for manipulating data with phpMyAdmin

Please check **www.PacktPub.com** for information on our titles